slow

mouth-watering recipes for
the slow cooker & crock pot

PENGUIN BOOKS
Published by the Penguin Group
Penguin Group (NZ), 67 Apollo Drive, Rosedale,
North Shore 0632, New Zealand (a division of Pearson New Zealand Ltd)
Penguin Group (USA) Inc., 375 Hudson Street,
New York, New York 10014, USA
Penguin Group (Canada), 90 Eglinton Avenue East, Suite 700, Toronto,
Ontario, M4P 2Y3, Canada (a division of Pearson Penguin Canada Inc.)
Penguin Books Ltd, 80 Strand, London, WC2R 0RL, England
Penguin Ireland, 25 St Stephen's Green,
Dublin 2, Ireland (a division of Penguin Books Ltd)
Penguin Group (Australia), 250 Camberwell Road, Camberwell,
Victoria 3124, Australia (a division of Pearson Australia Group Pty Ltd)
Penguin Books India Pvt Ltd, 11, Community Centre,
Panchsheel Park, New Delhi – 110 017, India
Penguin Books (South Africa) (Pty) Ltd, 24 Sturdee Avenue,
Rosebank, Johannesburg 2196, South Africa

Penguin Books Ltd, Registered Offices: 80 Strand, London, WC2R 0RL, England

First published by Penguin Group (NZ), 2010
1 3 5 7 9 10 8 6 4 2

Designed and typeset by seven.co.nz
Prepress by Image Centre Ltd
Printed in China through Bookbuilders, Hong Kong

Publisher Alison Brook
Managing Editor Kate Stockman

Thanks to:
A wonderful team of food assistants, Olwen Edwards, Mary-Lou McGarry, Sue Hamilton, Julie Wyatt and Tonita Burridge-Thorpe
My very patient nannies, Emma Douglas and Wendy Housley
The photographer and my dear friend, Alan Gillard
My gorgeous husband and children, Warwick, Jean-Luc and Olive-Rose, for being long-suffering taste-testers
Alison, Kate and the team at Penguin
The Warehouse, Tui Flower, Joan Gofton, French Country and many friends for the gorgeous props
New Zealand Beef & Lamb Marketing Bureau Inc.

ISBN 9780143203711

A catalogue record for this book is available
from the National Library of New Zealand.

www.penguin.co.nz

slow

allyson gofton

mouth-watering recipes for
the slow cooker & crock pot

Penguin Books

Friends who share recipes
are truly dear friends.

In memory of my dear friend, Ann B.

contents

It came orange, bright and gaudy like an over-ripe fruit of the same name. The crockery insert, which was not removable, was a rich brown but later would become pale fawn from overuse.

That was my mother's original crock pot, circa the 1970s. Its arrival came with great excitement, as the era of the electric self-help kitchen appliances was in full swing and anything that could possibly save you time cooking for the family – even back then – was welcomed with glee. It still lives, some 25 years later, though in my brother's home now – a testament to an exceptional piece of kitchenware. And while the recipes are a little more jazzy and the smells wafting through the home are a little more fragrant and spicy, Mum's old – if not antique – crock pot is still saving time, though for another busy generation.

Our techno-filled world is packed with culinary advice for today's cooks on how to make a little go a long way, how to have more dash than cash, how to travel the culinary world from our suburban home kitchens and, yes, how to save time. But we, being humans, juxtapose this with, 'But I want to cook, be involved – well at least on some level – in preparing the day's meal.' And so it is that crock pots and slow cookers are making a well-deserved revival. It has to be the ultimate fast-food cooker really: just pile in the ingredients, flip on the switch and walk out the door. It doesn't get much quicker or easier to produce a healthy and delicious meal. Couple this with all the exciting prepared sauces, pastes and spice and herb blends that adorn our ever-growing supermarkets and the meat and poultry cuts that we can select from, and it's evident that crock pot cooking has never been so exciting nor convenient as it is today.

Slow *has been an incredibly inspiring book to cook and write. The recipes are packed with flavour, and the many useful tips ensure successful slow cooking in our fast world.*

Enjoy.

Allyson

slow cooker & crock pot hints & tips

wattages

In writing Slow, my team and I have cooked with many different brands of slow cooker of different sizes, each with a different wattage. Without wanting to get too complicated, wattage is a measure of power, and so the higher the wattage, the more power transmitted to your slow cooker and the faster the food is cooked. I found that those slow cookers with a wattage range of 230–270 volts were best for cooking. On high they did not boil, but bubbles plopped evenly around the edge, while on low the sauces murmured along slowly, making all-day cooking possible without the worry of overcooking. Added to this dilemma are the sizes of the containers, the temperature of the foods when cooking started and so on. The times given in this book are a guide only, so you may need to amend cooking times to suit the capacity size and wattage of your slow cooker.

Allyson

general hints

Pre-warming the slow cooker or crock pot is a good idea. It's like pre-heating your oven; having the food go into a warmed slow cooker just assists with the timing. Pre-warm on low and for no longer than 15 minutes without anything inside the slow cooker.

All slow cookers will cook differently. This is because they almost always have a different wattage and therefore have varying levels of power.

When cooking on low, allow sufficient time – don't get caught short.

When cooking on high, be aware that some slow cookers simmer at a fairly high level and this may result in tough meat. All protein will become tough if it is boiled, so be mindful of this.

Meat dishes using tougher cuts of meat will have a nicer flavour and texture if they are simmered and not boiled. Cooking on low allows more time for flavours to develop, too.

If cooking from a conventional recipe do not add as much liquid (water, stock, wine, etc.). Liquids do not boil away in a slow cooker as they would on top of the stove. For the most part, 1 cup of liquid is usually sufficient for cooking with 1 kilogram of meat, though there will not be copious amounts of sauce. More liquid will be required if rice, pasta or dumplings are being added.

Should you wish to thicken any sauces or gravies, add a little flour mixed to a smooth paste with a little water, stirred in at the end of cooking. Cook, covered, on high, for an additional 30 minutes. Large pieces of meat or whole chickens can be removed to rest while the sauce or gravy thickens. For more ways to thicken your stews, casseroles etc., see page 19.

Pie crusts, mashed potato tops and the like, require baking. Transfer the casserole or braise to an ovenproof dish, top and bake in the oven as required (see pages 16–18 for ideas and recipes).

The ideal temperatures for meat cooked in a slow cooker are:
Pork – 71 °C
Lamb & beef (medium rare) – 55–60 °C
Lamb & beef (medium) – 60–65 °C
Lamb & beef (well done) – 70–75 °C

Frozen vegetables do not require pre-cooking. They can be stirred directly into the almost-cooked casserole. Allow an extra 30 minutes' cooking time on high.

Fish and shellfish can be cooked in a slow cooker, but given their delicate nature, add the fish in pieces to the slow cooker, once the sauce has been cooked. The fish can be cooked on low or high until it just flakes easily. Use medium-textured and firm-textured fish varieties such as alfonsino, blue cod, bluenose, dory, groper, John Dory, red gurnard, kahawai, mackerel, perch, orange roughy, tarakihi, trevally, snapper or tuna. Shellfish include prawns (best shelled), uncooked mussel meat, scallops and oysters (if you want to cook them, that is).

meats

Tough, economical cuts of meat cook to perfection in a slow cooker. Partnered with a selected assortment of ingredients, beef, lamb, pork or even sausages cook away to become invitingly tender and tasty. Especially welcome after a busy day.

Browning meat is optional when using a slow cooker. Where there is a *significant* improvement in flavour from browning the meat, the recipes here will feature the logo above. The necessary steps for this have been highlighted in the recipe.

Larger cuts of meat will benefit from standing time before carving. Transfer to a warmed plate and cover and stand, allowing about 5 minutes per 500 grams. The meat will not go cold and will be more succulent when carved.

Preferably, meats should be trimmed of fat as the fat will not 'cook' off as it would in an oven and may make the dish greasy in taste. If the meat has marbled fat or a layer of outer fat, do take the time to brown the meat and drain away any excess fat, unless otherwise stated in the recipe. This will improve the taste.

Large pieces of meat can be placed into the slow cooker with only a little liquid, but will tend to dry out around the edges, so it is advisable to always add some liquid. This is especially true for corned or pickled meats.

Dumplings can be cooked in casseroles. Just drop soup-spoon-sized balls of moist dough into the casserole towards the end of cooking. Once added, cover and cook on high for a further 60 minutes. Make sure you have plenty of hot liquid to cook dumplings in as they will soak up the sauce as they cook.

Sausages

The humble banger is usually a regular with most families and, if cooked correctly, they can be simmered along in the slow cooker with great success.

Browning is essential to avoid them having a boiled taste. Adding plenty of flavoursome ingredients like curry spices or pungent sauces such as soy, black bean, HP or Worcestershire will also help prevent that boiled taste.

Thick sausages are better than thin and they should *not* be pricked before browning as valuable juice will be lost.

chicken & poultry

Simmering chicken slowly in the slow cooker ensures the meat absorbs all the flavours it is being cooked with.

Chickens today are much more tender than those of the 1970s, when slow cookers were first popular. Many old recipes may have very long cooking times for chicken and, coupled with higher wattages today you may find that chicken – whole or in pieces – becomes overcooked. Use the cooking times in this book as a guide.

The best way to cook chicken is whole, stuffed or unstuffed, or leg and thigh portions with the bone in or out. I prefer the bone in as it adds flavour and helps keep the meat moist. Chicken breasts will of course cook in the slow cooker, but as they are leaner and normally a more expensive option, to my mind they are best used for faster styles of cookery.

I have found that if I leave a whole chicken on low all day, say while I am out at work from 8 a.m. to 5 p.m., the result is disappointing. The meat becomes overcooked, falls from the bone, and is stringy and dry, so preferably cook for less time to give a delicious result. I prefer to fill the slow cooker with bone-in leg and thigh portions.

Chicken will not 'brown-up' when cooking. It remains a dull creamy colour. Sprinkle on a little paprika, chopped herbs, ground black pepper or a favourite herb and spice rub to add colour and taste to the finished product.

Alternatively, take the time to dust the chicken with a little flour and brown the chicken in oil or butter in a frying-pan. Use two sets of tongs to turn the chicken gently to avoid splitting the skin. It will not affect the cooking time, but will ensure the chicken looks great when served.

The fat in poultry is mainly attached to the skin and while it is beneficial from a health point of view to remove the skin, the remaining meat is so lean it can dry out. Remove the skin before serving if wished.

Duck leg and thigh portions, especially wild duck, profit from the longer cooking times of the slow cooker.

Turkeys are too big to fit into a slow cooker, unless boned and stuffed. I think their flavour is better enjoyed when they have been roasted.

dried pulses

You could almost think that slow cookers were designed for cooking dried beans, peas and lentils. Without being boiled furiously, but slowly simmered with gutsy flavoured ingredients, dried pulses hold their shape beautifully and become well-flavoured and tender.

Dried pulses (except lentils) all require soaking overnight in 3–4 times the amount of water to pulses. Drain off the water and cook in fresh water or liquid without the lid on. Changing the water helps alleviate the wind-causing nature of the dried pulses.

Kidney & soy beans require 20 minutes' boiling time once soaked and *before* being placed in the slow cooker to cook to remove toxins. This step is essential.

Cooking time for pulses will vary depending on the size, freshness and percentage of dryness of the pulses. Many of our pulses are so well dried today, that they really do need 12 hours minimum soaking and long, slow cooking.

Old dried beans and pulses will not become tender no matter how long you cook them for. Use pulses within 6–9 months of purchase.

Do not add salt to dried pulses until after cooking has finished as salt prevents the beans from softening.

Acidic ingredients such as wine and tomatoes also slow down the cooking time of dried pulses, hence the long cooking time in some recipes.

Dried pulses need plenty of liquid to cook with and naturally the larger the bean or pea, the more liquid required.

If wishing to add pasta or rice, it is easiest to add this cooked at the end. The brands and styles of pasta and rice vary greatly today and absorb more or less water when cooking, making it hard to recommend appropriate cooking times.

Cooking rice in the slow cooker has varying results, so I recommend cooking rice in the more traditional ways.

vegetables

Adding vegetables to meat, poultry or pulse-based meals in the slow cooker certainly helps make the complete meal-in-a-pot. And cooking vegetables up for soups is a simple and tasty option in winter. Here are the more important things I have picked up while cooking the recipes for *Slow*.

Root vegetables such as potatoes, carrots, swedes and parsnips can take a deceptively long time to cook to tender, when added to a pot-roast-style meal. Ideally place them around the base of the slow cooker, so they can cook in the juices from the meat.

It may be worth considering pan-frying the vegetables for just a dash of time before adding to the slow cooker, to give them colour and get their cooking under way.

Root vegetables added to a casserole will cook well in the sauce or gravy, but again, large pieces will take time to cook until tender.

If vegetables such as parsnips have a large woody core, cut this out before cooking.

Onions, especially medium-sized baby onions (the ones that are too big to pickle) and large onions, also take a deceptively long time to soften.

Browning onions in oil in a hot frying-pan before adding to the slow cooker breaks down the cell walls somewhat and they cook much better, so do consider this step when cooking with onions.

With whole baby onions, another option is to pierce the onions with a fork or skewer through to the centre several times. This will help the heat to penetrate and soften the onion.

Leeks suffer from the same issue, so they are better softened and lightly browned in oil before cooking.

Garlic cloves, too, do not seem to soften if added whole without first being browned lightly. They are incredibly resistant to softening actually, so either brown or chop finely before adding.

Frozen vegetables do not require any pre-cooking. Add them to the slow cooker at the end of cooking time, cover with the lid and cook on high for about 20–30 minutes to heat the frozen vegetables through. Alternatively, they can be cooked in a little hot water or microwaved until hot, stirred in to the slow cooker and served immediately.

Leafy vegetables like spinach and silverbeet can be placed into the casserole or meal at the end of cooking time and heated – under cover – for 5–10 minutes on high until they have just wilted.

Whole mushrooms also take time to soften and soak up the flavours of the casserole, curry or sauce. And as mushrooms contain much water themselves, they will add a good amount of liquid to any dish they are cooked in.

Tomatoes are incredibly juicy, adding a significant amount of liquid to any dish. Peeling them is totally optional.

Eggplants benefit greatly from browning before being added to the slow cooker. Their flavour is much improved, though they will soften much more quickly if browned, so don't expect them to look sensational – go for taste!

Broccoli and cauliflower florets are best blanched and added to the casserole or dish in the last hour of cooking time if on low heat. (If on high, allow only 30 minutes.) This will prevent their stems from being stringy and tough and keep them looking lovely.

fruits, puddings & cakes

As slow-cooker cookery is an enclosed form of cookery and therefore moist-style, successful baking is limited to those goods that would normally be poached, steamed or cooked in a self-saucing-style recipe.

Milk- and cream-based puddings do not cook well and burn around the edges of the slow cooker. Though some dairy foods can be added at the end of cooking, it is best not to boil them. Follow the recipe given.

Steamed puddings will benefit from being on a trivet and having water in the slow cooker as you would normally, to transfer the heat more efficiently. You will not, though, get that 'bopping' noise that comes from a steamed pud cooking on the stove top.

Cover steamed puddings to prevent the water dripping off the lid into the puddings. If water gets into puddings, they will not rise as well and will have a heavy texture.

Stewed fruits are beautiful when cooked gradually in the slow cooker. If the slow cooker is filled with soft fruits such as ripe apricots, they will collapse under the weight so don't expect them to look their best, but they will taste wonderful.

Cooking sliced fruits such as apples for freezing is a cinch and they taste great. Pack the slow cooker firmly as the fruit will soften as it cooks. Only a tiny amount of water is required.

Self-saucing puddings are ideal to cook in a slow cooker, though the amount of pudding you cook will depend on the size of your slow cooker. Smaller 3-litre units are ideal for the standard recipe for a family of four. Larger 4.5–5-litre slow cookers are best for servings of 8 or more.

The water that forms on the lid when cooking a self-saucing pudding will trickle down the side and back into the sauce. If any should fall onto the sponge topping, the extra moisture will not make a major difference, given the amount of liquid already in the pudding.

top it

When your casserole or braise is cooked to tender perfection think about jazzing up its presentation, by transferring the dish to a casserole or pie dish and snuggling it under a topping. It's also a great way to jazz up reheated casseroles the next day. Here are a few basic ideas, with suggested quantities, that you can mix and mingle with the recipes in Slow. *Quantities are given to feed about 4–6 or to cover the top of a 20–24-cm pie, casserole or similar-style ovenproof dish.*

buttery mash

serves 4–5

Cook 600–750 grams peeled and diced floury potatoes in boiling salted water until tender. Drain and mash with ¼ cup cream or milk and 2–3 tablespoons butter. Season with salt and pepper.

variations

- Add 1–2 tablespoons chopped fresh herbs like chives, thyme, tarragon, parsley or dill.
- Add ½ cup crumbled feta or grated Cheddar.
- Mix in 1–2 tablespoons grated onion.
- Use cream cheese in place of butter.
- Add 2 tablespoons basil or sun-dried tomato pesto and ¼ cup grated Parmesan.
- Use mashed kumara or pumpkin in place of potatoes.

crouton sprinkle

for a 4.5–5 litre slow cooker

Decorate and serve the casserole or braise from the slow cooker. Just cut an average-sized sour dough or country-style bread loaf into 1–2-cm chunks and toss with melted butter or oil and grated Parmesan. Scatter onto a baking tray in one layer and fan bake at 180–190 °C for around 15 minutes or until golden. Toss with chopped parsley if wished and scatter on top of the meal in the slow cooker before serving.

filo ruffle

serves 5–6

Brush 12–16 sheets of filo pastry with melted butter and scrunch up. Place tightly packed on top of a cold cooked casserole in a pie dish and bake at 190 °C for 30–35 minutes or until the filling is hot and the pastry golden and well cooked.

variations

- Sprinkle sesame seeds on top of the filo ruffle.

grate scott potato top

serves 4–5

Coarsely grate 500 grams cold cooked potatoes and mix with ½ onion, grated, and ½–1 cup grated Cheddar-style cheese and bind with 1 well-beaten egg. Season lightly with garlic salt or lemon-pepper seasoning, scatter over a hot or cold casserole and bake until hot and golden.

variations

- Add chopped fresh herbs like thyme or rosemary or place 3–4 bay leaves on top before baking.
- Add ¼ cup basil pesto and ¼ cup pine nuts or chopped walnuts.
- Use a mix of leftover vegetables like kumara and pumpkin.
- Use feta or a crumbly-style blue cheese in place of the Cheddar-style cheese.

cheese & pastry crumble

serves 4–6

Grate 400-gram block semi-thawed savoury short crust pastry and mix with 1 cup grated Edam, Gouda or Colby cheese. Sprinkle over a cold cooked casserole and bake at 190 °C for 35–40 minutes or until hot and golden and the topping is cooked.

pancake pie

serves 4–5

Sift 1 cup of self-raising flour into a bowl and make a well in the centre. Beat 1 egg with ¾ cup milk and pour into the well, stirring to make a smooth batter. Stir in 25 grams melted butter. Pour evenly over a very hot casserole and bake at 180–190 °C for 30–35 minutes or until the pancake topping is cooked.

variations

- Add chopped herbs like thyme to the batter.
- Sift 1 teaspoon mustard or curry powder with the flour.

pastry

serves 4–6

Cover the pastry dish with 400 grams frozen pastry – savoury short crust or puff pastry – defrosted and rolled to a 3-mm thickness. For best results, place pastry over a cold filling with a pie funnel in the centre of the casserole. This will lift the pastry off the casserole, helping to avoid it becoming soggy.

variations

- Prepare different edgings around the pie.
- Brush with 1 egg yolk, beaten with 2 tablespoons milk for a golden baked pastry.
- Decorate with offcuts of leftover pastry.

savoury crumble

serves 4–5

Rub 50–75 grams softened butter into 2 cups fresh breadcrumbs and toss through ¼ cup loosely packed chopped fresh herbs like parsley or chives, ½–1 cup grated Cheddar-style cheese and 2 teaspoons prepared mustard. Sprinkle over the hot casserole and bake at 180 °C for 20–25 minutes or until hot and golden.

variations

- Use wholemeal breadcrumbs.
- Use half breadcrumbs and half crushed dry cracker crumbs.
- Use crumbled feta in place of Cheddar-style cheese.
- Vary the herbs, e.g. try tarragon, dill or oregano.
- Add 1–2 teaspoons mixed spice seasonings like Cajun or Mexican.
- Add 2 tablespoons za'atar (see recipe below).

french bread crust

serves 4–5

Cut ½ a long French bread stick into 1-cm-wide slices and spread generously with butter. Place the bread slices on top of the hot casserole in an overlapping manner. Sprinkle with a little grated cheese if wished and fan bake on high, at about 200 °C, until hot and golden.

variations

- Use garlic butter in place of standard butter.
- Use olive oil in place of butter – it will not brown as much.
- Layer the bread alternately with tomato or salami slices.
- Use half basil or sun-dried tomato pesto and half butter.

za'atar

makes 2 tablespoons

Toss or stir together 2 tablespoons crushed dried thyme (or ¼ cup chopped fresh thyme), 2 teaspoons ground sumac, 1 tablespoon toasted sesame seeds and ¼–½ teaspoon flaky salt. If using dried thyme, store the za'atar in an airtight container for a few weeks. If adding fresh thyme, use within 1–2 days.

gougère puff top

serves 6

For this savoury choux pastry, bring ¾ cup water and 100 grams butter to the boil. Stir in 1 cup flour and 1 teaspoon salt, remove from the heat and cool for 5 minutes. Beat in 4 eggs, one at a time, until the mixture is glossy, and stir in 1 cup grated Gruyère cheese. Place spoonfuls randomly over the top of a hot casserole in a pie dish and fan bake at 200 °C for 30–35 minutes until well risen, golden and the filling is hot.

thickening slow-cooked dishes

So the tomatoes were juicer than you had planned, or the extra wine in the bottom of the bottle went in to avoid waste and the resulting dish has too much sauce and needs thickening. There are many ways you can remedy the situation. I suggest that unless there is a swimming pool of liquid, 2–3 tablespoons flour will be sufficient for most dishes.

Flour and water paste

Mix standard white flour with sufficient water to make a smooth paste. It needs to be of pouring consistency to stir in easily to the hot sauce. Make sure there are no lumps as these will cook into white doughy lumps in the sauce. Use equal quantities of flour and water and stir slowly into the casserole. Cover and cook on high for about 30 minutes to thicken the sauce and to 'cook-out' the flour taste. The flour can also be mixed with wine or stock and can be added at the beginning or halfway through cooking time if wished.

Beurre manié

This is one of my favourite ways to thicken casseroles, sauces and soups. Work together twice the weight of soft butter to flour to make a smooth paste. Stir knobs into the hot casserole, cover and cook on high for 20–30 minutes to thicken the sauce and 'cook-out' the flour taste. The mixture melts its way into the casserole and the butter adds a velvety richness. Add beurre manié at the end of cooking time if thickening is required.

Cornflour and water paste

Mix equal quantities of cornflour and water together to make a smooth paste. Less cornflour is required to thicken sauces than wheat flour, though if cooked too long or reheated for too long, cornflour can break down and the sauce will lose its thickened quality. Stir into the casserole at the end of cooking time and cook on high for 30 minutes until thickened.

Rice flour and water paste

Make a thin paste with rice flour and water and stir in at the end of cooking time. It will behave similarly to cornflour (above), but gives people with gluten intolerance another option.

Egg yolk and cream liaison

Rich and delicious, this classic thickening method is particularly suited to thickening chicken casseroles or rich, creamy chicken or creamy vegetable-style soups. As a general rule, whisk together 2 egg yolks to ½ cup cream, stir evenly, add quickly into the hot sauce in the slow cooker and cook on low for about 15 minutes or until thickened. Do not allow to boil or you will have bits of scrambled egg throughout your lovely sauce.

Other thickening option

Add a little rolled oats, rice, red lentils or orzo pasta to the casserole at the beginning of cooking time – no more than 3–4 tablespoons – to help thicken an average-sized family casserole. Or try adding mashed potato or kumara – it's one way of adding vegetables to the family's meal!

Instant gravy powders

Easy to use, gravy powders come pre-flavoured to accompany chicken or red meats, and are often flavoured with herbs. They can be added at the beginning, stirred into the liquid ingredients to mix evenly, or at the end of cooking. If adding gravy powder at the end of cooking, mix with water or wine to a smooth paste and cook on high for an additional 30 minutes.

the slow-cook pantry

To make great-tasting meals easily in your slow cooker, keep a few 'great help' items in the pantry so you can throw a meal together in a jiffy. These are the things I keep on hand.

Garlic, ginger and chilli

Minced ready-to-go garlic, chilli and ginger are simply *fantastic*. Buy them in bottles, frozen pouches or tubes. If the garlic paste turns a deep yellow colour it has oxidised – throw it out and buy a new one.

Stock

Stock does make better-flavoured casseroles, soups, stews, braises or curries than just adding water. Stock cubes are just *fine*, though I find that if I use one cube or one teaspoon of stock powder per cup of water the stock is not as salty. Alternatively, buy the Tetra Pak-style products. Making your own is very therapeutic and worthy, but when time is of the essence, it's best to get some help.

Cook-in-style sauces

These are sold in jars, cans and pouches of around 500 grams in size, and they are *wonderful*. There's the tomato-based ones like bolognaise, or classic brown-sauce mixes like cottage-pie. Choose sauces that can be jazzed up with wine and herbs to create variety.

Curry pastes

Pre-made curry pastes allow us to cook internationally without ever having to leave home – *great stuff* – and there are so many to choose from. In a couple of spoonfuls you can go Indian, Thai, Malay, Indonesian, Sri Lankan and no doubt more. Pastes that are made with spices and herbs in an oil base will have a far better flavour than those mixed with water, so read the labels.

Canned tomatoes

These have become a pantry essential and they are *ideal* to add flavour and of course increase our vegetable intake. They come whole, diced, crushed, in purée, in juice and with plenty of flavour variants, like Indian, with pesto, etc. Keep your favourites on hand.

Soups

Canned condensed soups and dry packet mixes can form a *creative* basis to many dishes. Keep a selection that will mix and match with different meats.

Herbs

Keep dried on hand – they are easy to use and *benefit* from slow cooking where the flavours can be released. Fresh herbs add colour and flavour, so use when they are in season if you can.

Spices

Ground spices work just fine so long as they are not older than 12 months – after which time they lose much of their flavour. And don't forget spice blends, like garam masala – they are *power-packed* with flavour and can be added early or later in the cooking.

Bacon, salami and chorizo

The freezer is a store cupboard too and bacon, salami and chorizo-style sausages will add a touch of *panache* to many in-a-hurry casseroles. Have them pre-sliced or diced so you can add a handful at a time.

Frozen vegetables

These are *convenient* and a healthy way to add vegetables to our meals. A packet of simple frozen vegetables will help stretch a meal on a busy night, when you are in a hurry.

Instant gravy powders

Fantastically easy to use, gravy powder adds flavour and colour as well as thickening a dish. Keep a couple of flavour variants on hand.

meat cuts

To get the most delicious meal from your slow cooker, get to know the different cuts of meat and how they are best cooked. When buying meat to casserole or braise, picture the animal in your mind. The cuts from the forequarters and hindquarters – the parts of the animal that do the work – are the cuts to slow cook with. The cuts in the middle, primarily, are the cuts for fast cooking. Always ask the butcher what they have that might be nice as they will know what's out the back or what could be just right for the dish you plan to create.

cuts to pot-roast whole

Gently cooking a large cut of meat in the slow cooker is an economical way to enjoy a pot roast as you use cheaper cuts, and there'll be plenty of leftovers for sandwiches and salads the following days.

Key points are:

- Minimum-sized meat cut for the average-sized slow cooker I suggest is 1.5–2 kilograms. The cooking time ensures that if vegetables such as onions and potatoes are included in the recipe, they will be cooked when the meat is.
- Smaller-sized cuts of meat can be used for smaller households, though cooking time will be less and root vegetables will need to be cut into smaller pieces to cook until tender by the time the meat is cooked, or alternatively require cooking by another method first.
- Tie the meat at 2–3-centimetre intervals to ensure the meat keeps a good shape while cooking, and also to help make carving easier.
- Season the meat well before cooking.
- Browning the meat in a dash of oil in a heavy-based frying-pan will significantly enhance the colour and flavour of the finished dish. The meat will be brown and not a greyish colour when cooked, making it more appealing to the eye. The flavour is improved by the caramelising of the natural sugars in the meat and vegetables if being used.
- All large cuts of meat, regardless of the cooking style used, require standing time away from the source of the heat before carving, and slow-cooked meats are included in this. The rule of thumb is five minutes of resting time per 500 grams meat. Be assured the meat will not go cold on standing. Transfer to a warm plate or platter, cover and leave in a warm place – like the kitchen. Do not leave in a draft. If the meat has had

sufficient resting time, when carved it will be an even colour throughout, the juices will have been absorbed back into the meat fibres and won't flow all over the chopping board, and the meat will be meltingly tender, regardless of whether it is cooked rare or well-done.

Check with the butcher what he has at the time, but cuts that pot-roast to perfection are:

Beef
Thick flank (top rump); topside (trimmed of cap is best) and ask for the corner cut; sirloin; striploin; blade roll; bolar roast; fresh silverside; rump roast; whole chuck; Scotch fillet.

Lamb
Leg of lamb (short-cut leg of lamb is a better size for slow cookers); shoulder (boned and rolled or on the bone).

Pork
Shoulder (boned and rolled or on the bone); Scotch fillet; shoulder blade in the piece; rump; pork leg (usually a half leg as a full leg is too big to fit into most slow cookers).

Chicken, turkey
Whole (stuffed or unstuffed, boned and rolled with or without stuffing).

cuts to stuff, roll or stuff & roll

To create interest with large or cheaper cuts of meat, think about adding a stuffing. This can be a favourite bread stuffing, fruit and nuts, couscous, rice or even a prepared packet stuffing. Stuffings will add flavour, help the meat quantity stretch further and also help many cuts keep a good shape while cooking.

Key points are:

- Secure the stuffing inside the meat with string or toothpicks to prevent it from unrolling or falling open while cooking.
- If cooking a pocket pot roast, secure the opening with toothpicks or even sew up (my mum always had a spare darning needle in the kitchen and twine-like thread to sew up the pocket roast!).
- Browning is pretty much essential for colour and flavour, especially if there is a layer of fat on the outside. Meats like pork or lamb really do need browning.
- Allow the meat to rest to ensure that it is tender when carved and, more importantly, the stuffing doesn't fall out.
- If planning to serve the meat cold, season the stuffing well, as serving foods cold hides the flavour more than when served warm.

Check with the butcher what he has at the time, but some cuts to look out for that work well in a slow cooker include:

Beef
Brisket, well trimmed of excess fat; boned rib and paddle skirt. For a pocket roast, buy a topside or bolar pocket roast.

Lamb
Forequarter (boned); flap; leg of lamb (tunnel-boned).

Pork
Shoulder (boned); Scotch (trimmed only to eye or centre and then rolled in the skin and tied).

Chicken, turkey
Boned.

cuts to dice & casserole or braise

There are many beautiful cuts of meat to use in casseroling and braising, each with their own nuances, so it is certainly worth getting to know the way each of the cuts cook. You can easily vary the presentation of dishes depending on how you cut the meat.

Key points are:

- Have enough meat (and vegetables, etc.) to fill the slow cooker sufficiently, lest you arrive home to a very overcooked meal. This also means there are leftovers to freeze or have during the coming days.
- Cut the meat into good-sized pieces. I like the pieces to be 2.5 cm or larger to avoid overcooking and the meat becoming dry.
- Browning is recommended, though the choice is yours. Both the flavour and colour of the finished dish will benefit from browning the meat and vegetables.
- Casseroles can be mixed ready, refrigerated overnight and put on to cook the next day. If doing this, the ingredients will be cold from being refrigerated overnight, so extend the cooking times given in the recipes by about 2–3 hours on low and 1 hour on high.
- If the casserole or braise has been cooked on high, it would be wise to turn the heat off for around 15 minutes before serving, to allow the meat to rest. The meat will be more tender to eat.

Ideal cuts to simmer slowly for a meltingly tender result include:

Beef
Skirt; thick skirt; thick flank; chuck; mouse end (off the hind quarter); blade; cross-cut blade; oyster blade; bolar; oxtail; shin; good-quality gravy beef; tripe; kidneys.

Lamb
Round neck chops; best-end neck chops; shoulder chops; lamb necks (shoulder meat); shanks and knuckles; kidneys. Hogget – lamb aged between 15 and 30 months – is ideal for slow cooking.

Pork
Shoulder meat; pork knuckles; bacon bones, including bacon hocks; ham; ham bones.

Chicken, duck or turkey
Leg and thigh portions.

soup

- 3–4 medium-sized floury potatoes, peeled and chopped
- 1.5 kilograms pumpkin, peeled and chopped
- 1–2 onions, peeled and chopped
- 2 teaspoons minced garlic
- 6 cups water
- 1 tablespoon chicken stock powder
- 2 tablespoons cornflour
- 1 cup cream, crème fraîche or sour cream

classic pumpkin soup

makes about 8–9 cups
preparation time **30 minutes**
cooking time **low 5–6 hours, high 3–4 hours, plus extra 30 minutes**

For good pumpkin soup, choose a firm-textured pumpkin such as crown or buttercup. Each autumn, I make up pumpkin soup in large quantities and then add in toppings like prawns, basil or tomato pesto, smoked chicken and so on to vary the soup when I serve it. Pumpkin soup is loved by most people, so use this classic recipe to make your own bespoke versions.

Turn the slow cooker on to low to pre-warm while gathering and preparing the ingredients.

Into the slow cooker put the potatoes, pumpkin, onions, garlic, water and chicken stock powder. The water should cover the vegetables. Cover with the lid.

Cook on low for 5–6 hours or on high for 3–4 hours, or until the vegetables are tender.

Allow the soup to cool before carefully transferring to a food processor or blender and processing until smooth. Return to the slow cooker or a saucepan.

Mix the cornflour with the cream and stir into the soup. Cover with the lid and cook on high for 30 minutes or until the soup has thickened. If thickening in a saucepan on the stove, stir over a moderate heat for 4–5 minutes until thick and hot. Season with salt and pepper.

Serve in deep bowls with sour dough Parmesan croutons if wished.

sour dough Parmesan croutons

Cut a loaf of sour dough bread into chunky pieces and toss with plenty of olive oil or melted butter and finely grated Parmesan. Scatter one layer onto a baking paper-lined baking tray and bake at 200 °C for 15 minutes, or until golden and crispy.

variations

- **thai curry and coconut soup.** Add 2–3 tablespoons Thai red curry paste and 2 teaspoons minced ginger to the soup ingredients. Replace the cream with coconut cream and garnish with chopped coriander.
- **carrot, pumpkin and cumin soup.** Replace half the potato with carrots and add 2–3 teaspoons ground cumin with the vegetables. Use sour cream as the cream and decorate with a few toasted cumin seeds.

Continued on page 28

USHROOM

classic pumpkin soup *(continued)*

- **mussel and pumpkin chowder.** Add chopped cooked mussel meat to the finished soup and garnish with plenty of chopped parsley before serving.
- **pumpkin and pesto soup.** Omit the cream from the finished soup and stir in ½ cup basil pesto before serving garnished with sour cream and plenty of fresh basil leaves.
- **sweet potato and pumpkin.** Replace the pumpkin with orange-fleshed kumara.
- **pumpkin and vegetable chowder.** Before puréeing the soup, leave out a quarter of the pumpkin and potato pieces and cut into 1-cm chunks and set aside. Purée the remaining vegetables and return to the slow cooker with 1 cup frozen corn, 2 diced celery stalks, and 2–3 diced courgettes. Cover and cook for a further hour or until the vegetables are cooked. Stir in the reserved diced vegetables with the cream and season with herbs of your choice.
- **pumpkin, orange and tomato soup.** Replace three-quarters of the potatoes with juicy ripe tomatoes and purée when cooked. Stir in the grated rind and juice of 2 oranges.

blue cheese crostini

makes 16–18
preparation time **15 minutes**
cooking time **5–8 minutes**

150 grams blue-vein style cheese (or Stilton or Roquefort)
1 egg, separated
¼ cup cream
16–18 bread crostini

Preheat the oven to 200 °C fan grill.

Crumble the blue cheese into a bowl and then mash with a fork. Mix in the egg yolk and cream.

Whip the egg white in a small bowl until frothy and gently stir into the blue cheese mixture. Spread small spoonfuls on top of the crostini and fan grill in the preheated oven for 5–8 minutes until golden.

1 kilogram large mushrooms
2 medium-sized floury potatoes, peeled
8 shallots, peeled and sliced or 1 onion, peeled and sliced
1 teaspoon minced garlic
4 juniper berries, crushed
6 cups chicken, vegetable or light beef stock
1 cup port
1 cup cream or sour cream
1 tablespoon cornflour

mushroom & port soup

makes 10 cups
preparation time **10 minutes**
cooking time **low 5–6 hours, high 3–4 hours, plus extra 20–30 minutes**

Considering there's very little preparation involved in this recipe, it has an excellent flavour. In place of port, you can use pinot noir. Blue cheese is a classic partner with mushrooms, but rather than adding blue cheese to the soup, which can overheat and go stringy, make the crostini shown on the previous page.

Turn the slow cooker on to low to pre-warm while gathering and preparing the ingredients.

Chop the mushrooms and potatoes roughly and place into the pre-warmed slow cooker with the shallots or onion, garlic, juniper berries, stock and port. Stir to mix and cover with the lid.

Cook on low for 5–6 hours or on high for 3–4 hours, or until the vegetables are tender.

Purée the soup in a food processor or blender until smooth and return to the slow cooker.

Stir the cream or sour cream and cornflour together until smooth and stir into the soup. Cover with the lid and cook on high for a further 20–30 minutes or until the soup has thickened and is hot. Season with salt and pepper. Alternatively, return the soup to a saucepan to add the cream and cornflour and stir over a low heat only until thickened and hot. Do not boil.

Pictured on page 27

Serve with blue cheese crostini.

allyson's tips

- Oxtail imparts a magnificent beefy flavour, but as it is quite fatty, try and chill the finished soup overnight to easily lift off any excess fat. Reheat and serve.
- Cook poppadoms in the microwave to lower the fat level. Place 2–3 poppadoms in one layer and microwave for 45–60 seconds on high (100%) or until the poppadoms are cooked.

- 1 kilogram oxtail or meaty beef bones
- 2 onions, peeled and finely diced
- 2 carrots, peeled and finely diced
- 2 stalks celery, trimmed and finely diced
- 1 large eating apple, peeled, cored and finely diced
- 3 tablespoons flour
- 1–2 tablespoons curry powder
- ½ teaspoon ground pepper
- ¼ teaspoon ground mace or nutmeg
- ¼ teaspoon ground cloves
- ¼ cup tomato paste
- ¼ cup mango chutney
- 8 cups light beef stock or water
- ¼ cup short- or long-grain rice

mulligatawny

makes about 9–10 cups
preparation time without browning **30 minutes**
preparation time with browning **40 minutes**
cooking time **low 6–7 hours, high 3–5 hours, plus extra hour**

This is one of my favourite soups. It became popular during the time of the Raj. The name is Tamil in origin and literally translated means pepper water, though it is not a peppery hot soup, rather a rich, sweet curry-spiced beef soup.

Turn the slow cooker on to low to pre-warm while gathering and preparing the ingredients.

> ***If wishing to brown the ingredients:***
> *Heat a dash of oil or a knob of butter in a frying-pan and brown the beef oxtail or bones and onions very well.*

Into the pre-warmed slow cooker put the beef, onions, carrots, celery and apple.

Mix together the flour, curry powder, pepper, mace or nutmeg, cloves, tomato paste, mango chutney and beef stock or water to make a smooth mix. Pour over the beef and stir to mix the ingredients as well as possible. Cover with the lid.

Cook on low for 6–7 hours or on high for 3–5 hours.

Lift the beef bones from the slow cooker and when cool enough to handle pull the meat from the bones, discarding any fat. Return the meat to the slow cooker with the rice, cover and cook on high for a further hour.

I like to serve the mulligatawny in small bowls garnished with finely chopped tomato, red onion and coriander on top and a pile of poppadoms on the side if wished.

variation

- **chicken mulligatawny.** Use 2–4 chicken leg and thigh portions in place of the beef bones. Browning is optional.

allyson's tips

- Shallots are milder in flavour than onions, but if you do not have any, use peeled and finely chopped brown or red onion.
- Pick a plain sun-dried tomato paste without cheese. Alternatively, add ½ cup well-packed, sun-dried or semi-dried tomatoes, well drained of any oil.

- 1.5 kilograms large juicy tomatoes
- 6–8 shallots, peeled and sliced
- 1–2 stalks celery, trimmed and sliced
- 2 red capsicums, diced
- ¼ cup orzo pasta or rice
- ¼ cup sun-dried tomato paste
- 6 cups chicken stock
- 2 teaspoons sugar
- 1 cup loosely packed basil leaves

tuscan tomato soup

makes 12 cups
preparation time **30 minutes**
cooking time **low 5–6 hours, high 3–4 hours**

This simple tomato soup has a lovely fresh tomato flavour. Make it when juicy, sun-ripened beefsteak tomatoes are in plentiful supply and freeze to enjoy in winter when fresh tomatoes are more costly and have far less flavour.

Turn the slow cooker on to low to pre-warm while gathering and preparing the ingredients.

Cut a shallow cross just through the skin in the base of each tomato and cut out the core at the top. This will help the skin to split open and make peeling easier when blanched.

Blanch the tomatoes in boiling water for 1 minute and then plunge into cold water to arrest the cooking. Peel away the skin and cut the tomatoes into large chunks.

Put the tomatoes into the pre-warmed slow cooker with the shallots, celery, capsicums, orzo pasta or rice, tomato paste, chicken stock and sugar. Stir to mix as evenly as possible and cover with the lid.

Cook on low for 5–6 hours or on high for 3–4 hours, or until the tomatoes and shallots are soft.

Add the basil leaves and purée in a food processor, blender or mouli. Return to the slow cooker or a saucepan and season well with salt and pepper.

I like to serve this with crispy slices of grilled bacon or pancetta, a few basil leaves and a sprinkling of grated Parmesan.

- 3–4 large waxy potatoes, peeled and diced
- 200 grams pumpkin, peeled and diced
- 1 large onion, peeled and diced
- 2–4 rashers rindless bacon, finely chopped
- 3 teaspoons minced garlic
- ¼ cup short-grain rice
- 2 x 400-gram cans diced tomatoes in juice
- 8 cups chicken stock
- 310-gram can cannellini beans
- 200 grams green beans, sliced
- 2 courgettes, trimmed and diced

minestrone

makes 10–12 cups
preparation time **20 minutes**
cooking time **low 5–6 hours, high 3–4 hours, plus extra 30 minutes**

There are many versions of this traditional Italian winter vegetable and bean soup, though I also like it in late summer and early autumn so I can pile on lashings of freshly made basil pesto.

Turn the slow cooker on to low to pre-warm while gathering and preparing the ingredients.

Into the slow cooker put the potatoes, pumpkin, onion, bacon, garlic, rice and tomatoes. Stir in the stock – there should be enough liquid to just cover all the vegetables. Cover with the lid.

Cook on low for 5–6 hours or on high for about 3–4 hours, or until the vegetables are almost tender.

Drain the cannellini beans, rinse under cold running water and drain well. Add to the soup with the green beans and courgettes. Cover with the lid and cook a further 30 minutes on high or until the green beans are tender. Season if wished.

Serve the minestrone in large bowls. If wished, garnish with a generous spoonful of basil pesto or basil leaves.

variations

- Use carrots in place of pumpkin.
- Use 1 kilogram chopped fresh blanched tomatoes rather than canned tomatoes.
- Use flavoured canned tomatoes such as Italian-seasoned or tomatoes flavoured with garlic or basil.
- Use pancetta in place of bacon and try borlotti beans in place of cannellini beans.
- For a richer flavour, stir in 1 cup sun-dried tomato pesto – one without too much Parmesan.
- Stir in ¼ cup extra virgin olive oil before serving to add a gentle olive flavour and smooth texture to the soup.

- 1 kilogram Jerusalem artichokes
- ½ cup olive oil, virgin olive oil is nice here
- 1 onion, peeled and chopped
- 2 stalks celery, chopped
- 2 teaspoons minced garlic
- 1½ tablespoons chopped fresh sage
- 1 tablespoon chopped fresh thyme
- 5 cups good-flavoured chicken stock
- 1 cup cream

creamy artichoke soup

serves 8
preparation time **20 minutes**
cooking time **low 4–6 hours, high 3–4 hours, plus extra 20–30 minutes**

I first enjoyed this sensational soup created by chefs Al Brown and Steve Logan some years ago and it is truly delicious. If you have never been game enough to try this knobbly vegetable, then here's your chance. Originally, for this soup the Jerusalem artichokes were roasted, adding a caramelised sweet flavour, so be sure to brown them well – without burning them in the olive oil.

Turn the slow cooker on to low to pre-warm while gathering and preparing the ingredients.

Peel the artichokes and brown them in half the olive oil in a heavy-based frying-pan over a moderately high heat. Transfer them to the pre-warmed slow cooker.

Add the onion and celery to the frying-pan with the remaining oil and cook over a moderate heat for 8–10 minutes or until tender. Add the garlic and cook for one extra minute, being careful not to burn the garlic.

Add the vegetables and any olive oil to the slow cooker with the sage and thyme, pour in the chicken stock and cover with the lid.

Cook on low for 4–6 hours or on high for 3–4 hours, or until the artichokes are tender.

Purée the soup in a food processor, blender or mouli and return to the slow cooker. Stir in the cream, cover with the lid and cook for 20–30 minutes on high until hot. Season with salt and pepper before serving.

Serve drizzled with olive oil and garnished with fresh herbs.

- 1 onion, peeled and finely diced
- 50 grams butter
- 4 lemon grass stalks
- 1 leek, white part only, finely sliced
- 500 grams floury potatoes, peeled and diced
- 4 cups water
- 3–4 teaspoons chicken stock powder
- 1 cup milk
- ½ cup crème fraîche or sour cream
- 2 tablespoons finely chopped fresh chives

potato & lemon grass soup

serves 6–8
preparation time **20 minutes**
cooking time **low 5–6 hours, high 3–4 hours, plus extra 30 minutes**

Potatoes are so rarely thought of as a vegetable to make into soup, but good-flavoured floury potatoes make a tasty soup. Vichyssoise is a classic potato and leek soup, created by a French chef in the early 1900s – served chilled, it is garnished simply with chives. The trick here is to cook the onion until soft in the frying-pan before piling into the slow cooker as it will not cook to be tender otherwise. The addition of lemon grass adds a sweet, refreshing flavour and the soup can be served hot or cold.

Turn the slow cooker on to low to pre-warm while gathering and preparing the ingredients.

Cook the onion in the butter in a frying-pan over a moderate heat for about 12–15 minutes, stirring occasionally until the onion is soft. Try not to brown the onion.

Hit the lemon grass stalks with a mallet or the handle base of a cook's knife to bruise them. This allows the flavours to come through during cooking.

Into the pre-warmed slow cooker put the onion and butter from the pan with the lemon grass stalks, leek, potatoes, water and chicken stock powder and stir as well as possible to mix the ingredients evenly. Cover with the lid.

Cook on low for 5–6 hours or on high for 3–4 hours, or until the potato is tender.

Remove the lemon grass stalks and purée the ingredients in a food processor or with a blender until smooth. Return to the slow cooker with the milk, crème fraîche or sour cream and chives and cover with the lid.

Cook on high for 30 minutes before serving hot with a drizzle of olive oil (lemon-scented is nice here) and a few extra chives. Alternatively, allow the soup to chill and serve cold.

- 2 large leeks, trimmed
- 1.5–1.6-kilogram whole chicken
- 1 onion, peeled and sliced
- 1 bouquet garni, optional
- 10 cups water or light chicken stock
- 1 cup chopped prunes
- ¼ cup Madeira, port or sweet sherry
- 1 cup chopped celery leaves
- ¼ cup chopped fresh thyme

cock-a-leekie soup

serves 8–10
preparation time **20 minutes**
cooking time **low 5–6 hours or high 3–4 hours**

In the days of cock fighting the fugie or loser was made into a cock-a-leekie, which might seem a rather inglorious end to a hard life, but such a scrawny and tough bird added enormous amounts of flavour to this soup, though little meat I should imagine. The soup should be so thick with well-cooked leeks that it looks more like a stew than a soup. Some purists are against the prunes, but I like the sweetness they and the Madeira bring. And for a wee bit more Scottish tradition, serve freshly baked oat scones on the side.

Turn the slow cooker on to low to pre-warm while gathering and preparing the ingredients.

Cut the leeks in half lengthwise and wash under running water to remove any grit caught in the layers. Slice finely.

Rinse the chicken well and place into the slow cooker. Scatter the leeks and onion around the chicken and sit the bouquet garni, if using, on top. Pour in the water or chicken stock and season well with salt and pepper. Cover with the lid.

Cook on low for 5–6 hours or on high for 3–4 hours, or until the chicken is tender.

While the chicken is cooking, soak the prunes in the Madeira, port or sweet sherry.

Carefully remove the chicken from the slow cooker and, when cool enough to handle, pull the meat from the chicken, discarding the bones and skin.

Tear the chicken into small pieces and return to the slow cooker with the prunes and Madeira, port or sweet sherry, celery leaves and thyme, and season with salt and pepper.

Serve the cock-a-leekie in deep bowls with richly buttered, warm oat scones (page 40).

allyson's tips

- Celery leaves are full of flavour, so don't throw them away as they can add great flavour to soups, salads and sauces.
- Madeira is a fortified sweet wine that was first made on the Portuguese island of Madeira in the north Atlantic. It is a delicious wine to use in both sweet and savoury foods where dried fruits like prunes or raisins are also included.

cock-a-leekie soup with oat scones
(page 40)

2½ cups self-raising flour
½ teaspoon salt
½ cup oat bran, Scotch or rolled oats
50 grams butter, diced
1¼ cups milk

oat scones

makes 16
preparation time **10 minutes**
cooking time **10–12 minutes**

Preheat the oven to 220 °C. Place the oven rack in the upper half of the oven but not right at the top. Lightly grease a baking tray or line with baking paper.

Sift the self-raising flour and salt into a mixing bowl. Stir in the oat bran or oats.

Use your fingertips to rub in the butter until the mixture resembles breadcrumbs.

Make a well in the centre of this mixture and stir in the milk, using a knife to form a soft dough.

Turn out onto a lightly floured bench, knead gently and pat out until 2-cm thick. Cut the dough into 16 squares or rounds and place on the prepared tray. Brush with milk to glaze.

Bake in the preheated oven for 10–12 minutes or until the scones are well-risen and a dusty golden colour.

Transfer to a cake rack, cover loosely with a clean tea towel and stand for 2–3 minutes before serving warm with butter.

Pictured on previous page

1 cup finely grated Edam, Gruyère or Colby-style cheese
1 egg, beaten
2 tablespoons packet onion soup mix
4 sheets pre-rolled frozen flaky puff pastry, defrosted

onion 'n' cheese pastry straws

makes about 40
preparation time **10 minutes**
cooking time **12–15 minutes**

Onion soup mix is a pantry cupboard staple, if not for the ubiquitous reduced cream dip, then to jazz up a casserole. It is also perfect to include in these simple-to-make cheese straws. They are great to serve with soup or have as part of a nibble platter.

Preheat the oven to 200 °C. Lightly grease 1–2 baking trays or line with baking paper.

Mix the cheese, egg and onion soup mix together. Spread half of the mixture over one sheet of pastry and top with a second sheet. Roll firmly once or twice with a lightly floured rolling pin to join the layers together.

Use a wetted knife to cut into long 0.5–1-cm-wide strips. Twist the strips and place on the prepared trays. Press the ends of the strips to the trays or baking paper to prevent the strips from unravelling when baking. Repeat with the remaining ingredients.

Bake in the preheated oven for 12–15 minutes or until the straws are lightly golden and cooked. Transfer to a cake rack to cool, and store in an airtight container.

2 cups self-raising flour
½ teaspoon salt
50 grams butter, chilled and diced
100 grams Gruyère cheese, finely diced
1 tablespoon finely chopped fresh rosemary
¾–1 cup milk
beaten egg or milk, to glaze
extra grated cheese, optional

rosemary & gruyère scones

makes 10–12
preparation time **10 minutes**
cooking time **10–12 minutes**

Preheat the oven to 230 °C. Grease a baking tray or line with baking paper. Place the oven rack towards the top of the oven.

Sift the flour and salt into a large bowl. Use your fingers to rub the butter into the dry ingredients until it looks like crumbs. Stir in the cheese and rosemary and make a well in the centre.

Pour in ¾ cup milk and mix quickly with a knife to make a soft dough, adding the remaining milk if required. Turn the dough out onto a lightly floured bench and knead very lightly. Roll out or press out to 2-cm thickness.

Cut into 4-cm rounds or squares and place on the prepared tray. Brush with beaten egg or milk to glaze and sprinkle with a little extra grated cheese if wished.

Bake in the preheated oven for 10–12 minutes until well risen, golden and cooked.

Transfer to a cake rack. Cover the scones with a clean tea towel for a few minutes (this will soften the crust of the scones a little) and serve warm.

allyson's tips

- 500 grams split peas equals 2½ cups.
- For good flavour, you require a 1-kilogram ham bone.

pea & ham soup with Gruyère cheese scones (page 41)

- 500 grams green or yellow split peas, rinsed and drained well
- 1 large ham bone
- 2 onions, peeled and chopped
- 2 stalks celery, washed and sliced
- 2 potatoes, peeled and diced
- 8 cups water or light chicken or vegetable stock
- 2 bay leaves or 1 bouquet garni
- 1 tablespoon chopped fresh rosemary or sage

pea & ham soup

serves 8–10
preparation time **10 minutes**
cooking time **low 7–9 hours, high 4–5 hours**

This classic soup is ideal to cook in a slow cooker.

Turn the slow cooker on to low to pre-warm while preparing the ingredients.

Scatter the split peas into the slow cooker. Add the ham bone, onions, celery, potatoes, water or stock, bay leaves or bouquet garni and stir to mix the ingredients.

Cover and cook on low for 7–9 hours or on high for 4–5 hours.

Carefully remove the ham bone, cover and set aside until cool. Pull away and discard any thick skin. Pull the meat off the bone and shred or chop. Remove the bay leaves or bouquet garni.

Using a potato masher, mash the soup ingredients to make a chunky soup. Stir in the shredded ham and season with the rosemary or sage, and salt and pepper to taste.

Serve hot, accompanied with rosemary and Gruyère cheese scones (page 41) if wished.

variations

- Use 2–3 bacon bones in place of the ham bone or a mix of both.
- If using bacon bones, serve the soup in bowls, sprinkled with crispy cooked and diced bacon.
- Add ½–1 cup cream before serving.

- 2 red onions, peeled and finely chopped
- 2 teaspoons minced garlic
- 7-cm piece ginger, peeled and finely shredded or 1½ tablespoons minced ginger
- 2 teaspoons ground turmeric
- 2 tablespoons curry powder
- 1.5 kilograms juicy, ripe tomatoes
- 1 cup red lentils
- 3 teaspoons vegetable or chicken stock powder
- 6 cups water

curried fresh tomato & lentil soup

serves 8–10
preparation time **20 minutes**
cooking time **low 5–6 hours, high 3–4 hours**

Choose juicy, ripe tomatoes to make this stunning-tasting, Indian curry-inspired soup.

Turn the slow cooker on to low to pre-warm while gathering and preparing the ingredients.

Heat a good dash of oil in a frying-pan and cook the onions for about 10 minutes or until they begin to soften. Add the garlic, ginger, turmeric and curry powder and cook for a further 2–3 minutes or until fragrant.

Transfer to the pre-warmed slow cooker.

Cut a small shallow cross, just through the skin, in the base of the tomatoes and cut out the core in the top. Blanch the tomatoes in boiling water for 1 minute and then plunge into cold water. Peel away the skin.

Chop the tomatoes roughly and add to the slow cooker with the lentils, vegetable or chicken stock powder and water. Stir to mix evenly and cover with a lid.

Cook on low for 5–6 hours or on high for 3–4 hours, or until the lentils are tender.

Serve in wide bowls garnished with lime wedges to squeeze into the soup, chopped fresh coriander to sprinkle in, and piles of crisp poppadoms if wished.

Front: curried fresh tomato & lentil soup
Rear: parsnip soup with feta crostini
(page 46)

- 750 grams parsnips, peeled and roughly chopped
- 1 large floury potato, peeled and roughly chopped
- 1 onion, peeled and finely chopped
- 4 rashers lean rindless bacon, finely chopped
- 1 teaspoon minced garlic
- 6 cups chicken stock
- 6 sun-dried tomato halves in oil, well drained
- ½ cup cream or sour cream, optional

garnish

- 4 rashers rindless bacon, finely diced
- 4 sun-dried tomato halves in oil, well drained
- ¼ cup walnuts, chopped, optional
- 2 tablespoons chopped fresh parsley

parsnip soup

serves 8–10
preparation time **15 minutes**
cooking time **low 5–6 hours, high 3–4 hours**

Parsnips are sweet and tasty and, cooked up with sun-dried tomatoes, bacon and onion, they make a fabulous winter soup.

Turn the slow cooker on to low to pre-warm while preparing the ingredients.

Into the slow cooker put the parsnips, potato, onion, bacon, garlic, stock and sun-dried tomatoes and stir to mix evenly. Cover with the lid.

Cook on low for 5–6 hours or on high for 3–4 hours or until the parsnips are tender. Cooking time will vary considerably with the age of the parsnips – older parsnips are much woodier and will take longer to cook.

Purée the soup in a food processor or blender or through a mouli until smooth. Return to the slow cooker and stir in the cream or sour cream if using. Season with salt and pepper.

For the garnish, cook the bacon in a dash of oil until crispy and brown. Drain on absorbent paper. Finely dice the sun-dried tomatoes and toss with the bacon, walnuts if using and parsley.

Serve the soup sprinkled with a little of the garnish and accompanied with feta crostini.

- ½ French stick or 1 small ciabatta loaf
- ¼ cup olive oil or 100 grams butter, melted
- 100–150 grams feta, crumbled

feta crostini

serves 8–10
preparation time **5 minutes**
cooking time **7–10 minutes**

Preheat the oven to 180 °C fan grill.

Cut the bread into 1-cm-wide slices. Brush both sides with oil or melted butter.

Place on a baking tray and fan grill for 7–10 minutes or until the feta begins to soften a little. If wished, add a few parsley sprigs and/or diced sun-dried tomatoes on top and season with pepper.

- 2–3 chicken leg and thigh portions, skin removed
- 2 onions, peeled and finely diced
- 2 large carrots, peeled and finely diced
- 3 stalks celery, trimmed and finely diced
- 1 waxy potato, peeled and finely diced, optional
- ½ cup split green peas or yellow peas
- ½ cup pearl barley
- 1 tablespoon chicken stock powder
- 1 bouquet garni, optional
- 10 cups water
- 1 cup frozen peas and corn mix
- 1 cup loosely packed, chopped fresh parsley

family chicken & vegetable soup

serves 10
preparation time **20 minutes**
cooking time **low 5–6 hours, high 3–4 hours, plus extra 30 minutes**

A winter stand-by. I've used leg and thigh portions as getting hold of chicken carcasses is far too hard these days, and it is nice to have some meat to pull off the bones and return to the soup too.

Turn the slow cooker on to low to pre-warm while gathering and preparing the ingredients.

Place the chicken into the pre-warmed slow cooker. Add the onions, carrots, celery, potato if using, split peas, barley, chicken stock powder and bouquet garni if using.

Pour in the water – there should be sufficient water to just cover the chicken and vegetables. Cover with the lid.

Cook on low for 5–6 hours or on high for 3–4 hours, or until the chicken is cooked.

Carefully remove the chicken pieces and, when cool enough to handle, pull the meat off the bones, tear into bite-sized pieces and return to the soup.

Add the frozen peas and corn to the soup, cover with the lid and cook on high for a further 30 minutes to cook the frozen vegetables and ensure the soup is hot.

Stir in the parsley and season with salt and pepper. Remove the bouquet garni before serving.

Serve in deep bowls with the onion 'n' cheese pastry straws (page 41).

variations

- Add 1 cup minced or finely diced ham with the peas and corn.
- Replace the potato, split peas, barley and stock powder with a purchased packet of soup pre-mix. They come pre-flavoured for minestrone, pea and ham, chicken and corn and more. Look for them in the supermarket, near where packet soups are sold.
- For a bacon flavour, add 2–3 bacon bones when cooking.
- Replace the parsley with ¼ cup chopped fresh thyme.
- Mix 2 tablespoons of cornflour with 1 cup cream until smooth and stir into the soup with the frozen peas and corn for a cream-style version. Cover and cook on high for 30 minutes before serving.

beef

allyson's tips

- Double the recipe and freeze half for another time. Add additional cooking time – 2 hours on low or 1 hour on high.
- For mushrooms, use whole button mushrooms or chunkily diced flat mushrooms.
- If you do not have pickling onions, use 2 large onions, peeled and diced.

750 grams lean beef for casseroling
8–10 pickling-size onions, peeled
2–4 rashers bacon, trimmed of rind
125 grams mushrooms
1–2 teaspoons minced garlic
1 bouquet garni, optional
¼ cup tomato paste
2 tablespoons flour
2½ cups beef stock or water

family beef potato-topped casserole

serves 5–6
preparation time without browning **20 minutes**
preparation time with browning **30 minutes**
cooking time **low 6–7 hours, high 3–4 hours**

A classic basic that can be easily altered to make your own version, with your family's favourite flavours.

Turn the slow cooker on to low to pre-warm while gathering and preparing the ingredients.

Cut the beef into 3-cm pieces. Halve the pickling onions if large and dice the bacon.

> ***If wishing to brown the ingredients:***
> *Brown the beef and pickling onions well in a dash of oil in a hot frying-pan.*

Put the beef, onions, bacon, mushrooms, garlic and bouquet garni if using into the pre-warmed slow cooker.

Mix together the tomato paste, flour and stock or water to make a smooth paste. Pour into the beef and vegetables and stir to mix. Season well with salt and pepper. Cover with the lid.

Cook on low for 6–7 hours or on high for 3–4 hours, or until the beef and onions are tender. Serve as is, or under a mashed potato top (see page 17) and accompany with seasonal vegetables.

variations

- Replace beef with lamb or hogget.
- Use wine in place of stock.
- Add a 400-gram can of chopped tomatoes.
- Add 1–2 teaspoons Vegemite for a great flavour.
- Replace 1 cup of stock or water with a 400-gram can condensed tomato soup.
- Add 2 cups frozen mixed vegetables once cooked. Cover and allow a further 30 minutes' cooking time on high to cook the vegetables and bring the casserole back up to temperature.
- Add 1 x 32-gram packet French onion soup mix for extra flavour. Stir into the liquid ingredients.

1.5-kilogram piece corned beef
1 onion, quartered
1 orange, quartered
½ teaspoon whole cloves
2 tablespoons golden syrup

family corned beef

serves 8–10
preparation time **10 minutes**
cooking time **low 7–9 hours, high 4–6 hours**

Turn the slow cooker on to low to pre-warm while gathering and preparing the ingredients.

If the corned beef is encased in plastic wrap, undo and rinse to remove any excess brine.

Place the corned beef into the pre-warmed slow cooker and scatter the onion, orange and cloves around the corned beef.

Pour the golden syrup on top and then add sufficient tap cold water to cover the beef. Cover with the lid.

Cook on low for 7–9 hours or on high for 4–6 hours, or until tender.

Remove the corned beef from the liquid and place on a warm plate. Cover and leave to rest for 10 minutes before carving and serving with either mustard sauce or white sauce with parsley, (both opposite). If planning to serve the corned beef cold, turn the slow cooker off and leave it to cool for 2–3 hours in the cooking liquid before removing and refrigerating.

1 teaspoon minced ginger
50 grams butter
4 tablespoons flour
2 cups chicken stock
2 tablespoons prepared mustard
1–2 teaspoons brown sugar

mustard sauce

serves 8–10
preparation time **5 minutes**
cooking time **10 minutes**

Gently pan-fry the ginger in the butter in a heavy-based saucepan for 2–3 minutes. Stir in the flour and cook for 1–2 minutes or until frothy. Gradually add the chicken stock, stirring continuously until the sauce thickens. Add the mustard and brown sugar and season with salt and pepper before serving.

50 grams butter
¼ cup flour
2 cups milk
2 tablespoons grated or very finely chopped onion
3–4 tablespoons chopped fresh parsley

white sauce with parsley

serves 8–10
preparation time **10 minutes**
cooking time **10 minutes**

Melt the butter in a heavy-based saucepan and add the flour. Cook for 1–2 minutes over a moderate heat, stirring regularly to prevent burning. It is at this stage that you must cook the flour to burst the starch grains so that the sauce will not end up with a raw flour taste.

Remove from the heat and gradually stir in the milk to make a thin, smooth sauce. Return to the heat, add the onion and stir over a low heat until the sauce has thickened. Simmer for 2–3 minutes, stirring regularly. Add the parsley and season with salt and white pepper.

- 1.5–2-kilogram piece of corned beef with a good fat layer
- 1 onion, peeled and halved
- 2 carrots, washed and chopped
- 1 bay leaf
- 1 tablespoon whole cloves
- ½ cup brown sugar
- 1 teaspoon mustard powder
- 1 teaspoon ground cinnamon
- ½ teaspoon ground allspice
- juice of one lemon

spiced sugar-glazed corned beef

serves 10–12
preparation time **10 minutes**
cooking time **7–9 hours**
resting time **2–3 hours**
roasting time **1 hour**

This corned beef requires double cooking. First it is gently simmered in a flavoursome stock and then richly glazed and baked to tender perfection. For the finest result, make sure you leave the beef to cool in the liquid before roasting.

Turn the slow cooker on to low to pre-warm while gathering and preparing the ingredients.

Put the corned beef into the pre-warmed slow cooker. Scatter the onion, carrots and bay leaf around the meat. Add sufficient cold water to cover the beef. Cover with the lid.

Cook on low for 7–9 hours (it is not recommended to cook this on high).

Turn off and leave the corned beef to cool in the liquid for 2–3 hours. At this stage the corned beef can be well-wrapped and refrigerated overnight.

Preheat the oven to 180 °C. Line a deep-sided baking tray with foil.

Place the meat on the prepared tray. Stud the beef with the whole cloves. Mix the brown sugar, mustard powder, cinnamon and allspice together with the lemon juice and spread half of mixture over the beef.

Bake in the preheated oven for 1 hour, basting with the remaining glaze occasionally.

Serve with your favourite vegetables. The mustard sauce on the previous page is an ideal accompaniment to this dish. Keep leftovers well wrapped and use in sandwiches or salads.

allyson's tip

- The cut of meat photographed is called the silverside. It is a lean fillet portion with an even covering of fat, ideal for this recipe.

allyson's tip

- A little sherry adds a unique flavour to this down-to-earth casserole. You can vary the finished flavour of the dish by using a dry, medium-dry or sweet sherry. Sherry should not bc considered Grandmother's tipple, as the authentic drop from Jerez on the south-west coast of Spain is truly a delectable fine wine. Have a glass well-chilled to accompany this stew if having with friends.

750 grams lean beef for casseroling
750 grams waxy potatoes, peeled if wished
1 large onion, peeled and roughly chopped
2 large juicy tomatoes, diced, optional
½–1 cup stuffed green olives, halved
2–3 teaspoons minced garlic
400-gram can diced tomatoes in juice or Mexican-style tomatoes
1½ cups beef stock or water
¼ cup sherry
2 tablespoons paprika
¼ cup chopped fresh parsley

spanish beef & potato stew

serves 6
preparation time without browning **15 minutes**
preparation time with browning **25 minutes**
cooking time **low 6–7 hours, high 3–4 hours**

B

Serve warm crusty bread with this gutsy-flavoured stew to mop up the juices.

Turn the slow cooker on to low to pre-warm while gathering and preparing the ingredients.

Cut the beef and potatoes into 2-cm dice.

If wishing to brown the ingredients:
Brown the beef and onion well in a dash of oil in a hot frying-pan. This will be best done in 2–3 batches.

Into the pre-warmed slow cooker put the beef, potatoes, onion, fresh tomatoes, olives and garlic.

In a jug, stir together the canned tomatoes, stock or water, sherry and paprika. Pour into the slow cooker, stir to mix and cover with the lid.

Cook on low for 6–7 hours or on high for 3–4 hours without lifting the lid. Once the cooking time is finished, check the beef for tenderness and continue to cook if required. Season well with salt and pepper.

Season the stew scattered with a little parsley and extra olives if wished.

variations
- Use pork in place of beef.
- Use smoked paprika for an earthy flavour.
- Add 2 teaspoons dried oregano when cooking.
- Add 2 sliced and pan-fried chorizo sausages to the beef when cooking.
- Add ¼–½ teaspoon saffron threads for a very authentic Spanish taste.

1 kilogram lean beef for casseroling
2–3 onions, peeled and diced
4 rashers rindless bacon, diced
12–18 prunes
1 tablespoon minced garlic
pared rind one large orange
about 4 sprigs fresh thyme or ¼ teaspoon dried thyme
¼ cup flour
2 cups Guinness
2 cups beef stock

beef & guinness casserole

serves 6–8
preparation time without browning **15 minutes**
preparation time with browning **25 minutes**
cooking time **low 7–8 hours, high 4–5 hours**

B

Including the pared rind of one orange in this classic dish adds a hint of sweetness under the rich, warm flavours of the Guinness.

Turn the slow cooker on to low to pre-warm while gathering and preparing the ingredients.

Cut the beef into 2–3-cm pieces.

If wishing to brown the ingredients:
Brown the beef, onions and bacon well in a dash of oil in a hot frying-pan. This will be best done in several batches to avoid the ingredients stewing rather than browning.

Into the pre-warmed slow cooker put the beef, onions, bacon, prunes, garlic, orange rind and thyme.

Mix together the flour, Guinness and stock to form a smooth mix and pour over the beef. Stir to mix well and cover with the lid.

Cook on low for 7–8 hours or on high for 4–5 hours. Season well with salt and pepper. Serve with seasonal vegetables.

500 grams lean beef mince
½ cup raw or uncooked long-grain rice
¼ cup chopped fresh herbs (parsley, chives, oregano, marjoram, etc.)
1 large onion, peeled and finely diced
1 large carrot, peeled and finely diced
1 x 550-gram can or jar of your favourite cook-in-style sauce
1½ cups beef stock or water

porcupine meatballs

serves 5–6
preparation time **20 minutes**
cooking time **low 6–7 hours, high 3–4 hours**

Family food with ease. Adding the rice to the meatballs will bulk them out as well as adding carbohydrates. For parents, add in a little basil pesto when serving.

Turn the slow cooker on to low to pre-warm while gathering and preparing the ingredients.

Mix together the mince, rice and herbs with a good seasoning of salt and pepper. Take dessertspoonfuls of mixture and roll firmly into balls and set aside.

Into the pre-warmed slow cooker put the onion and carrot.

Mix together the cook-in-style sauce and beef stock or water and pour into the slow cooker. Stir to mix evenly with the vegetables.

Sit the porcupine balls on top and cover with the lid.

Cook on low for 6–7 hours or on high for 3–4 hours. Serve with your favourite vegetables.

variations

- Use lamb or pork mince in place of beef.
- Use half-cooked brown rice in place of raw white rice.
- Add or vary the vegetables with whatever is to hand – celery, parsnip, yams and mushrooms all go well here.

6 dried bay leaves
¾ cup coarse or flaky salt
1 teaspoon whole allspice
1 teaspoon ground mace or nutmeg
½–1 teaspoon ground cloves
1 teaspoon ground white pepper
¼ –½ teaspoon dried thyme
1.75-kilogram brisket in one piece, unrolled
50 grams butter
1 onion, peeled and finely chopped
330-millilitre bottle dark beer

salted spiced brisket

serves 10
preparation time without browning **10 minutes**
preparation time with browning **20 minutes**
marinating time **overnight**
cooking time **low 7–9 hours, high 3–5 hours**

Salted rolled brisket is a cut that was very popular some years ago, though it has fallen out of favour today as it is thought to be too fatty. But ask for lean brisket and take the time to salt the meat for 24 hours ahead of cooking it for a tasty cold cut of meat for the summer months.

Crush half the bay leaves and set the remaining half aside.

Mix together the crushed bay leaves, salt, allspice, mace or nutmeg, cloves, white pepper and thyme in a very large bowl.

Turn the brisket over in the salt mixture, rubbing the mix into the meat well.

Cover with plastic wrap and leave in a cool place, away from warmth and direct sunlight for 24 hours, turning two or three times if possible.

Turn the slow cooker on to low to pre-warm while preparing the rest of the recipe.

Remove the beef from the mix, which will now be quite wet – the salt draws the moisture out of the meat. Rinse quickly to remove excess salt and pat dry on a paper towel. Roll the meat up firmly and secure with string.

If wishing to brown the meat:
Heat a good dash of oil in a large frying-pan and brown the beef on all sides as well as possible. Do not leave the brisket too long in one place in the frying-pan as it is apt to burn from the salt and spices.

Heat the butter in a frying-pan or saucepan and cook the onion over a moderate heat for 5–6 minutes until it begins to soften. Add the remaining bay leaves and the beer and simmer until reduced by half.

Pour into the pre-warmed slow cooker and sit the beef in the middle. Cover with the lid.

Cook on low for 7–9 hours or on high for 3–5 hours or until the beef is well-done. Remove the beef from the slow cooker and place in a deep bowl. Cover with a lid or a couple of layers of foil and place a moderately heavy weight in the middle. This will press the meat, making it a lovely firm texture which can be sliced thinly later. Once cool, refrigerate overnight.

Serve thinly sliced with salads or in sandwiches.

- 750 grams lean beef for casseroling
- 1 medium-sized eggplant
- 1 red capsicum, diced
- 1 onion, peeled and diced
- ¼ cup pitted black olives, chopped
- ¼ cup sun-dried tomatoes, chopped
- 2–3 teaspoons minced garlic
- 1 tablespoon capers
- 1 tablespoon chopped fresh oregano
- ¼ cup tomato paste
- 2 tablespoons flour
- 1½ cups beef stock
- ¼ cup red wine

tuscan beef casserole

serves 5–6
preparation time without browning **15–20 minutes**
preparation time with browning **25–30 minutes**
cooking time **low 6–8 hours, high 3–5 hours**

This Tuscan-inspired casserole is enjoyable as is or nestled under a rich Parmesan pastry pie top. To make the pies, allow the beef mixture to cool well before putting it into a large pie dish or individual dishes. Particularly tasty on a winter's night accompanied with a gutsy red wine.

Turn the slow cooker on to low to pre-warm while gathering and preparing the ingredients.

Cut the beef into 2–3-cm pieces and the eggplant into 1-cm dice. There is no need to peel it.

> ***If wishing to brown the ingredients:***
> *Brown the meat, eggplant, capsicum and onion in a dash of oil in a hot frying-pan. This is best done in batches.*

Into the pre-warmed slow cooker put the meat, eggplant, capsicum, onion, olives, sun-dried tomatoes, garlic, capers and oregano.

In a jug, mix together the tomato paste, flour, stock and wine to make a smooth mix. Pour into the slow cooker and stir to mix all the ingredients evenly together and cover with the lid.

Cook on low for 6–8 hours or on high for 3–5 hours.

Serve with seasonal vegetables or create into pies using the rich Parmesan pastry (see page 64).

tuscan beef pie

- 1 x quantity of Tuscan beef casserole (see page 63)
- 1 x quantity of rich Parmesan pastry
- beaten egg or milk to glaze

serves 5–6
preparation time **15 minutes**
cooking time **20–25 minutes**

Preheat the oven to 200 °C. Place the oven rack just above the centre.

Transfer the Tuscan beef casserole to a large 6-cup capacity pie dish or 5–6 individual pie dishes.

Roll the dough out to 3-mm thickness. Cut sufficient 1-cm-wide strips of pastry to run around the edge of the pie dish or dishes.

Brush the edges with water – this ensures the pastry strips stay in place. Press the pastry strips on.

Roll the remaining pastry over the pie and press firmly onto the pastry edge. Trim the edges and use the trimming to cut out decorations for the pie top if wished.

For individual pies, divide the pastry evenly into 5–6 portions before rolling each out to cover the pie dishes.

Brush with beaten egg or milk for a golden top.

Bake in the preheated oven for 20–25 minutes or until the pastry is golden and cooked and the filling is hot. Serve with your favourite winter vegetables.

rich parmesan pastry

- 2 cups flour
- ½ teaspoon salt
- 200 grams butter, chilled and diced
- ½ cup finely grated Parmesan
- 1 egg yolk
- 3–4 tablespoons chilled water

makes 450 grams
preparation time **10 minutes**

Sift the flour and salt into a bowl. Use your fingertips to rub in the butter until the mixture resembles coarse crumbs. Stir through the cheese and make a well in the centre.

Mix the egg with 3 tablespoons of the water and pour into the well. Use a knife to cut the ingredients together, adding the extra water if required.

Turn out onto a floured bench, knead lightly to bring together. Wrap and refrigerate until required.

food processor method

✤ Pulse the flour, salt and butter together until the mixture resembles crumbs. Pulse in the egg yolk and water until the mixture forms small, moist beads of dough. Turn out onto a floured bench, bring together, knead lightly and refrigerate before use.

allyson's tips

rich Parmesan pastry

- In place of Parmesan, use pecorino or an aged Gouda.

allyson's tips

- If time permits, chill the cooked braise overnight to allow excess fat to rise to the top and be easily lifted off. Reheat to serve. If reheating in the slow cooker, allow about 1½ hours on high.
- Basic seasoned flour is prepared from plain flour with a seasoning of salt, pepper and dry mustard. A ¼ teaspoon ground cloves in the seasoned flour would go well with oxtail.

- about 2 kilograms meaty oxtail, cut into joints and trimmed
- about ½ cup seasoned flour
- 2–3 tablespoons oil
- 2 carrots, peeled and sliced
- 2 large onions, peeled and chopped
- ¼–½ cup raisins or currants
- 4 teaspoons minced garlic
- 2 bay leaves, crushed
- 1 tablespoon chopped fresh thyme or ½ teaspoon dried thyme
- 1 teaspoon celery salt or celery seeds
- 2 cups red wine
- 1 cup port
- 2 tablespoons tomato paste
- 1 tablespoon balsamic vinegar

braised oxtail

serves 6–8
preparation time without browning **30 minutes**
preparation time with browning **40 minutes**
cooking time **low 7–8 hours, high 4–6 hours**

B

Oxtail does involve more work to cook than most other cuts, mainly because it is best to refrigerate the casserole overnight to allow the fat to set on top. This can then be lifted off. I like this richly flavoured oxtail recipe served under a fluffy-baked puff pastry pie topping (see over the page) with roasted parsnips.

Turn the slow cooker on to low to pre-warm while gathering and preparing the ingredients.

Toss the oxtails in the seasoned flour, shaking off the excess.

If wishing to brown the ingredients:
Heat a good dash of oil in a large heavy-based frying-pan and, when hot, brown the oxtail pieces well. Do this in batches to prevent the oxtail from stewing. The browner the oxtail, the more flavoursome the finished dish. Set aside.

Brown the carrots and onions in any remaining oil. Add an extra dash of oil if required.

Into the pre-warmed slow cooker put the oxtail, carrots, onions, raisins or currants, garlic, bay leaves, thyme and celery salt or seeds.

In a jug stir together the red wine, port, tomato paste and balsamic vinegar. Pour into the slow cooker and stir as well as possible to mix the ingredients. Cover with the lid.

Cook on low for 7–8 hours or on high for 4–6 hours.

Use a flat wide spoon to lift the fat off the top of the braise.

Serve the oxtail with your favourite vegetables. Alternatively, pull the meat from the bones and return to the casserole to serve.

1 x quantity of braised oxtail (see page 67), cold
400-gram block frozen flaky puff pastry, defrosted
beaten egg or milk to glaze

braised oxtail pie

serves 6–8
preparation time **20 minutes**
cooking time **25 minutes**

Have the oxtail braise made and cold.

Pull the meat from the bones and return to the braise. Transfer the mixture to an 8-cup capacity pie dish.

Push a pie funnel into the centre of the pie dish.

On a lightly floured board, roll the pastry out to 3-mm thickness.

Cut a 1–1.5-cm-wide strip long enough to be placed onto the edge of the pie dish. Brush the edge with water and press the strip firmly onto the edge. Brush the pastry strip with beaten egg or milk to glaze.

Roll the larger piece of pastry over the top and press firmly on to the pastry strip. Trim the edge and press firmly together, without squashing the edges as this will prevent the pastry from rising. Any leftover pieces can be used to decorate the pie if wished.

Brush the pie with beaten egg or milk to glaze, being careful not to brush the edges of the pastry as this glues the layers of the pastry somewhat and the pastry will not rise as well when baking.

Chill the pie for 30 minutes while preheating the oven to 220 °C fan bake. Place the oven rack just above the centre.

Bake the pie in the preheated oven for 20–25 minutes until the pastry is well risen and golden and the pie is bubbling hot.

Serve hot with your favourite vegetables.

1 kilogram lean beef for casseroling
2 rindless rashers bacon, finely sliced
1 onion, peeled and finely diced
2 stalks celery, diced
2 carrots, peeled and finely diced
250 grams button mushrooms, sliced
1 teaspoon minced garlic
535-gram can of your favourite cook-in-style sauce
2 cups beef stock

dumplings
1¼ cups self-raising flour
1 tablespoon butter
1–2 teaspoons chopped fresh thyme, optional
½ cup milk

beef with dumplings

serves 6
preparation time without browning **20 minutes**
preparation time with browning **30 minutes**
cooking time **low 6–7 hours plus 1 hour on high, high 4 hours**

Dumplings are incredibly popular in my home, be they sweet or savoury. The kids love them cooked with the gravy – they think of them as a treat, yet they are so easy. The first dumplings were probably prepared from bread dough and often they replaced the meat altogether for many poor people. Today, with self-raising flour, they're quick, easy to make and make a bright, breezy change to a family casserole.

Turn the slow cooker on to low to pre-warm while gathering and preparing the ingredients.

Cut the beef into 2–3-cm sized pieces.

If wishing to brown the ingredients:
Heat a dash of oil in a frying-pan and, when hot, brown the beef well. This will be best done in batches to prevent the meat from stewing. Set aside. Brown the bacon and onion if wished.

Into the pre-warmed slow cooker put the beef, bacon, onion, celery, carrots and mushrooms.

In a jug, stir together the garlic, cook-in-style sauce and stock. Pour into the slow cooker and stir as well as possible to mix. Cover with the lid.

Cook on low for 6–7 hours or on high for 3 hours.

Add the dumplings, cover with the lid and continue cooking for a further hour on high. If possible, turn the dumplings halfway through the cooking time.

Serve the casserole with dumplings and seasonal green vegetables.

dumplings
Sift the flour into a bowl and rub in the butter until well mixed. Stir in the thyme if using. Make a well in the centre and pour in the milk, stirring to make a moist scone-like dough.

Divide evenly into 12 pieces and, with floured hands, roll each into a ball.

variations
- Make the dumplings with half of the flour being wholemeal self-raising flour.
- Vary the herb used in the dumplings.
- Add ½ cup grated Cheddar-style cheese.

allyson's tips

- Mexican chilli powder seasoning is a blend of paprika, cumin, garlic, chilli and more. If you do not have any to hand, but have plain chilli powder, use only 1–1½ teaspoons chilli powder.
- Use chuck steak, cut into small 1-cm cubes or less, in place of the mince.

- 1½ cups dried kidney beans
- 750 grams lean, coarsely minced beef
- 2 onions, peeled and finely diced
- 1 tablespoon minced garlic
- 400-gram can diced tomatoes in juice
- 150 grams mushrooms, diced
- 1½ tablespoons paprika
- 1 tablespoon Mexican chilli powder seasoning
- 1 teaspoon ground cumin
- 2 cups beef stock or water

avocado cream

- 2 avocados
- 125-gram tub sour cream
- 2 tablespoons chopped fresh coriander
- 2 teaspoons ground coriander
- 1 teaspoon ground cumin

mexican beef 'n' beans

serves 10–12
soaking time **overnight**
preparation time without browning **30 minutes**
preparation time with browning **40 minutes**
cooking time **low 6–7 hours, high 3–4 hours**

Tacos are great family food. Making the filling in a slow cooker means you can use plenty of dried beans. Pre-soaked kidney beans, though, must be boiled rapidly for 20 minutes before putting into the slow cooker.

Cover the kidney beans with water. Allow 3–4 times the amount of water to beans and leave overnight or for at least 12 hours.

Drain well. Place the beans into a large saucepan and cover with fresh water. Bring to the boil and boil rapidly, uncovered, for 20 minutes. Drain well. (At this stage, the beans can be refrigerated in an airtight container for 1–2 days).

Turn the slow cooker on to low to pre-warm while gathering and preparing the remaining ingredients.

> ***If wishing to brown the ingredients:***
> *Brown the mince and onions well in a dash of oil in a hot frying-pan. This will be best done in 2–3 batches to avoid the meat from stewing. Set aside.*

Into the pre-warmed slow cooker put the kidney beans, mince, onions, garlic, tomatoes, mushrooms, paprika, Mexican chilli powder seasoning, cumin and stock or water. Stir well and cover.

Cook on low for 6–7 hours or on high for 3–4 hours, or until the beans are tender.

Season with salt and pepper and serve with rice or in tacos, or as nachos with the avocado cream to accompany.

avocado cream

Halve, stone and peel the avocados. Place the pulp in a bowl with the sour cream and mash with a fork or potato masher to make a smooth or chunky cream – the texture is up to you. Season with the cumin and salt and the fresh and ground coriander to taste.

variations

- Vary the beans and adjust cooking time to suit, larger beans will take longer and may require more beef stock or water.
- Use Mexican-flavoured tomatoes.
- Add 2 tablespoons chopped Jalapeño peppers. These are sold bottled in brine, or occasionally you will find them fresh around February/March.

1.5 kilograms lean beef for casseroling
2 onions, peeled and finely sliced
500 grams button mushrooms, finely sliced
8–10 gherkins, finely sliced
1 tablespoon flour
1½ cups beef stock
½ cup brandy
250-gram tub sour cream
1 tablespoon prepared mustard

beef stroganoff

serves 8–10
preparation time without browning **20 minutes**
preparation time with browning **30 minutes**
cooking time **low 7–8 hours, high 3–4 hours**

A classic beef stroganoff is prepared from the tail-end of the beef fillet. It's quickly cooked, with a generous knob of butter, flambéd with brandy and finished with sour cream. This slow-cooker version combines all the classic ingredients but simmers slowly, producing a rich-flavoured dish. I always add shredded gherkins for a touch of piquancy.

Turn the slow cooker on to low to pre-warm while gathering and preparing the ingredients.

Cut the beef into thin strips or slices. Season with pepper.

If wishing to brown the ingredients:
Heat a good knob of butter in a large frying-pan and brown the meat well over a moderately high heat. This will be best done in batches. Add more butter if required. Set the beef aside and cook the onion until lightly brown.

Into the slow cooker put the beef, onions, mushrooms and gherkins.

Mix together the flour, stock and brandy and pour into the slow cooker. Stir to mix as well as possible and cover with the lid.

Cook on low for 7–8 hours or on high for 3–4 hours.

Stir in the sour cream and mustard and season with salt and pepper. Serve the stroganoff over pasta or beside mashed potato and your favourite vegetables.

variation

- Use boneless chicken thigh portions in place of beef. Be sure to brown the chicken for best flavour.

- 2 kilograms pre-cut beef steak and kidney mix
- 2–3 large onions, peeled and diced
- 250–500 grams mushrooms, sliced
- ½ cup beef-flavoured gravy powder
- 3 cups mild-flavoured beef stock or water
- ½–1 teaspoon ground black pepper

steak & kidney casserole

serves 8–10
preparation time without browning **15 minutes**
preparation time with browning **30 minutes**
cooking time **low 6–7 hours, high 3–4 hours**

This recipe can be halved, as it will feed a mountain of people, but I find it easier to make up more than a basic family quantity as you can freeze the leftovers for use at a later date.

Turn the slow cooker on to low to pre-warm while gathering and preparing the ingredients.

> ***If wishing to brown the ingredients:***
> *Heat a good dash of oil in a frying-pan and brown the beef steak and kidney mix over a high heat. Do this in small batches to prevent the beef and kidneys from stewing. Set aside. Add extra oil to the pan and cook the onions until golden. Stir 1 cup of stock or water into the pan and scrape all the sediment off the base of the pan as this will add heaps of flavour.*

Into the pre-warmed slow cooker put the beef and kidneys, onions, mushrooms, gravy powder, stock or water and pepper. Stir to mix and cover with the lid.

Cook on low for 6–7 hours or on high for 3–4 hours, or until the beef is tender.

Serve as a cobbler, under a savoury scone topping (as pictured), as a pie under a flaky puff pastry case, as cottage pie-style, under a mashed potato crust or simply as is with vegetables and plenty of mashed potatoes to mop up the gravy with.

variations

- Add ¼–½ cup tomato paste.
- Use 2 cups red wine and 1 cup beef stock.
- Use 1½ cups beer and 1½ cups beef stock.
- Stir in a dozen oysters, shelled of course, just before serving to have a taste of the past, when oysters were so cheap they were put in meat dishes to stretch the meat!
- Add 1 tablespoon of curry powder and ¼ cup Worcestershire sauce for a twist.

1 x quantity of steak and kidney casserole (see page 74)
2 cups self-raising flour
2 teaspoons dry mustard powder
50 grams butter, diced
¼ cup chopped fresh herbs like sage, parsley and thyme
¾ cup milk

steak & kidney cobbler

serves 8–10
preparation time **20 minutes**
cooking time **15–20 minutes**

A quick and easy twist on a pie.

Preheat the oven to 220 °C.

Turn the steak and kidney casserole into a large ovenproof dish, reheating if necessary until piping hot. This can be done in the microwave or oven.

Sift the flour and mustard powder into a bowl. Use your fingertips to rub in the butter until the mixture looks like crumbs. Stir through the herbs and make a well in the centre.

Pour in the milk and stir quickly with a knife to make a soft dough. Turn out on a lightly floured surface and knead lightly. Press out with floured hands to about 1.5–2-cm thickness.

Cut into rounds or squares and place the pieces on top of the piping hot steak and kidney casserole, preferably around the edges. Brush with milk to glaze if wished.

Bake in the preheated oven for about 15–20 minutes or until the scones are cooked. Serve piping hot.

variations

- Sprinkle the scones with a little grated cheese before baking.
- Use half wholemeal flour – make sure it is self-raising wholemeal flour or, if not, add 2 teaspoons baking powder per cup of wholemeal flour.

- 1.5 kilograms beef for casseroling, in one piece
- 8–10 long rashers streaky bacon
- 2 onions, peeled and finely sliced
- 2 tablespoons flour
- 2 cups beef stock
- ¼ cup whisky
- 1 tablespoon prepared mustard, Dijon is nice here
- 1 teaspoon minced garlic
- ½ cup cream or sour cream

highland beef & bacon braise

serves 6
preparation time without browning **30 minutes**
preparation time with browning **40 minutes**
cooking time **low 6–8 hours, high 3–5 hours**

A touch of the angels' drink – whisky – adds warmth to this simple beef dish.

Turn the slow cooker on to low to pre-warm while gathering and preparing the ingredients.

Cut the beef into 3-cm-size chunks. Use the back edge of a heavy knife such as a cook's knife to stretch the bacon rashers a little. This will keep them thin and easy to wrap around the beef pieces.

Cut each rasher in half crosswise and wrap one piece around a cube of beef. Secure with a toothpick. Repeat with remaining ingredients.

If wishing to brown the ingredients:
Heat a dash of oil or a knob of butter in a large heavy-based frying-pan and brown the bacon-wrapped beef pieces in the hot pan. Turn carefully to avoid the bacon from sticking to the bottom of the pan. Cook the onions until lightly browned if wished.

Into the pre-warmed slow cooker put the beef and onions.

Mix together the flour, stock, whisky, mustard and garlic to make a smooth mix and pour over the beef. Stir to mix the ingredients as evenly as possible. Cover with the lid.

Cook on low for 6–8 hours or on high for 3–5 hours.

Stir in the cream or sour cream and season with pepper before serving with your favourite vegetables.

variation

- Use Madeira or brandy in place of whisky.

allyson's tip

- Cooking a pot roast to perfection may seem daunting and while meat cooked on low in a slow cooker takes a long time to 'overcook', using a thermometer will take any worry away. See page 9 for temperatures for beef, lamb and pork.

- 2-kilogram piece of beef for pot roasting (see pages 21–22)
- 2 onions, peeled and quartered or 8 small pickling-size onions, peeled
- 2 carrots, peeled and halved crosswise
- 2–3 stalks celery, chopped roughly
- 1 apple, cored and thickly sliced
- 1 bouquet garni
- 2 cups beef stock
- 1 tablespoon cornflour

country beef pot roast

serves 8–10
preparation time without browning **20 minutes**
preparation time with browning **30 minutes**
cooking time **low 6–7 hours, high 4–5 hours**

A simple pot roast, ideal for weekday meals.

Turn the slow cooker on to low to pre-warm while gathering and preparing the ingredients.

A large piece of meat is best tied to keep shape. Using string, tie the meat securely in several places.

> ***If wishing to brown the ingredients:***
> *Heat a good dash of oil in a large frying-pan and, when hot, brown the beef well on all sides. Browning the meat will give the finished pot roast a good colour as well as adding flavour. Brown the onions, carrots and celery if wished.*

Into the pre-warmed slow cooker put the beef, vegetables, apple and bouquet garni, and pour in the stock. Season well with salt and pepper and cover with the lid.

Cook on low for 6–7 hours or on high for 4–5 hours, or until the meat is cooked.

Carefully lift the meat from the slow cooker, place on a warm plate, cover and rest for 20 minutes before carving and while making the gravy.

Mix the cornflour with a little water to make a smooth paste. Stir into the slow cooker, cover and cook a further 20–30 minutes until thickened.

The beef will rest during this time, making carving easier and it also ensures the meat will be juicy when carved.

Serve the beef thinly sliced with the vegetables and gravy.

allyson's tip

- Use an instant gravy powder that goes well with beef.

1 kilogram lean beef mince
1–2 onions, peeled and finely diced
1–2 teaspoons minced garlic
¼ cup instant gravy powder
1 cup water or red wine
½ cup tomato paste
2 x 400-gram cans diced tomatoes in juice
1 teaspoon dried thyme
1 teaspoon dried oregano

bolognaise mince

serves 8–10
preparation time without browning **20 minutes**
preparation time with browning **40 minutes**
cooking time **low 4–5 hours, high 2–3 hours**

I like to prepare a good-sized quantity of this mince to have on hand in the freezer for those mid-week meals. A basic recipe can so easily be varied too, just jazz it up to suit your family.

Turn the slow cooker on to low to pre-warm while gathering and preparing the ingredients.

> ***If wishing to brown the ingredients:***
> *Heat a dash of oil in a frying-pan and brown the mince well in batches, breaking up with the back of a spoon as it browns. Add a dash more oil to the frying-pan and cook the onion for 10 minutes over a moderate heat until browned and softened. Add the garlic and cook a further minute.*

Into the pre-warmed slow cooker put the mince, onion and garlic.

In a jug, mix together the instant gravy powder to a smooth paste with the water or red wine, before adding the tomato paste, tomatoes, thyme and oregano.

Stir into the beef mince and cover with the lid.

Cook on low for 4–5 hours or on high for 2–3 hours. Season with salt and pepper before serving.

Serve tossed through spaghetti or use as the base for a pie or mixed with pasta and turned into a favourite pasta bake.

Any leftover mince will freeze well in an airtight container. Use within 6 months.

variations

- Use flavoured canned tomatoes.
- Add 3–4 finely diced and crispy cooked rashers of bacon.
- Add 100 grams of shredded salami.
- Add more garlic, or stir in the pulp of one roasted garlic bulb at the end of cooking time.

½ x quantity of Bolognaise mince (see page 81)
2–3 cups cooked pasta shapes
2–4 courgettes, trimmed and thinly sliced
2–3 large tomatoes, thinly sliced
1 cup grated Cheddar-style cheese

pasta bake

serves 4–6
preparation time **15 minutes**
cooking time **35–40 minutes**

Preheat the oven to 180 °C.

Mix the Bolognaise mince with pasta shapes and pile into an ovenproof dish. Pan-fry the courgette slices on each side in a knob of butter until golden. Place on top of the mince and then cover with the tomato slices. Scatter over the cheese.

Bake in the preheated oven for 35–40 minutes until the cheese has melted and the dish is piping hot.

variations

- Stir in ½–1 cup roughly torn basil leaves.
- Stir in ½ cup sliced black olives.
- Add ½ cup halved stuffed olives.
- Add 4–5 finely sliced anchovy fillets.
- Stir in 100–200 grams tomato or red capsicum pesto.
- Add chopped sun-dried or semi-dried tomatoes or red capsicums.

- 250–350 grams mushrooms, finely diced
- 1 teaspoon minced garlic
- 1 cup prepared stuffing mix
- 1 egg
- 1.75-kilogram piece of beef topside
- 1 cup beef stock
- 1 cup red wine
- ½ teaspoon dried sage
- 4 carrots, peeled and thickly sliced
- 8 baby onions, peeled and halved
- ¼ cup instant gravy powder
- Worcestershire sauce, optional

pocket topside pot roast

serves 8–10
preparation time **20 minutes**
cooking time **low 6–7 hours, high 3–4 hours**

Topside is a lean piece of meat that the butcher would traditionally cut a pocket in. Stuffing could then be tucked into the pocket to add flavour.

Turn the slow cooker on to low to pre-warm while gathering and preparing the ingredients.

Cook mushrooms in a knob of butter in a hot frying-pan until well-softened and all the juices have evaporated. Add the garlic and cook for one minute only.

Transfer the mushrooms to a bowl and stir in the stuffing mix and egg. Mix well.

Place one hand flat on top of the topside to ensure the meat does not move. Using a long, thin-bladed knife, make a deep cut into the meat on one side to make a pocket. If you can, turn the pointed end of the knife wider inside the topside so that the cut is wider inside than on the outside face. This allows more space for stuffing on the inside and helps prevent the stuffing falling out.

Fill the pocket with the stuffing. Secure the front with skewers or toothpicks.

Place the beef into the pre-warmed slow cooker. Pour over the stock and wine. Season with dried sage and salt and pepper if wished. Put the carrots and onions around the meat and cover with the lid.

Cook on low for 6–7 hours or on high for 3–4 hours, or until the meat is tender.

Carefully lift the beef from the slow cooker to a warm plate, cover and leave to rest for 20 minutes before carving.

Mix the gravy powder with sufficient water to make a thick smooth paste. Stir into the slow cooker, cover and cook on high for 20–25 minutes or until the sauce has thickened. Alternatively, thicken the juices in a saucepan.

Season with a dash of Worcestershire sauce if using, and salt and pepper.

Serve the beef finely carved across the grain – this way the beef is far more tender to eat – with carrots, onions, mashed potatoes and your favourite greens.

1–1.5 kilograms lean beef for casseroling
1 teaspoon each salt and ground black pepper
2–3 tablespoons oil
2 onions, peeled and diced
2 teaspoons minced garlic
3 tablespoons Massaman curry paste
2 medium orange-fleshed kumara, peeled and diced
400-gram can coconut milk
1½ cups beef stock
1–1½ cups frozen peas
2 tablespoons chopped fresh coriander

thai beef & sweet potato curry

serves 6
preparation time without browning **20 minutes**
preparation time with browning **25 minutes**
cooking time **low 5–6 hours, high 3–4 hours, plus extra 15–20 minutes**

Where Thailand borders Malaysia, there is a blending of cuisines. This recipe is redolent of the curries there.

Turn the slow cooker on to low to pre-warm while gathering and preparing the ingredients.

Cut the beef into 2–2.5-cm pieces and season with salt and pepper.

If wishing to brown the ingredients:
Heat a dash of oil in a large frying-pan and cook the onions and garlic over a medium heat for 4–5 minutes until tender and lightly browned. Set aside.

Heat a further dash of oil in the frying-pan and brown the meat quickly over a high heat. This may be best done in 2–3 batches. With the last batch of meat, add the curry paste and cook until fragrant.

Into the slow cooker put the beef and curry paste, onions, garlic, kumara, coconut milk and stock and cover with the lid.

Cook on low for 5–6 hours or on high for 3–4 hours. Stir in the peas and coriander, re-cover and continue cooking on high for a further 15–20 minutes.

Serve in bowls garnished with shredded coconut and chopped tomatoes. Accompany with steamed rice and prawn crackers.

variations
- Use pork or boneless chicken leg and thigh portions in place of beef.
- Use potato or pumpkin in place of kumara.
- Add 3–4 bruised lemon grass stalks or 2–3 kaffir lime leaves to add a sweet lemon and lime note, particularly nice with pork.

allyson's tip

- Massaman curry paste has a rich flavour that comes from a blend of ingredients including chilli, cinnamon, nutmeg, white pepper, cardamom, lemon grass, galangal and of course chillies and garlic. It's available at specialty Asian food shops. Alternatively, use Penang or Thai red or green curry paste.

allyson's tips

- Do not try to add sausages to a very hot pan as this causes sausages to burst.
- Do not prick sausages before cooking as this causes the juice and thus the flavour to run away.

- 8–10 thick beef sausages
- 2 onions, peeled and sliced
- 2–3 carrots, peeled and sliced
- 1 teaspoon minced garlic
- ½ cup gravy powder
- 3 cups water
- ¼ cup orange juice
- ¼ cup redcurrant jelly
- 1 tablespoon Worcestershire sauce

cumberland sausages

serves 6–8
preparation time without browning **10 minutes**
preparation time with browning **20 minutes**
cooking time **low 5–7 hours, high 3–4 hours**

B

Orange juice, redcurrant jelly and Worcestershire sauce are essential ingredients in a Cumberland sauce. It was one of Queen Victoria's most preferred sauces and it's particularly nice with a good beef sausage.

Turn the slow cooker on to low to pre-warm while gathering and preparing the ingredients.

If wishing to brown the ingredients:
Place the sausages into a moderately low heated frying-pan and brown evenly. Set aside. Add the onions and carrots to the pan, with a dash of oil if required, and cook for 4–5 minutes over a moderately high heat until lightly browned. Add the garlic and cook a further minute.

Into the pre-warmed slow cooker put the sausages, onions, carrots and garlic.

Stir together the gravy powder, water, orange juice, redcurrant jelly and Worcestershire sauce to make a smooth sauce. Pour over the sausages and cover with the lid.

Cook on low for 5–7 hours or on high for 3–4 hours.

Serve the sausages with your favourite vegetables.

variations

- Use thick pork or venison sausages.
- Use port jelly in place of redcurrant jelly.
- Add 1–2 teaspoons prepared mustard with the sauce ingredients.

8–10 thick beef sausages
2 capsicums, thickly sliced
3 stalks celery, thickly sliced
3 apples, peeled and thickly sliced
1 onion, peeled and thinly sliced
1 cup sultanas
432-gram can pineapple chunks in juice
½–¾ cup of your favourite Indian curry paste
2 cups water

curried sausages

serves 4–6
preparation time without browning **15 minutes**
preparation time with browning **20 minutes**
cooking time **low 6–7 hours, high 3–4 hours**

A quick no-fuss recipe that makes good use of pre-made curry pastes. Use your favourite.

Turn the slow cooker on to low to pre-warm while gathering and preparing the ingredients.

If wishing to brown the ingredients:
Brown the sausages in a frying-pan over a moderate to low heat until well browned on all sides.

Into the pre-warmed slow cooker put the sausages. Scatter over the capsicums, celery, apples, onion and sultanas.

Mix together the pineapple chunks with the juice, curry paste and water and pour over the sausages and vegetables. Stir to mix as evenly as possible and cover with the lid.

Cook on low for 6–7 hours or on high for 3–4 hours.

Serve with mashed potatoes or rice and garnish with cashew nuts if wished.

variations
- Use canned peach slices in juice in place of the pineapple.
- Add 2–3 tablespoons chopped fresh coriander before serving.

- 1½ cups lima beans
- 50 grams butter
- 1.5-kilogram piece beef brisket
- 1 onion, peeled and chopped
- 2–3 cloves garlic, crushed, peeled and sliced
- ½ cup pearl barley
- 4–5 medium-sized waxy potatoes, peeled and chopped
- 2 carrots, peeled and thickly sliced
- 1 turnip or small swede, peeled and diced, optional
- 1 bay leaf, crushed
- 2 tablespoons flour
- 1 teaspoon paprika
- ½ teaspoon ground black pepper
- ½ teaspoon ginger
- ¼ teaspoon ground cinnamon
- 5 cups water or beef stock

cholent

serves 8
soaking time **overnight**
preparation time without browning **30 minutes**
preparation time with browning **40 minutes**
cooking time **low 9–10 hours, high 5–6 hours**

Cholent is a classic Jewish dish developed as a response to religious requirements and eaten since around the Middle Ages. A slow cooker is ideal for cooking cholent.

Soak the lima beans in plenty of water overnight. Allow 3–4 times the amount of water to beans.

Turn the slow cooker on to low to pre-warm while preparing the ingredients.

> ***If wishing to brown the ingredients:***
> *Heat the butter in a heavy based frying-pan and brown the brisket well on all sides. Set aside. Add the onion and stir over a moderate heat until well softened. Add the garlic to the pan and cook for an extra minute or two.*

Drain the beans well and scatter into the base of the pre-warmed slow cooker. Add the pearl barley, onion and garlic and sit the beef on top.

Add the potatoes, carrots, turnip or swede if using and bay leaf.

Mix together the flour, paprika, pepper, ginger, cinnamon and water or stock and pour over the ingredients in the slow cooker. The liquid needs to cover the beef and vegetables. Cover with the lid.

Cook on low for 9–10 hours or on high for 5–6 hours.

To serve, lift the meat from the slow cooker. Slice and arrange on a platter.

Use a slotted spoon to place the vegetables, beans and barley over the meat. Pour over a little of the cooking juices and garnish the whole dish with chopped parsley if wished. Serve the remaining juice on the side.

- 1 kilogram lean beef for casseroling
- 1½ teaspoons ground turmeric
- 1½ teaspoons ground coriander
- 1 teaspoon ground cumin
- ½ teaspoon chilli powder
- 1 tablespoon minced ginger
- 1 teaspoon minced garlic
- ¼ cup oil
- 4 large waxy potatoes, peeled and cut into large pieces
- 3 red onions, peeled and thickly sliced
- 3 cups beef stock or water
- 1 bay leaf, optional
- 1 cup dried plump apricots
- 1 teaspoon garam masala

bengali beef & onions

serves 6–8
marinating time **overnight**
preparation time without browning **15 minutes**
preparation time with browning **30 minutes**
cooking time **low 6–7 hours, high 3–4 hours**

An adaptation from one of my favourite food writers, Madhur Jaffrey. Her books on regional Indian cookery are my favourite travel guides whenever I visit this colourful and exotic country. This dish should have plenty of thin flavoursome sauce, perfect for mopping up with warm naan bread.

Cut the beef into large, chunky 4-cm-sized pieces and place in a lidded container.

Sprinkle over the turmeric, coriander, cumin, chilli powder, ginger and garlic and pour over the oil. Rub well to coat the beef with the spice mix, cover and refrigerate overnight to marinate the beef.

Turn the slow cooker on to low to pre-warm while gathering and preparing the remaining ingredients.

> ***If wishing to brown the ingredients:***
> *Heat a dash of oil in a large frying-pan and brown the beef well in batches, adding more oil if necessary. The beef and spices will have soaked up the oil used in the marinade, so more oil will be required.*

Place the beef into the pre-warmed slow cooker and scatter over the potatoes and onions.

Pour in the stock or water and add the bay leaf if using. Cover with the lid.

Cook on low for 6–7 hours or on high for 3–4 hours, until the meat and vegetables are tender.

Add the apricots and garam masala and season with salt and pepper and a pinch of sugar before serving.

variations

- Add large chunks of peeled apple or pears to add a little sweetness.
- Use curry powder in place of the spices. It will be less authentic in flavour, but will still taste great.
- Vary the vegetables, using kumara or parsnips to replace the potatoes.
- Add 2–3 ripe chunky diced juicy tomatoes about 30 minutes before serving.

allyson's tips

- For a sweeter-style garam masala, delicious with this dish, grind 1 cinnamon stick, 12 whole cardamoms and 10–12 whole cloves together in a mortar and pestle or mini food mill. Alternatively, use ground spices.
- Use the plump Turkish apricots here, as they are less acidic in flavour.

- 1 kilogram lean beef for casseroling
- 2 rashers rindless bacon
- 1 onion, peeled
- 4 stalks celery, trimmed
- ½ cup currants or chopped prunes
- 3 tablespoons flour
- 330-millilitre bottle dark beer
- 1 cup beef stock
- ½ teaspoon ground nutmeg or mace
- grated rind and juice of one orange
- 300-gram (approximately) bottle or can whole peeled chestnuts

beef with chestnuts & currants

serves 6–8
preparation time without browning **20 minutes**
preparation time with browning **30 minutes**
cooking time **low 5–7 hours, high 3–4 hours, plus extra 15 minutes**

Chestnuts are increasingly more available here. Their season is late autumn to winter, but canned chestnuts are a good alternative and easier to use. Their inclusion in this casserole adds a delightful texture and taste.

Turn the slow cooker on to low to pre-warm while gathering and preparing the ingredients.

Cut the meat into chunky 3-cm-sized pieces. Slice the bacon, onion and celery thickly.

If wishing to brown the ingredients:
Heat a dash of oil in a frying-pan and, when hot, brown the beef, bacon, onion and celery well. This will be best done in batches.

Into the pre-warmed slow cooker put the beef, bacon, onion, celery and currants or chopped prunes.

In a jug, mix together the flour, beer, stock, nutmeg or mace and orange rind and juice to make a smooth sauce. Pour over the beef and stir to mix evenly. Cover with the lid.

Cook on low for 5–7 hours or on high for 3–4 hours, or until the meat is tender. Drain the chestnuts if required and stir them into the casserole. Cover and cook for a further 15 minutes to allow the chestnuts to warm through.

Serve the casserole with your favourite seasonal vegetables or simply with warm, buttered bread.

allyson's tip

- Even though schnitzels come thinly sliced, it is always a good idea to flatten them a little. This way you get two beef olives from each schnitzel and the meat is not so thick when rolling.

- 2 cups fresh breadcrumbs
- 75 grams butter, chilled and grated
- ½ teaspoon celery seeds, crushed, optional
- ½ teaspoon dried thyme
- ½ teaspoon dried oregano
- grated rind 2 lemons
- 10–12 beef schnitzels
- 1–2 onions, peeled and sliced
- 1 cup chopped prunes
- ¼ cup flour
- 2½ cups beef stock
- ¼ cup redcurrant jelly, optional
- ¼ cup HP or Worcestershire sauce

beef olives

serves 8–10
preparation time without browning **30 minutes**
preparation time with browning **45 minutes**
cooking time **low 6–7 hours, high 3–4 hours**

The name does not have any association with the olives that you pick off a tree. Rather, beef olives are a very old dish – in fact from medieval times – when they were referred to as 'aloes', from the French word *alou* meaning lark. It was thought that these braised little goodie bags of beef and stuffing looked like little birds prepared for the table, especially if they were minus their heads! Whatever you call them, beef olives are a great family dish.

Turn the slow cooker on to low to pre-warm while gathering and preparing the ingredients.

Mix together the breadcrumbs, butter, celery seeds, thyme, oregano and lemon rind.

Place one schnitzel on top of a piece of damp plastic wrap on a chopping board. Sprinkle the meat with a little water and cover with a second sheet of plastic wrap. Hit firmly with a mallet or rolling pin to flatten the schnitzels so they are an even thickness. The dampened plastic will help prevent the meat from tearing. Repeat with remaining schnitzels. Cut the schnitzels in half cross-wise.

Place a spoonful of stuffing on each piece of beef and roll up to enclose the filling. Secure with a toothpick.

If wishing to brown the ingredients:
Heat a dash of oil in a frying-pan and brown the beef olives until well browned. Brown the onion if wished.

Into the pre-warmed slow cooker put the beef olives, onion and prunes.

In a jug mix together the flour, stock, redcurrant jelly if using and HP or Worcestershire sauce, and pour over the beef olives. Cover with the lid.

Cook on low for 6–7 hours or on high for 3–4 hours. Serve the beef olives with seasonal vegetables.

variations

- Use a bought pre-made dried stuffing mix – it's easy.
- Add sliced celery and carrots with the onion.
- Use pork schnitzels in place of beef schnitzel.
- Wrap the beef olives in bacon rashers before securing with a toothpick and browning.
- Add a can of chopped tomatoes.
- Use a can of your favourite cook-in-style sauce with ½ cup water in place of the flour and stock.

1 kilogram honeycomb tripe
75 grams butter
1 onion, peeled and diced
4 tablespoons flour
3 cups milk (whole, not lite or trim)
1 cup chopped fresh parsley

tripe with onion & parsley

serves 6–8
preparation time **15 minutes**
cooking time **low 6–7 hours, high 3–4 hours**

Tripe seems to be one of those foods that divides us, you either hate or love it. Internationally, there are plenty of well-known tripe dishes. Tripes à la mode de Caen from Normandy featuring cider and calvados, or Pepperpot from the US with its origins in the West Indies and containing plenty of pepper, or Busecca from Milan, where it is simmered with white beans, pancetta, vegetables and plenty of tomatoes and served with Parmesan. But for most of us, the classic north England dish of tripe with onion and parsley seems to be the preferred choice and the slow cooker ensures it is tender and keeps that well-recognised smell under wraps while it cooks.

Turn the slow cooker on to low to pre-warm while gathering and preparing the ingredients.

Cut the tripe into 2–3-cm pieces. Place into the slow cooker and cover with cold water. Cook on low for around 4–5 hours or on high for 2–3 hours or until the tripe is tender.

When the cooking time is almost up, heat the butter in a large saucepan with the onion and cook over a low heat for around 7–8 minutes, until the onion has softened, stirring regularly.

Stir in the flour and cook for 2 minutes, stirring regularly until the mixture is frothy. Gradually stir in the cold milk and cook, stirring constantly until the sauce is smooth and thick.

Drain the tripe and discard the cooking water. Return the tripe to the slow cooker, stir in the white sauce and cover with the lid.

Cook on low for a further 2 hours or on high for 1 hour. Season with the parsley and salt and pepper and serve ladled over thick slices of toasted sour-dough bread or as a pie under a pile of buttery mashed potato.

variation

- Add 2 tablespoons curry powder into the butter and flour for a curried recipe.
- Add 2 tablespoons prepared Dijon or French mustard to the white sauce for a hot mustard twist.
- Sprinkle liberally with finely chopped, crisply cooked bacon rashers when serving and garnish with a few chopped capers.

dorset steak & sausage stew

serves 6–8
preparation time without browning **20 minutes**
preparation time with browning **30 minutes**
cooking time **low 5–7 hours, high 3–4 hours**

beef
1 kilogram lean beef for casseroling
¼ cup flour
1 tablespoon brown sugar
1 teaspoon dry mustard
1 teaspoon beef stock powder
¼ teaspoon pepper

sausage meatballs
250 grams beef sausage meat
½ cup fresh breadcrumbs
¼ cup currants or sultanas
1 tablespoon chopped fresh thyme or ½ teaspoon dried thyme

sauce
1 onion, peeled and diced
1 cup beef stock
½ cup port or red wine
2 tablespoons redcurrant or port wine jelly
4–6 whole cloves

Britain is home to so many regional dishes. This one is from one of my mother's old cookbooks, jazzed up for today. It combines both meat and sausages in a very enjoyable stew that has the tiniest hint of cloves, which are a hark back to the early days of the spice trade. Cloves were one of the first commodity spices available and it is a spice that works well with beef.

Turn the slow cooker on to low to pre-warm while gathering and preparing the ingredients.

Cut the beef into large 4-cm-sized pieces. Mix together the flour, sugar, mustard, stock powder and pepper. Toss the meat in the seasoned flour mix to coat. This is easiest done in a plastic bag. Shake off the excess and keep any remaining seasoned flour.

In a separate bowl, mix together the sausage meat, breadcrumbs, currants or sultanas and thyme and mix well. Take dessertspoon-sized pieces and roll into balls. Toss in the remaining seasoned flour.

If wishing to brown the ingredients:
Heat a good dash of oil in a frying-pan and, when hot, brown the beef and sausage meatballs well.

Into the pre-warmed slow cooker put the beef, sausage meatballs, onion, stock, port or red wine, redcurrant or port wine jelly and cloves and stir as well as possible to mix. Cover with the lid.

Cook on low for 5–7 hours or on high for 3–4 hours.

Serve the stew with seasonal vegetables.

variations

- Use the meat from lamb or pork sausages. Buying flavoured sausages will vary the flavours here too.
- Use marmalade and medium-sweet sherry in place of redcurrant or port wine jelly and port or red wine.
- Add vegetables like carrots, parsnips, leeks and mushrooms. to make a one-pot meal.
- Replace the cloves with 2 blades of mace.

6–8 rindless rashers streaky bacon
1.6–1.75 kilogram cross-cut blade, in one piece
handful fresh thyme sprigs
25–50 grams butter
1 onion, peeled and finely chopped
1 cup Madeira or Port
2 tablespoons instant gravy power

cross-cut blade pot roast with madeira gravy

serves 8–10
preparation time without browning **15 minutes**
preparation time with browning **25 minutes**
cooking time **low 6–7 hours, high 3–4 hours**

B

Normally this cut of beef is sold diced for braising or casseroling, but I find that it makes an exceptional pot roast when cooked in one piece. The flavour of the beef is superb and it is meltingly tender – so long as it is cooked only to medium. Roast a few vegetables in the oven to accompany this pot roast for a fabulous economical meal.

Turn slow cooker on to low to pre-warm while gathering and preparing the ingredients.

Place the rashers of bacon randomly over the beef and arrange the thyme on top. Secure the bacon and thyme with string.

If wishing to brown the ingredients (I strongly recommend browning for this recipe):
Heat a good dash of oil in a large heavy-based frying-pan and brown the meat on all sides as evenly as possible. Brown well as this will ensure a good flavour. Set aside. Add the butter to the frying-pan and cook the onion over a low heat for 5–8 minutes until it has softened. Add the Madeira or Port and simmer until reduced by half.

Into the pre-warmed slow cooker put the onion and Madeira or Port and sit the beef on top. Season well with pepper and cover with the lid.

Cook on low for 6–7 hours or on high for 3–4 hours. I used a meat thermometer to ensure I cooked the meat to medium (60–65 °C).

Lift the beef from the slow cooker, place on a warm platter and cover. Allow to rest while preparing the gravy.

Make the cooking juices up to 2 cups with water and place into a saucepan, with the gravy powder. Cook over a low heat, stirring constantly until thickened.

Serve the beef thinly sliced with your favourite vegetables and the Madeira gravy.

variation

- Red wine can be used in place of Madeira or Port though the finished gravy is much thinner in flavour.

allyson's tips

- Braai is a barbecue in South Africa, so the spice blend or mix is a general seasoning used for red meats, pork and chicken. If you cannot find any South African brands in the international section of the supermarket, use another favourite barbecue-style seasoning mix.
- The chutney you use will also vary the flavour of the finished dish. Look for one that includes dried fruits for an authentic bobotie.

- 1 kilogram lean beef for casseroling
- 2 onions, peeled and finely chopped
- 2 tablespoons brown sugar
- 2 tablespoons South African-style braai 'n' grill spice blend
- 2 teaspoons ground ginger
- 2 teaspoons curry powder
- 1 cup raisins or sultanas
- 1 cup spicy fruit-style chutney
- ¼ cup Worcestershire sauce
- ¼ cup tomato paste
- ½ cup beef stock

custard

- 1½ cups milk
- 4 eggs
- 1 tablespoon fresh thyme leaves

bobotie

serves 8
preparation time **20 minutes**
cooking time **low 6–7 hours, high 3–4 hours, plus 1 hour extra if including custard**

This traditional South African dish combines finely diced beef in a rich sweet and sour sauce under a canopy of egg and milk custard. It's great in summer served with a crisp salad, or on cooler nights with mashed pumpkin or kumara.

Turn the slow cooker on to low to pre-warm while gathering and preparing the ingredients.

Cut the beef into small 1–1.5-cm dice.

> ***If wishing to brown the meat and onions:***
> *Heat a good dash of oil in a large frying-pan and brown the beef in batches over a high heat. Cook the onion for 3–4 minutes until it begins to soften. Add the brown sugar, spice blend, ginger and curry powder and continue cooking for a further 2–3 minutes when the mix is very fragrant.*

Into the pre-warmed slow cooker put the beef, onions, brown sugar, spice blend, ginger, curry powder, raisins or sultanas, chutney, Worcestershire sauce, tomato paste and stock. Stir well to mix the ingredients evenly and cover with the lid.

Cook on low for 6–7 hours or on high for 3–4 hours.

The bobotie can be enjoyed as is at this stage with your favourite vegetables if wished.

To cover with the custard, beat the milk, eggs and thyme together and carefully pour over the bobotie in the slow cooker and cover with the lid. Cook on high power for an extra hour or until the custard has set.

Alternatively, transfer the meat to a large 8-cup capacity ovenproof dish and pour the egg mixture on top. Bake in a 180 °C oven for 30–35 minutes or until the custard has set. The dish can also be presented in smaller individual serving-sized dishes. Baking time will be a few minutes less.

variations

- Use lamb in place of beef.
- Use curry paste in place of powder and double the amount for a spicier bobotie.

12 thick beef sausages
2 onions, peeled and chopped
1–2 teaspoons minced garlic
2 tablespoons flour
1 tablespoon coarsely cracked black pepper
1 cup red wine
1 cup beef stock

sausages in pepper gravy

serves 6
preparation time without browning **10 minutes**
preparation time with browning **20 minutes**
cooking time **low 5–6 hours, high 3–4 hours**

A simple family dish that's perfect mid-week.

Turn the slow cooker on to low to pre-warm while gathering and preparing the ingredients.

> ***If wishing to brown the ingredients:***
> *Heat a dash of oil in the frying-pan and brown the sausages over a moderately low heat to avoid them splitting. Brown the onions if wished.*

Into the pre-warmed slow cooker put the sausages, onions and garlic. In a jug mix together the flour, pepper, wine and stock to make a smooth sauce and pour over the sausages. Cover with the lid.

Cook on low for 5–6 hours or on high for 3–4 hours, or until the sausages and onions are tender.

Serve with your favourite seasonal vegetables.

2 kilograms lean beef for casseroling
2 onions, peeled and diced
2 carrots, peeled and diced
2 green capsicums, diced
2 leeks, trimmed and thickly sliced, optional
¼ cup seasoned flour
2 cups beef stock
400-gram can condensed tomato soup

french bread slices

½ French bread stick
1–1½ cups grated Cheddar-style cheese

tomato & beef casserole

serves 8
preparation time without browning **15 minutes**
preparation time with browning **25 minutes**
cooking time **low 7–8 hours, high 4–5 hours**

B

Only a few simple ingredients are needed to make this tasty family casserole.

Turn the slow cooker on to low to pre-warm while gathering and preparing the ingredients.

Trim the beef of any excess fat and cut into largish pieces, about 3–4-cm cubes.

If wishing to brown the ingredients:
Heat a dash of oil in a frying-pan and brown the beef well on both sides. Set aside. Add the onions to the pan with an extra dash of oil if required and cook for about 5 minutes.

Into the pre-warmed slow cooker put the beef, onions, carrots, capsicums and leeks. Stir together the flour, stock and condensed soup and pour into the slow cooker. Stir to mix as evenly as possible and cover with the lid.

Cook on low for 7–8 hours or on high for 4–5 hours, or until the meat is tender.

Serve the casserole straight from the slow cooker as is, or topped with the cheese-grilled French bread slices.

french bread slices

Cut the bread into 1-cm-wide slices and place on a baking tray. Place under a hot grill until lightly browned. Turn the pieces over and scatter the cheese evenly over the top of the bread slices. Return to the grill until the cheese has melted and turned lightly golden.

variations

- Add 150–250 grams mushrooms, sliced or diced.
- Add 1 tablespoon paprika and ½ teaspoon cayenne pepper.
- Add 4–6 slices bacon, finely diced.
- Use red wine in place of stock.
- Make with lamb or hogget in place of beef.
- Add 1 tablespoon curry powder with the soup.

1 ox tongue
1 orange, halved
1 bouquet garni
1 onion, peeled and halved
2 tablespoons golden syrup or brown sugar
¼ cup chopped fresh basil or parsley
¼ cup sliced sun-dried tomatoes in oil, well drained
¼ cup chopped black olives
2 tablespoons chopped capers
1 tablespoon of your favourite prepared mustard
1 cup white wine
3 teaspoons gelatin

olive crumble
½–1 cup black or green olives, pitted
2 chargrilled red capsicums
1 tablespoon capers
¼ cup diced sun-dried tomatoes
2 tablespoons chopped fresh parsley
2 tablespoons chopped fresh basil
½ teaspoon minced garlic
3–4 tablespoons olive oil
2 tablespoons vinegar or lemon juice

tuscan ox tongue terrine

serves 8–10
chilling time **overnight**
preparation time **10 minutes**
cooking time **low 6–8 hours, high 3–5 hours**
cooling time **1 hour**

Yes tongue – now that's a dish from your grandmother's past. It's delicious and very cheap and easy to turn into a snazzy terrine with flavours of olives, capers and sun-dried tomatoes. Just great with crackers or in a sandwich – try it!

Turn the slow cooker on to low to pre-warm while gathering and preparing the ingredients.

Wash the tongue – they usually come vacuum-packed in brine – and place in the slow cooker.

Add the orange halves, bouquet garni, onion and golden syrup or brown sugar and pour in enough tap water to cover. Cover with the lid.

Cook on low for 6–8 hours or on high for 3–5 hours, or until the tongue is tender when pierced with a skewer or fine-bladed knife.

Turn the slow cooker off and allow the tongue to cool for an hour in the liquid. Lift the tongue out, strain and reserve half a cup of the cooking liquid. (If the skin will not come off easily, then the tongue is not cooked properly and will need additional cooking time.)

Carefully peel away the thick outer skin. Cut the tongue into 2-cm dice and place in a large bowl with the basil or parsley, sun-dried tomatoes, olives, capers and mustard. Season well with pepper and mix.

Stir the wine in with the half cup of reserved cooking liquid and sprinkle over the gelatin. Allow to swell then dissolve over hot water or by heating in the microwave for 10–15 seconds.

Transfer the seasoned tongue to a 6-cup capacity loaf tin and pour over the gelatin and wine mix. Cover with plastic wrap and place a small weight on top. Refrigerate overnight. Serve sliced with olive crumble and mayonnaise on freshly sliced crusty bread.

olive crumble
Chop the olives, capsicums and capers finely and toss with the sun-dried tomatoes, parsley, basil, garlic, olive oil and vinegar or lemon juice. Stand for 10 minutes before serving. Recipe makes about 2 cups.

1 tablespoon tamarind pulp
¼ cup water
1.5 kilograms lean beef for casseroling
2 stems lemon grass
2 onions, peeled and diced
1–1½ tablespoons minced garlic
1 tablespoon minced ginger
8 dried chillies or 1 tablespoon Sambal Oelek
6 whole cardamom pods or 1 teaspoon cardamom seeds
2 teaspoons ground coriander
1 teaspoon ground cumin
½–1 teaspoon ground laos, optional
½ teaspoon ground cinnamon
1 teaspoon salt
2 cups coconut milk

fresh cucumber relish
1 tablespoon tamarind pulp
¼ cup water
1 fresh telegraph cucumber
2 tablespoons grated palm or brown sugar
¼ red onion, finely diced
½–1 teaspoon finely chopped lemon grass
2 tablespoons chopped fresh mint

beef rendang with fresh cucumber relish

serves 8
preparation time without browning **20 minutes**
preparation time with browning **30 minutes**
cooking time **low 7–8 hours, high 4–5 hours**

This Malaysian beef dish is traditionally quite dry. The meat is cooked slowly in coconut milk and spices, so that by the end of cooking the meat has absorbed all the liquid. I prefer a saucier dish to mop up rice with, but if you'd prefer a more authentic version, use 1 cup of coconut milk only.

Turn the slow cooker on to low to pre-warm while gathering and preparing the ingredients.

Knead the tamarind pulp into the water until murky and thick. Scoop or strain out the seeds and fibre and reserve the thick liquid.

Cut the beef into index finger-sized pieces. Trim the lemon grass where the white bulbous end changes colour to green. Finely slice the white part. Discard or use the green stem for flavouring soups, stock or rice.

If wishing to brown the ingredients:
Brown the beef in a good dash of oil. This will be best done in batches to avoid the meat from stewing.

Into the pre-warmed slow cooker put the beef, tamarind water, lemon grass, onions, garlic, ginger, chillies or Sambal Oelek, cardamom pods or seeds, coriander, cumin, laos if using, cinnamon, salt and coconut milk. Stir to mix as well as possible. Cover with the lid.

Cook on low for 7–8 hours or on high for 4–5 hours.

Taste and season with additional salt if required before serving with boiled rice and the cucumber relish.

fresh cucumber relish
Knead the tamarind and water together until the mixture is murky and thick. Sieve to remove any fibre or seeds and reserve the liquid.

Trim the cucumber, chop into ½-cm dice and place in a bowl with the tamarind water, palm or brown sugar, onion, lemon grass and mint. Season with salt before serving.

allyson's tips

- Traditionally the meat is not browned, but for our tastes, you may prefer to do this step.
- Bruise the long green lemon-grass stems with the handle of a knife. Tie in a knot and place in a teapot, pour on boiling water and stand for 3 minutes before serving this for a refreshing tisane (herbal tea).
- Laos is the Indonesian name for galangal. It is a member of the ginger family and the rhizome is the part eaten. It has a ginger, pine and pepper flavour and is highly aromatic and pungent. It is available frozen or dried from Asian food shops.
- Sambal Oelek is a paste of crushed chillies, vinegar and salt, though some brands may include other flavours such as garlic and sugar.

chicken

leek & tarragon chicken pies
(page 118)

2–3 leeks, trimmed and halved lengthwise
6–8 chicken leg and thigh portions
1½ cups chicken stock or white wine
1 tablespoon minced garlic
1 teaspoon dried tarragon
1–1½ cups roughly chopped pitted prunes
¼–½ cup cream

chicken, leek & tarragon braise

serves 6
preparation time without browning **10 minutes**
preparation time with browning **20 minutes**
cooking time **low 6–7 hours, high 4–5 hours**

B

This braise boasts fabulous winter flavours from the leeks and prunes and all that's required on the side is a bowl of steaming hot, fluffy mashed potatoes.

Turn the slow cooker on to low to pre-warm while gathering and preparing the ingredients.

Wash the leeks thoroughly to remove any grit that hides between the layers. Shake dry and slice finely.

> ***If wishing to brown the ingredients:***
> *Brown the chicken pieces and leeks well in a dash of oil or a hearty knob of butter in a hot frying-pan until well browned. This will be best done in batches to avoid the ingredients from stewing.*

Place the chicken and leeks into the pre-warmed slow cooker. Mix together the chicken stock or wine, garlic and tarragon and pour over the chicken. Scatter over the prunes.

Cover and cook on low for 6–7 hours or on high for 4–5 hours. Stir in the cream and season with salt and pepper before serving.

variations

- Replace all the chicken stock or water with ¾ cup vermouth or dry sherry and ¾ cup chicken stock.
- Add ½ cup chopped ham with the chicken.
- Use a whole chicken in place of chicken pieces and amend cooking time to suit.
- Pull the meat from the chicken and turn into a pie (see page 118).

1 x quantity of chicken, leek and tarragon braise (see page 117), cold
3–4 sheets frozen pre-rolled flaky puff pastry, defrosted
beaten egg or milk to glaze

leek & tarragon chicken pies

serves 6–8
preparation time **15 minutes**
cooking time **15–20 minutes in the oven**

Jazz up the braise by serving under a flaky pie crust.

Preheat the oven to 220 °C. Place the oven rack just above the centre.

Pull the chicken meat from the bones, discarding the skin and bones. Return the meat to the sauce and mix well. Divide the mixture evenly among 6–8 small pie-style dishes or one large 6–8-cup capacity pie dish.

Place the pastry sheets on a lightly floured board. Cut out pieces large enough to cover the top of the individual pies, without any overhang. If required to re-roll the pastry, place the scraps on top of each other and roll out – do not knead as the layers in the puff pastry will not cook or be able to rise and the result will be a heavy and doughy pastry top.

If making one large pie, place 2 sheets of pastry on top of each other and roll out large enough to cover the pie.

Brush with beaten egg or milk to glaze. Cut a cross in the centre to allow the steam to escape.

Bake in the preheated oven for 15–20 minutes until the pastry is well browned and golden and the filling is piping hot. Allow an extra 10 minutes' cooking time for a larger pie.

1.5–1.6-kilogram whole chicken
1–2 carrots, peeled and sliced
1 onion, peeled and diced
1 bay leaf or bouquet garni
1 cup water

sauce
75 grams butter
6 tablespoons flour
400-gram can corn kernels, well drained
½ cup cream, optional
¼ cup chopped parsley, optional

ivy's chicken

serves 6
preparation time **10 minutes**
cooking time **low 5–6 hours, high 3–4 hours**

When I was younger, chickens were mostly a bit on the tough side and as a result they were served more often boiled or poached and in an accompanying sauce. My mum always cooked her chicken in a simple flavoured stock, which was later turned into a white sauce with the addition of corn and occasionally bacon, or made into a curry, using good old Keen's curry powder – either way we loved it.

Turn the slow cooker on to low to pre-warm while gathering and preparing the ingredients.

Wash the chicken and pat dry. Place the chicken into the pre-warmed slow cooker and scatter in the carrot and onion and add the bay leaf or bouquet garni. Pour in the water and cover with the lid.

Cook on low for 5–6 hours or on high for 3–4 hours, or until the chicken is tender. Carefully remove the chicken from the slow cooker and place on a warm plate and cover. The chicken can be served at this stage with your favourite sauce or chilled with salad or in sandwiches.

Heat the butter in a large saucepan and, when hot, stir in the flour and cook for 1–2 minutes, stirring constantly until the mixture is frothy. Ladle in the chicken stock and vegetables from the slow cooker and cook, stirring until the sauce is thick.

Stir in the corn, cream and parsley if using. Tear the meat from the chicken in chunky pieces and fold into the sauce. Serve over rice or mashed potatoes.

variations

- **ham and chicken.** Add 1 diced ham steak with corn.
- **chicken 'n' potato pie.** Pile the chicken and sauce into a deep pie- or lasagne-style dish and top with mashed potato. Bake at 180 °C until the pie is hot and golden.
- **bacon and corn.** Pan-fry 4–5 rashers bacon until crispy and stir in with the corn. Use cream-style corn if wished.
- **curry.** Add extra 25 grams butter to the sauce and add 2 tablespoons of your favourite curry powder with the flour. Omit the corn.
- **cheese mornay.** Beat 2 egg yolks into the cream before stirring into the dish, with 1 cup grated Cheddar-style cheese.

allyson's tips

- If a curry is too 'chilli hot', stir ½–1 cup of plain unsweetened yoghurt into the curry before serving. Do not allow the curry to boil once added, as the yoghurt will curdle and while the dish will not be ruined, it will look awful.
- There is no need to soak lentils overnight, but it is a good idea to rinse them before cooking.

chicken & lentil curry

serves 8
preparation time **15 minutes**
cooking time **low 6–7 hours, high 3–4 hours, plus extra 20–30 minutes**

2 cups light-flavoured chicken stock or water
1 tablespoon tamarind pulp
8 chicken leg and thigh portions
1–2 red onions, peeled and thickly sliced
1 cup red lentils
400-gram can chopped tomatoes
2 tablespoons curry powder
1 tablespoon minced garlic
1 tablespoon minced ginger
2 teaspoons ground coriander, optional
2 teaspoons ground cumin, optional
3–4 bunches fresh spinach

The flavours of this simple curry are delicious. This easy recipe is one of my favourites in *Slow*.

Turn the slow cooker on to low to pre-warm for 15–20 minutes while gathering and preparing the ingredients.

Mix the stock or water and tamarind pulp together, kneading the tamarind until the water is murky. Strain to remove any fibrous material from the tamarind and set the brownish stock or water aside.

Remove the skin from the chicken if wished.

Scatter the onion and lentils into the pre-warmed slow cooker. Sit the chicken pieces on top.

Stir together the tamarind water with the tomatoes, curry powder, garlic, ginger and the coriander and cumin if using. Pour over the chicken and cover with the lid.

Cook on low for 6–7 hours or on high for 3–4 hours.

Tear the spinach leaves from the coarser stems. Rinse the leaves and stir into the curry. Cook on low for a further 20–30 minutes or until the spinach has just wilted and the curry is hot.

Serve sprinkled with a little chopped onion and chopped fresh coriander or toasted cashew nuts before serving with plenty of rice on the side.

variations

- Use Indian-spiced canned tomatoes – they are great with this dish.
- Use an Indian curry paste in place of curry powder.
- Add ½–1 teaspoon chilli powder for a curry with more kick.

8 chicken leg and thigh portions
3 tablespoons flour
1 tablespoon paprika
½ teaspoon ground white pepper
12 cloves garlic, crushed, peeled and sliced thickly
2 carrots, peeled and sliced
2 parsnips, peeled and sliced
1 tablespoon fresh rosemary leaves, stems removed
1½ cups chicken stock or water

country garlic chicken

serves 6–8
preparation time without browning **15–20 minutes**
preparation time with browning **30 minutes**
cooking time **low 6–7 hours, high 4–5 hours**

A simple dish that makes the most of winter vegetables. Some herbs withstand long slow cooking better than others as their flavours do not become overcooked or grass-like. Such herbs include thyme, oregano and sage, so do try these in place of rosemary to vary this family-friendly dish.

Turn the slow cooker on to low to pre-warm while gathering and preparing the ingredients.

Remove the skin from the chicken if wished. The chicken portions can be cut in half if need be to fit into the slow cooker.

Place the chicken pieces into a clean plastic bag with the flour, paprika and white pepper, and toss to coat.

> ***If wishing to brown the ingredients:***
> *Heat a good dash of oil or a knob of butter in a heavy-based frying-pan and brown the chicken pieces well on all sides.*

Into the pre-warmed slow cooker put the garlic, carrots and parsnips. Sit the chicken pieces on top and scatter over the rosemary leaves. Season well with salt and pepper. Pour in the chicken stock and cover with the lid.

Cook on low for 6–7 hours or on high for 4–5 hours. Serve the chicken simply with the sauce from the slow cooker, with the carrots and parsnips and your favourite seasonal vegetables.

variations

- Add half a 32-gram packet of onion soup or tomato soup mix to the flour and paprika for tossing the chicken portions in.
- Add 3–4 diced rashers of bacon. These can be pan-fried if wished. Use the bacon fat to brown the chicken, it will add extra flavour.
- Add a finely chopped onion or leek.
- Add 2–3 tablespoons Worcestershire or HP sauce before serving – scrumptious.
- Use a whole chicken in place of portions. Stuff the chicken with a rosemary-spiked simple bread stuffing. A stuffing will add flavour and help the chicken retain a good shape while cooking.

allyson's tip

- Make sure the carrots and parsnips are placed into the slow cooker first as they will cook better.

allyson's tips

- New season baby potatoes are delicious if used here.
- Use Italian parsley leaves as they are softer to eat whole.

1.5–1.6-kilogram whole chicken
1 tablespoon flour
1–2 medium-sized leeks, trimmed
¼ cup olive oil, virgin or extra virgin is nice here
12–16 small waxy potatoes
2 cloves garlic, crushed, peeled and sliced
½ cup dry white wine
1 cup large green olives, not stoned
1 cup grated mozzarella
½ cup finely grated Parmesan
1 cup freshly picked parsley leaves

golden braised chicken with olives

serves 5–6
preparation time without browning **20 minutes**
preparation time with browning **30 minutes**
cooking time **low 4–6 hours, high 3–4 hours**

This simple recipe looks so elegant when presented, it is hard to believe it was cooked in a slow cooker.

Turn the slow cooker on to low to pre-warm while gathering and preparing the ingredients.

Wash the chicken and pat it dry, especially the cavity. Season the cavity with salt and pepper. Tie the legs of the chicken together and twist the wings under the body. This will help the chicken keep a good shape when cooking. Sift the flour over the chicken evenly.

Cut the leeks in half crosswise.

> ***If wishing to brown the ingredients:***
> *Heat the oil in a heavy-based frying-pan and, when hot, brown the chicken as well as you can on all sides. Brown the leeks and potatoes too.*

Into the pre-warmed slow cooker put the chicken, oil, leeks, potatoes, garlic, wine and olives and cover with the lid.

Cook on low for 4–6 hours or on high for 3–4 hours or until the chicken is cooked.

Turn the oven on to 200 °C fan grill.

Carefully lift the chicken from the slow cooker and place on a warm serving platter, cover and set aside while finishing the dish.

Using a slotted spoon, lift the potatoes and olives from the slow cooker and place into an ovenproof lasagne-style dish. Scatter over the mozzarella and Parmesan and place under the preheated grill until the cheeses have melted and become golden brown.

Arrange the potatoes and olives around the chicken. Cut the leek into thick slices and add to the platter. Stir the parsley into the cooking juices in the slow cooker and season.

Serve the chicken with the cooking juices and vegetables.

If wished, the juices can be thickened with 1–2 tablespoons of cornflour, mixed to a thin paste with water. The quickest way is to transfer the juices to a saucepan and cook on top of the stove.

variation

- Use 6 chicken leg and thigh portions in place of a whole chicken.

chicken and marinade
- 12 chicken drumsticks
- 2 tablespoons lemon juice
- ½ teaspoon salt
- 1½ tablespoons yellow food colouring
- 1 tablespoon red food colouring
- 1 cup plain unsweetened yoghurt
- ½ onion, peeled, minced or finely chopped
- 1 tablespoon minced ginger
- 2 teaspoons minced garlic
- 1 green chilli, finely chopped
- 2 teaspoons garam masala

sauce
- 2 x 400-gram cans Indian spiced tomatoes
- 1 tablespoon shredded fresh ginger
- 1 teaspoon garam masala
- 1 teaspoon ground cumin
- 1 green chilli, diced (de-seeded if wished)

to finish
- 100–150 grams butter
- ½ cup cream

butter chicken

serves 6
preparation time without browning **30 minutes**
preparation time with browning **40 minutes**
marinating time **preferably overnight, 4 hours minimum**
cooking time **low 6–8 hours, high 4–5 hours**

I love to make my own butter chicken as it has a much lighter texture and fresher flavours. You can taste the spices – they are not hidden under a cloyingly thick tomato purée and cream sauce.

Use a sharp knife to cut 2–3 deep gashes through to the bone in each chicken drumstick. Mix the lemon juice and salt together and work into the chicken.

Mix the food colourings together and use to paint each drumstick. This will give the chicken a more authentic red-colour look of tandoori chicken.

Place the chicken pieces into a lidded container in a single layer. Mix together the yoghurt, onion, ginger, garlic, chilli and garam masala, pour over the chicken pieces and turn the chicken to coat in the marinade. Cover and refrigerate overnight or for at least 4 hours.

Turn the slow cooker on to low to pre-warm while preparing the remainder of the butter chicken.

Remove the chicken from the marinade and use a pastry brush to brush off excess marinade.

If wishing to brown the chicken:
Heat a dash of oil in a heavy-based frying-pan and, when hot, brown the chicken pieces really well – only a few at a time to prevent the pieces from stewing.

Into the pre-warmed slow cooker put the chicken pieces. Mix together the sauce ingredients and pour over the chicken. Turn the pieces to coat in the sauce and cover with the lid. It may look as if there is not going to be enough sauce, but there will be once the chicken is cooked.

Cook on low for 6–8 hours or on high for 4–5 hours, or until the chicken pieces are tender.

Transfer the chicken from the slow cooker to a warm plate, cover and set aside. Add the butter and cream to the sauce and stir until the butter has melted. Return the chicken pieces to the sauce and turn to coat. If time permits, cover with the lid and cook on high for a further 30 minutes so that the sauce can reheat.

Serve with pilaf rice, naan bread and a favourite chutney.

variation
- Use 10 lamb shoulder chops or 6 lamb shanks in place of chicken drumsticks and amend the cooking time to suit.

allyson's tips

- If you do not wish to use food colouring, omit this step altogether. The chicken will still taste fantastic, but it won't be that authentic red colour.
- Indian-spiced tomatoes are great for this dish. If you do not have them, use two cans chopped tomatoes in juice with 1–2 tablespoons of your favourite curry powder or paste.

- 1.5–1.6-kilogram whole chicken
- 1 whole orange or red-skinned apple
- 1 stalk celery, sliced
- 1 carrot, peeled and sliced
- 1 onion, peeled and sliced
- ½ teaspoon dried oregano, marjoram or thyme, optional
- 1 cup water, chicken stock or white wine

basic slow-cooker chicken

serves 5–6
preparation time **5 minutes**
cooking time **low 5–6 hours, high 3–4 hours**

This poached-style chicken can be served simply with a favourite sauce or gravy. It's a particularly good recipe for people following a diet plan, and an ideal way to cook a whole chicken for pasta.

Turn the slow cooker on to low to pre-warm while gathering and preparing the ingredients.

Rinse the chicken well and pat dry.

Place the orange or apple into the chicken cavity. Season the chicken well with salt and pepper.

Scatter the celery, carrot and onion into the base of the slow cooker. Sprinkle over the dried herbs if using.

Sit the chicken on top and pour the water, stock or wine over the chicken and cover with the lid.

Cook on low for 5–6 hours or high for 3–4 hours, or until the chicken is cooked. Carefully lift the chicken from the slow cooker and serve as wished.

Use the stock remaining in the slow cooker to make a sauce, gravy or soup, or to freeze for use at a later date.

- 1 x quantity of basic slow-cooker chicken
- 2 oranges
- 4 cups cooked pasta shapes
- 4–6 stalks celery, sliced
- 2–3 cups salad leaves
- 1 cup loosely packed fresh mint or basil leaves
- 1 cup roughly chopped celery leaves

honey dressing

- ¼ cup cider or white wine vinegar
- ¼ cup oil, olive oil is nice here
- ¼ cup runny honey
- 1 tablespoon of your favourite prepared mustard

celery, chicken & orange salad

serves 6
preparation time **15 minutes**

Serve the salad just warm – the flavours are more pronounced than when the salad is served chilled.

Pull the meat from the chicken, discarding the bones and skin. Pull the meat into chunky pieces and place in a large bowl.

Grate the rind from the oranges and add to the bowl. Use a small sharp knife to trim away all of the bitter white pith on the oranges, chop the orange flesh and add to the chicken.

Add the pasta, celery, salad leaves, mint or basil and celery leaves and pour in the dressing. Toss well to mix. Serve soon after dressing.

honey dressing
Place the vinegar, oil, honey and mustard into a screw-topped jar, seal and shake to mix well.

allyson's tips

- Boiling ¾ cup dry orzo pasta in plenty of salted water will give you 1½ cups cooked.
- The paprika will colour up the chicken, which would otherwise stay a cream colour when cooked in the slow cooker. Alternatively, brown in oil before cooking.
- Do not be tempted to stuff the chicken and refrigerate overnight. This is a great way to get food bugs! And also, make sure the stuffing is cold when you fill the chicken cavity to prevent any food nasties.

1½ cups cooked orzo pasta
2 tablespoons chopped anchovies
1½ tablespoons minced garlic
1 tablespoon chopped capers
¼ cup chopped fresh parsley
¼ cup chopped pitted black olives
1.5–1.6-kilogram whole chicken
400-gram can chopped tomatoes in juice
½ cup white wine, chicken stock or water
about 1 teaspoon paprika, optional

italian tomato & olive chicken

serves 6
preparation time **20 minutes**
cooking time **low 6–7 hours, high 4–5 hours, plus extra 15–20 minutes**

Loaded with gutsy flavours, a basket full of grilled, intensely flavoured garlic bread slices is all that is needed to accompany this dish.

Turn the slow cooker on to low to pre-warm while gathering and preparing the ingredients.

Mix together the pasta, anchovies, garlic, capers, parsley and olives. Season well with pepper.

Rinse the chicken well and pat the cavity dry with absorbent paper towel.

Use a half to a third of the pasta mixture to stuff the chicken cavity firmly. Set the remaining mix aside in a lidded container in the fridge.

Tie the legs of the chicken together to secure the filling and ensure the chicken keeps a good shape when cooking. Tuck the wings underneath the chicken.

Pour the canned tomatoes and wine, stock or water into the pre-warmed slow cooker. Sit the chicken on top of the sauce and sprinkle with the paprika if using. Cover with the lid.

Cook on low for 6–7 hours or on high for 4–5 hours before lifting the lid to see if the chicken is cooked. Wiggle the end of the chicken's drumstick, if it moves freely the chicken is cooked. If not, cover and cook a further 30–45 minutes and test again.

Once cooked, carefully remove the chicken to a warm serving plate and cover.

Stir the reserved pasta stuffing mix into the hot sauce that has accumulated in the slow cooker. Cover with the lid and cook on high for 15–20 minutes to reheat the sauce. Season with pepper and add a little fresh parsley, or basil for a fresh herby flavour if wished.

Carve the chicken into chunky pieces and accompany with a hearty serving of the stuffing and sauce.

variations

- Use cooked rice in place of orzo pasta.
- Use smoked paprika if wished for a smoky Spanish-inspired dish.
- Add 2–3 tablespoons basil pesto to the sauce before serving.
- Add 1 tablespoon chopped fresh rosemary to the pasta stuffing mix.
- Use green olives in place of black.

creole spice seasoning

¼ cup flaky salt
2 tablespoons powdered garlic
1 tablespoon paprika
2 tablespoons ground black pepper
1 tablespoon ground white pepper
½ teaspoon cayenne pepper

Stir together the salt, garlic, paprika, black, white and cayenne pepper. Keep in an airtight container.

- 8 chicken leg and thigh portions
- 2–4 smoked chorizo-style sausages, finely sliced
- 2 stalks celery, sliced
- 1 green capsicum, diced
- 1 onion, peeled and sliced
- 400-gram can diced tomatoes in juice
- 1 cup chicken stock
- 1 tablespoon Creole spice seasoning
- 1 tablespoon chopped fresh thyme

- 150 grams lean pork mince
- 150 grams chicken livers, trimmed and diced
- 2 cups long-grain rice
- ½ onion, peeled and finely diced
- 1 green capsicum, finely diced
- 1 stalk celery, finely diced
- 1 teaspoon Creole spice seasoning
- 3 cups chicken stock or water
- 2–3 spring onions, trimmed and sliced

cajun chicken stew

serves 6–8
preparation time without browning **20 minutes**
preparation time with browning **30 minutes**
cooking time **low 6–7 hours, high 3–5 hours**

Cajun dishes nearly always begin with or contain the 'Holy Trinity'; green capsicums, onions and celery. These vegetables, along with the peppery Creole spice seasoning, form the basis of many traditional Cajun and Creole dishes. The flavours are unique and this dish would work just as well with pork.

Turn the slow cooker on to low to pre-warm while gathering and preparing the ingredients.

> ***If wishing to brown the chicken:***
> *Brown the chicken pieces in a dash of oil in a hot frying-pan.*

Into the pre-warmed slow cooker put the chicken, chorizo sausages, celery, capsicum, onion, tomatoes, stock, Creole spice seasoning and thyme and cover with the lid.

Cook on low for 6–7 hours or on high for 3–5 hours.

The chicken can be served in pieces or the meat pulled from the chicken portions and returned to the sauce to serve with the dirty rice.

dirty rice

serves 6–8
preparation time **15 minutes**
cooking time **20 minutes**

So named because it looks rather messy and brownish when cooked, but tastes sensational.

Heat a dash of oil in a lidded frying-pan and, when hot, add the pork mince and chicken livers and pan-fry over a high heat until browned. Set aside.

Add a dash more oil to the pan and cook the rice and onion for 2–3 minutes until the rice turns from opaque to white.

Return the mince and chicken livers to the pan with the capsicum, celery and Creole spice seasoning. Stir in the stock or water, cover and turn to the lowest heat to simmer for 10 minutes.

Turn off the heat but do not lift the lid. Stand the rice for 5 minutes before lifting the lid and forking through the spring onions. Season with salt if wished.

1.5–1.6-kilogram whole chicken
¼ cup olive oil, virgin olive oil is nice here
1 large juicy lemon, thinly sliced
1 onion, peeled and finely sliced
1 cup raisins
100 grams quince paste, sliced
1 teaspoon dried oregano
1 cup chicken stock
2–3 bunches spinach, washed

herbed chicken in quince jus

serves 4–5
preparation time without browning **20 minutes**
preparation time with browning **30 minutes**
cooking time **low 5–6 hours, high 3–4 hours, plus extra 10–15 minutes**

This dish has been inspired by the flavours of Greece. Serve it simply with a generous pile of steaming hot-buttered or olive-oil-soaked orzo pasta and a chilled glass of wine for a delightfully casual meal.

Turn the slow cooker on to low to pre-warm while gathering and preparing the ingredients.

Rinse the chicken and pat the cavity dry. Tie the chicken legs together so it keeps a good shape while cooking.

If wishing to brown the chicken:
Heat the oil in a deep, heavy-based frying-pan and, when hot, add the chicken and brown as well as possible on all sides.

Into the pre-warmed slow cooker layer the lemon and onion. Scatter over the raisins, quince paste and oregano.

Sit the chicken on top and pour in the chicken stock and olive oil. Season with salt and pepper and cover with the lid.

Cook on low for 5–6 hours or on high for 3–4 hours.

Lift the chicken from the slow cooker, place on a warm plate and cover.

Tear the coarse stems from the spinach leaves and rinse the leaves. Shake well to remove excess water and add to the slow cooker. Stir to mix as evenly as possible. Sit the chicken on top of the spinach, cover and cook on high for 10–15 minutes or until the spinach leaves have wilted.

Carve the chicken into generous portions and serve on grilled eggplant slices with some of the sauce and spinach.

variation

✣ Use 6 chicken leg and thigh portions in place of a whole chicken. A little extra cooking time may be required.

¼ cup Worcestershire sauce
3 tablespoons mustard powder
3 tablespoons mango chutney or brown sugar
6 chicken leg and thigh portions
3–4 waxy potatoes, washed and roughly chopped
2–3 carrots, peeled and sliced
2 onions, peeled and sliced
1–2 teaspoons minced garlic
2 cups chicken stock or water
3 tablespoons instant gravy powder

sweet devilled chicken casserole

serves 6
preparation time without browning **15 minutes**
preparation time with browning **25 minutes**
Marinating time **preferably overnight, 4 hours minimum**
cooking time **low 5–7 hours, high 3–4 hours, plus extra 30 minutes**

Devilling food has long fallen out of fashion over the years, probably in part because other flavourings and condiments have become available. It once referred to foods cooked with hot fiery spices or condiments. Mustard was and still is a key ingredient in devilling foods (being one of the earliest, readily available condiments), especially in devilled kidneys. Foods that were reheated were regularly devilled – served in a fiery hot sauce or coating. I quite like the flavours of devilled foods, especially where they include Worcestershire sauce – a hark back to the day of the Raj.

Mix together the Worcestershire sauce, mustard powder and chutney or brown sugar.

Put the chicken into a sealable bag and pour in the marinade. Seal and turn to coat evenly. Alternatively, place the chicken in a dish, coat with the marinade and cover. Allow the chicken to marinate overnight if possible or for at least 4 hours.

Turn the slow cooker on to low to pre-warm while gathering and preparing the remaining ingredients.

If wishing to brown the chicken:
Remove the chicken from the marinade, reserving the marinade. Brown the pieces on both sides in a dash of oil in a frying-pan.

Into the pre-warmed slow cooker put the chicken and marinade, potatoes, carrots, onions, garlic and stock or water and cover with the lid.

Cook on low for 5–7 hours or on high for 3–4 hours, or until the chicken and vegetables are all well cooked.

Carefully transfer the chicken from the slow cooker to a warm plate and cover.

Mix the gravy powder with a little water to make a smooth thick paste and stir into the slow cooker. Sit the chicken back on top and cover. Cook on high for an extra 30 minutes to thicken the sauce.

Serve the chicken with the vegetables and gravy, garnished with fresh herbs.

variations

- Use beef in place of chicken. Use about 1.5 kilograms of diced cross-cut blade or chuck steak. Cooking time will be similar.

allyson's tip

- For the best flavour, use a gravy powder that is suited to serve with chicken or light meats as opposed to beef, which will be too strong.

allyson's tip

- Apricot nectar is available in most supermarkets, though it might take a bit of looking for. If you cannot find it, measure the syrup or juice from the can of apricots and make up to 750 ml with a mango/orange blend of fruit juice. Avoid apple-based juices as they will be very sweet and acidic.

8 chicken leg and thigh portions
2 x 32-gram packets onion soup mix
750-millilitre bottle apricot nectar
400-gram can apricots, well drained

1970s apricot chicken

serves 8
preparation time without browning **15 minutes**
preparation time with browning **30 minutes**
cooking time **low 5–6 hours, high 3–4 hours**

Every so often there's one recipe that hits the culinary news waves and somehow embodies the era in which it was published. Apricot chicken was the 1970s homemaker's saving grace. Packet soups became acceptable and helped take the stress out of, and add variety to, family meals and the apricot nectar was a great twist. If you could put it all in the slow cooker – dinner was hassle-free!

Turn the slow cooker on to low to pre-warm while gathering and preparing the ingredients.

If wished, cut the leg and thigh portions in half.

> ***If wishing to brown the chicken:***
> *Heat a dash of oil in a heavy-based frying-pan and quickly brown the chicken pieces.*

Put the chicken into the pre-warmed slow cooker.

Stir together the soup mix and apricot nectar, pour over the chicken and cover with the lid.

Cook on low for 5–6 hours or on high for 3–4 hours, or until the chicken is tender.

Add the apricots and season with salt and pepper before serving with plenty of creamy mashed potatoes. Garnish with chopped fresh chives.

variations

- Add a sliced onion and 1–2 teaspoons minced garlic. Brown in a dash of oil in a frying-pan to add a sweet caramelised-onion flavour.
- Brown and add 4–6 finely sliced rashers of bacon with the chicken.
- Stir in ½ cup sour cream before serving.
- Replace 1 cup of apricot nectar with ½ cup medium-sweet sherry.

allyson's tip

- Chicken leg and thigh portions on the bone will tolerate being a little overcooked, unlike chicken breast. My preference is the thigh portions, bone-in for this recipe.

- 10–12 chicken pieces, bone-in (drumsticks or thighs are best here)
- 8–10 pickling-sized onions, peeled and halved if large
- 8 rashers rindless bacon, diced
- 250 grams button mushrooms, halved
- 2–3 teaspoons minced garlic
- 1 tablespoon chicken stock powder
- 1 bouquet garni, optional
- ¼ cup tomato paste
- 2 tablespoons flour
- 2 cups red wine
- 1 cup water

coq au vin

serves 4–6
preparation time without browning **20 minutes**
preparation time with browning **30 minutes**
cooking time **low 6–7 hours, high 3–4 hours**

The traditional Coq au Vin, chicken in red wine, was prepared with an older bird. Thus it was simmered long and slow until the meat fell from the bones – perfect for slow cookers. However, today we do not get older birds which makes the cooking time less and the flavour not so intense, hence the inclusion of the chicken stock powder.

Turn the slow cooker on to low to pre-warm while gathering and preparing the ingredients.

> ***If wishing to brown the ingredients:***
> *Brown the chicken in a knob of butter or a little oil in a heavy-based frying-pan over moderately high heat until the chicken pieces are well browned on all sides. Set aside. Add the onions and bacon to the pan and brown evenly.*

Into the pre-warmed slow cooker put the chicken, onions, bacon, mushrooms, garlic, stock powder and bouquet garni, if using.

In a jug, stir together the tomato paste, flour, wine and water to make a smooth sauce. Pour over the chicken and cover with the lid.

Cook on low for 6–7 hours or on high for 3–4 hours, or until the chicken is tender.

Serve with your favourite potato dish and other seasonal vegetables.

variations

- Use 2 diced medium-sized onions in place of the baby onions.
- Use pancetta in place of bacon.
- Use white wine in place of red wine.
- Vary the wine flavour with different reds, but always choose a quality wine.

- 2–3 medium-sized fennel bulbs
- 1.5–1.6-kilogram whole chicken
- 1 onion, peeled and thinly sliced
- 4–6 cloves garlic, crushed, peeled and sliced or 2 teaspoons minced garlic
- ½ cup puy lentils
- ¼ cup currants
- 1½ cups chicken stock
- ½ teaspoon paprika

fennel braised chicken with puy lentils

serves 5–6
preparation time without browning **15 minutes**
preparation time with browning **25 minutes**
cooking time **low 5–7 hours, high 3–4 hours**

B

A simple and elegant recipe, ideal to share with friends at any time of the year.

Turn the slow cooker on to low to pre-warm while gathering and preparing the ingredients.

Slice the fronds off the top of the fennel bulbs, chop finely and set aside. Slice the fennel bulbs finely.

Rinse the chicken well and pat dry with an absorbent paper towel, especially the cavity of the chicken.

If wished, tie the chicken legs together and tuck the chicken wings under the chicken; this will ensure the chicken keeps a good shape during cooking.

> ***If wishing to brown the chicken:***
> *Heat a good dash of oil in a large, heavy-based frying-pan and, when hot, carefully brown the whole chicken on all sides as well as possible.*

Into the pre-warmed slow cooker put the chicken, sliced fennel bulbs, onion, garlic, puy lentils, currants and stock. Sprinkle with the paprika and half the reserved fennel fronds and cover with the lid.

Cook on low for 5–7 hours or on high for 3–4 hours.

Serve the chicken in chunky portions with the braising liquid and vegetables. Garnish with the remaining fennel and some shredded lemon rind if wished.

variations

- Use brown or green lentils in place of puy lentils, but not red lentils.
- Use barley in place of lentils.
- Use half chicken stock and half white wine or vermouth.
- Add 3–4 tablespoons cream before serving.
- Stuff the chicken with a lemon and currant spiked bread-based stuffing. Add extra cooking time, about 1–2 hours on low and 40–60 minutes on high.
- 5–6 leg and thigh pieces can be used in place of the whole chicken.

allyson's tip

- Puy lentils are smallish green-blue lentils that originated in central France and have reached culinary cult status here in recent time, invariably in part to their AOC status, which is a guarantee of place of origin qualification. They retain their shape and flavour when cooked, imparting a sweet flavour with a hint of smokiness.

- 1.5–1.6-kilogram whole chicken
- 4 lemon grass stalks
- 1½ teaspoons minced ginger
- 1–2 teaspoons minced garlic
- 1 teaspoon minced chilli or Sambal Oelek
- 1½ teaspoons ground coriander
- 2 cups chicken stock
- 400-millilitre can coconut cream
- 1 tablespoon fish sauce, optional
- 150–200 grams thin dried egg noodles
- 1 red capsicum
- 150 grams mange-tout (sugarsnap peas)
- 3–4 spring onions, trimmed and sliced
- 2 tablespoons chopped fresh coriander
- 1 tablespoon chopped fresh mint

chicken laksa braise

serves 6
preparation time **15 minutes**
cooking time **low 5–6 hours, high 3–4 hours**

A whole chicken cooked gently in thick, creamy coconut cream with spices and flavourings from South-East Asia is an easy way to make a mouth-watering laksa-style braise with ease.

Turn the slow cooker on to low to pre-warm while gathering and preparing the ingredients.

Rinse the chicken well and pat dry with a paper towel, especially the cavity.

Cut the lemon grass in two, crosswise just where the white bulbous end begins to turn green.

Bruise the green stalks with the heel of a heavy cook's knife and place them into the cavity of the chicken with half of the minced ginger.

Place the chicken into the pre-warmed slow cooker. Finely slice the remaining lemon grass and add to the slow cooker with the remaining ginger, garlic, chilli or Sambal Oelek, ground coriander, stock, coconut cream and fish sauce, if using, and cover with the lid.

Cook on low for 5–6 hours or on high for 3–4 hours, or until the chicken is tender. Carefully remove the chicken from the slow cooker, place on a plate and cover.

Cook the noodles in boiling salted water for 4–5 minutes or until tender. Drain well and chop roughly.

Add the noodles, capsicum, mange-tout, spring onions, fresh coriander and mint to the slow cooker. Cover and cook on high for 30 minutes to allow the vegetables time to heat through but remain crispy.

Break the chicken into pieces and serve in deep bowls with the noodles and a large ladle of coconut-infused cooking liquid.

variation

✤ Use 5–6 chicken leg and thigh portions in place of a whole chicken.

6–8 duck leg and thigh pieces
2 large onions, peeled and thinly sliced
4 cloves garlic, crushed, peeled and sliced
2 tablespoons sugar
¼–½ cup orange marmalade
¼ cup orange juice
1 cup chicken stock
2 tablespoons chopped fresh thyme
1–2 oranges

braised duck with orange & caramelised onions

serves 6–8
preparation time with browning **20 minutes (browning is essential here)**
cooking time **low 5–6 hours, high 2–3 hours**

B

With duck I prefer to cook the breast portions, which are best cooked quickly, separately from the leg and thigh portions which are better braised or cooked slowly. Orange and thyme are classic partners as they balance the duck's richness.

Turn the slow cooker on to low to pre-warm while gathering and preparing the ingredients.

Heat a dash of oil in a frying-pan and, when very hot, place the duck pieces into the pan, skin-side down to brown very well. Turn once and transfer to the pre-warmed slow cooker.

Drain most of the fat from the pan, leaving about 3 tablespoons. Add the onions and cook over a moderately high heat for 12–15 minutes, until the onions are well browned but not burnt. Stir regularly to prevent the onions from burning.

Add the garlic to the pan and cook only for a minute. Stir in the sugar and, when the sugar has melted, add the onions to the slow cooker.

Mix together the marmalade, orange juice, stock and thyme and pour over the duck. Cover with the lid.

Cook on low for 5–6 hours or on high for 2–3 hours, without lifting the lid.

To serve, grate the rind from the oranges with a zester or coarse grater and reserve. Use a sharp knife to cut away all the bitter white pith. Cut the orange into pieces. Add the orange rind and flesh. Season the duck with salt and pepper and extra fresh thyme if wished before serving. Mashed kumara makes an excellent accompaniment to the duck.

variations

- Use red onions for a sweeter onion flavour.
- Add 3–4 crushed juniper berries; they are great with game or rich meats.
- For an Asian influence, add 2–3 star anise.
- Replace ¼ cup stock with ¼ cup port or Madeira.
- Add 1–2 diced bacon steaks or rashers to the onions when browning.

12 chicken thigh portions, bone-in
1 onion, peeled and chopped
1 red capsicum, chopped
1 teaspoon minced garlic
1 ham steak, diced
10 stuffed olives, halved
2–4 tablespoons raisins
1 tablespoon capers, well rinsed
1 bay leaf
500 grams waxy potatoes, peeled and diced
400-gram can diced tomatoes in juice
1½ cups chicken stock
1 tablespoon wine or cider vinegar
2 cups frozen peas

caribbean chicken stew

serves 6
preparation time without browning **20 minutes**
preparation time with browning **30 minutes**
cooking time **low 5–7 hours, high 4–4½ hours, plus extra 20–30 minutes**

This all-in-one dish is ideal for mid-week family eating.

Turn the slow cooker on to low to pre-warm while gathering and preparing the ingredients.

> ***If wishing to brown the chicken:***
> *Heat a dash of oil in a large frying-pan and, when hot, brown the chicken pieces well on all sides.*

Into the pre-warmed slow cooker put the chicken pieces, onion, capsicum, garlic, ham, olives, raisins, capers and bay leaf. Scatter the potatoes over the top.

Mix together the tomatoes, stock and vinegar and pour over the chicken. Cover with the lid.

Cook on low for 5–7 hours or on high for about 4–4½ hours, or until the chicken is cooked.

Place the peas in a colander and pour boiling water over them. Scatter the peas into the slow cooker, cover with the lid and cook on high for a further 20–30 minutes, or until the peas are hot and tender.

Serve the Caribbean chicken with plenty of boiled rice.

1.5–1.6-kilogram whole chicken
½ cup light soy sauce
¼ cup dark soy sauce
2 tablespoons honey
2 tablespoons sugar
½ cup dry sherry
pared rind one orange
2 star anise, crushed
2 teaspoons minced ginger
1 teaspoon minced garlic
1 teaspoon sesame oil

soy & star anise braised chicken

serves 6
preparation time **20 minutes**
marinating time **preferably overnight, 4 hours minimum**
cooking time **low 5–7 hours, high 3–4 hours**

Allowing the chicken to marinate in a gutsy Chinese spiked soy sauce-based marinade overnight will enhance the flavour of the finished dish. Rather than serving with your favourite mix of stir-fry vegetables, remove from the cooking sauce, chill and take to a picnic. Pull the meat off in chunks and stuff into baps with salad greens, sweet chilli sauce and a handful of crunchy honey-roasted peanuts for salad rolls with a difference.

Wash the chicken and pat dry, especially the cavity. Place the chicken in a resealable bag. Mix together the soy sauces, honey, sugar, sherry, orange rind, star anise, ginger, garlic and sesame oil. Pour into the bag and seal.

Turn the chicken to coat evenly in the mixture and refrigerate overnight or for at least 4 hours.

Turn the slow cooker on to low to pre-warm. Place the chicken and marinade from the bag into the slow cooker and cover with the lid.

Cook on low for 5–7 hours or on high for 3–4 hours or until the chicken is cooked.

Carefully remove the chicken from the slow cooker onto a warmed serving platter. Cover and keep warm. Transfer the sauce from the slow cooker to a saucepan and simmer until reduced by a third. Glaze the chicken with a little of the sauce and place the remaining sauce into a serving jug.

Serve the chicken with your favourite stir-fried vegetables and the sauce on the side.

variation

- Use 6 chicken leg and thigh portions in place of whole chicken.

allyson's tip

- For a simple vegetable stir-fry, toss spring vegetables such as baby carrots and asparagus in a hot frying-pan in a dash of oil with plenty of shredded fresh ginger. When crisp-tender, toss through a handful of sesame seeds and season with a dash of soy sauce.

8 chicken leg and thigh portions
2 onions, peeled and finely sliced
2 teaspoons minced garlic
4 large juicy fresh tomatoes, roughly chopped
½–1 cup black olives
1 bouquet garni
1 tablespoon fresh rosemary or thyme leaves
400-gram can tomato purée or diced tomatoes in juice
½ cup red or dry white wine
½ cup chicken stock
2 tablespoons tomato paste
3 anchovy fillets, finely chopped

chicken cacciatore

serves 8
preparation time without browning **20 minutes**
preparation time with browning **30 minutes**
cooking time **low 6–7 hours, high 3–4 hours**

The word *cacciatore* is Italian for hunter, and any dish with this name will usually contain tomatoes, onions, mushrooms, herbs and wine. It was a favourite dish of the 1970s – I remember cooking it at the Tech college I attended. Its ease of preparation and use of simple, good-flavoured ingredients makes it a dish worth bringing back to life. I've added anchovies for an extra punch.

Turn the slow cooker on to low to pre-warm while gathering and preparing the ingredients.

Cut the chicken leg and thigh portions in half if wished.

> ***If wishing to brown the ingredients:***
> *Heat a good dash of oil or a knob of butter in a heavy-based frying-pan and brown the chicken pieces well on all sides. This will be best done in batches to avoid the chicken from stewing. The browner the chicken, the more flavour the finished dish will have. Once the chicken pieces are all browned, add the onions and garlic and a dash more oil if required and brown lightly.*

Into the pre-warmed slow cooker put the chicken, onions, garlic, fresh tomatoes, olives, bouquet garni and rosemary or thyme. In a jug, mix together the tomato purée or tomatoes in juice, wine, stock, tomato paste and anchovies. Pour over the chicken and cover with the lid.

Cook on low for 6–7 hours or on high for 3–4 hours, or until the chicken is tender. Serve the chicken with pasta.

Alternatively, lift the chicken from the slow cooker and, when cool enough to handle, pull the meat from the bones. Return the meat to the slow cooker (discard the bones) and stir to mix. Toss through plenty of hot, freshly cooked chunky-style pasta, with slow-cooked tomato halves. Add extra fresh rosemary leaves if wished. Have grated Parmesan on hand for guests to grate on their bowls of pasta as they please.

variations

- Add a few slices of thin-cut salami. Choose a chilli- or garlic-spiced salami for the fabulous flavour it will add.
- Use bacon in place of salami – 4–5 diced rashers would be ideal and they can be pan-fried with the chicken until brown.
- Make a mixed-meat cacciatore, replacing half the chicken in weight with beef, lamb or pork and including a few slices of salami or a chorizo-style sausage.

12 chicken drumsticks
1 tablespoon paprika
1 tablespoon onion salt
1 teaspoon garlic powder
2 bacon steaks, thinly sliced, optional
2 onions, peeled and sliced
250–350 grams button mushrooms, halved
420-gram can condensed tomato soup
½ cup water
½–1 cup sour cream, optional

paprika chicken

serves 6–8
preparation time without browning **20 minutes**
preparation time with browning **30 minutes**
cooking time **low 6–7 hours, high 3–5 hours**

Most family pantry cupboards have at least one, if not two, cans of condensed tomato soup – ready for that feed-the-family-in-a-hurry emergency. Use it here to make this easy family-style casserole.

Turn the slow cooker on to low to pre-warm while gathering and preparing the ingredients.

In a plastic bag or large lidded container, put the chicken drumsticks with the paprika, onion salt and garlic powder and shake to mix evenly. At this stage, the chicken can be refrigerated overnight if wished.

If wishing to brown the ingredients:
Heat a dash of oil in a heavy-based frying-pan and, when very hot, brown the chicken drumsticks quickly and evenly. Do not overcrowd the pan as the chicken will stew and not brown. Brown the bacon and onions if wished.

Into the pre-warmed slow cooker put the chicken, bacon, onions and mushrooms. In a jug, mix together the condensed tomato soup and water and pour over the chicken pieces. Turn the pieces to coat as well as possible and cover with the lid.

Cook on low for 6–7 hours or on high for 3–5 hours, or until the chicken drumsticks are well cooked. Gently mix in the sour cream if using and season with pepper.

Serve with your favourite seasonal vegetables or a baked potato and crisp salad.

variations

- In place of bacon steaks, use 3–4 bacon rashers or 1 ham steak.
- Use 1 x 400-gram can diced tomatoes and ½ cup tomato paste in place of condensed soup. Try a flavoured variant like tomatoes with garlic.
- Add ¼ cup chopped fresh parsley or chives before serving.

- 1.5–1.6-kilogram whole chicken
- 1 sprig fresh tarragon or ½ teaspoon dried tarragon
- 1 tablespoon flour
- 1 cup Champagne or sparkling wine
- 250 grams mascarpone
- 2 teaspoons cornflour
- 3–4 tablespoons prepared mild-style mustard
- 1 tablespoon finely chopped fresh tarragon or 1 teaspoon dried tarragon

carrier chicken

serves 5–6
preparation time without browning **10 minutes**
preparation time with browning **15 minutes**
cooking time **low 5–7 hours, high 3–4 hours, plus extra 15–20 minutes**

Robert Carrier was one of the earliest British celebrity chefs, hitting fame for his love of French-style cuisine in the 1970s. He loved Champagne – well who doesn't? – and this is an adaptation of a recipe from one of his books, which I was given as a budding young chef to inspire me along my way. The flavours of tarragon, mustard, chicken and cream are classics and the dish is stunning, if not a little calorific!

Turn the slow cooker on to low to pre-warm while gathering and preparing the ingredients.

Wash the chicken and pat dry, especially the cavity. Season the cavity with salt and pepper and place the tarragon into the centre. Tie the legs of the chicken together and twist the wings under the body of the chicken. This will help the chicken keep a good shape when cooking. Sift the flour over the chicken evenly.

If wishing to brown the chicken:
Heat a good knob of butter in a heavy-based frying-pan and, when hot, brown the chicken as well as you can on all sides. Browning adds flavour and colour.

Into the pre-warmed slow cooker put the chicken and Champagne or sparkling wine and cover with the lid.

Cook on low for 5–7 hours or on high for 3–4 hours, or until the chicken is tender.

Carefully remove the chicken from the slow cooker and place on a warm serving platter. Stir the mascarpone and cornflour together and stir into the slow cooker with the mustard and second measure of tarragon. Cover with the lid and cook on high for a further 15–20 minutes until the sauce is hot.

Carve the chicken and serve with a generous spoonful of the creamy mustard and tarragon sauce. Alternatively, pull the chicken meat from the bones and return to the sauce. Transfer to an ovenproof dish or dishes and cover with mashed potato (see buttery mash, page 16). Bake at 180 °C until hot and golden.

allyson's tip

- If buying fresh tarragon, make sure it is French tarragon and not Russian, which looks the same but is a wolf in sheep's clothing – it has no flavour. When out of season, use dried tarragon. It is one of the herbs that, when dried, retains its flavour well.

1.5–1.6-kilogram whole chicken
2 tablespoons flour
50 grams butter
1½ cups chicken stock
1 bouquet garni
3 egg yolks
½ cup cream
2 tablespoons cornflour
250–350 grams fresh asparagus spears, blanched
1–2 tablespoons chopped fresh tarragon or chervil

chicken & asparagus fricassée

serves 5–6
preparation time without browning **10 minutes**
preparation time with browning **15 minutes**
cooking time **low 5–7 hours, high 3–4 hours, plus extra 20–30 minutes**

B

This is a classic fricassée. A dish cooked simply in stock with a few flavourings like a bouquet garni. The finished sauce is thickened with egg yolks and cream – it is delicate and delicious. I have, though, added a little cornflour to prevent anyone overcooking the sauce and scrambling the egg yolks.

Turn the slow cooker on to low to pre-warm while gathering and preparing the ingredients.

Rinse the chicken well under running cold water and pat dry using absorbent paper, especially the chicken cavity.

Sift the flour over the top of the chicken and, if wished, tie the legs together so the chicken holds its shape.

> ***If wishing to brown the chicken:***
> *Heat the butter in a heavy-based frying-pan and, when hot, carefully brown the chicken as well as possible on all sides.*

Into the pre-warmed slow cooker put the chicken, butter, stock and bouquet garni and cover with the lid.

Cook on low for 5–7 hours or on high for 3–4 hours, or until the chicken is well cooked. Carefully lift the chicken from the slow cooker and transfer to a plate, cover and keep warm.

Mix together the egg yolks, cream and cornflour to make a smooth paste and stir into the slow cooker with the cooking juices. Cover and cook on high for 20–30 minutes or until the sauce has thickened.

Alternatively, cook the sauce in a saucepan over a low heat, stirring constantly until thickened.

Tear or cut the chicken into large pieces and return to the slow cooker with the asparagus and tarragon or chervil and turn gently to coat in the hot sauce. Serve immediately with your favourite seasonal vegetables.

variations

- **mushroom.** Slice 250 grams button mushrooms finely and cook in a generous knob of butter in a moderately hot frying-pan until soft and no moisture remains. Stir into the sauce with the egg yolks and cream.
- **corn.** Add one well-drained can of corn kernels with the egg yolks and cream and season with herbs such as chives or parsley.
- Use 6 leg and thigh portions in place of a whole chicken.

ginger crust pastry

1¼ cups plain flour
¼ teaspoon baking soda
¼ teaspoon cream of tartar
1 teaspoon ground ginger
¼ teaspoon mixed spice
125 grams butter, chilled and diced
2 tablespoons brown sugar
3–4 tablespoons water

Sift the flour, baking soda, cream of tartar, ginger and mixed spice into a bowl. Rub in the butter and stir in the sugar. Make a well in the centre.

Cut in sufficient water to make a stiff dough. Turn out onto a lightly floured bench and bring together. Wrap in plastic wrap and refrigerate until needed.

- 2 cups pinot noir
- 12 chicken thigh portions, bone-in
- 2 bacon steaks or 6 rashers of bacon, diced
- 6 large flat mushrooms, quartered
- ¼ cup tomato paste
- 1–2 tablespoons chopped fresh thyme, optional

rich pinot chicken with mushrooms

serves 5–6
preparation time without browning **20 minutes**
preparation time with browning **30 minutes**
cooking time **low 6–7 hours, high 3–4 hours**

Simmering the pinot noir until it is reduced by half ensures that this chicken dish has a warm, mellow, gutsy wine flavour. I like to serve it blanketed under a sweetish ginger crust pastry – the flavours work well together and the finished tart looks stunning. The pastry also works well with beef and pork dishes, cooked in red wine.

Turn the slow cooker on to low to pre-warm while gathering and preparing the ingredients.

Put the pinot noir into a small saucepan and simmer over a moderate heat until reduced to 1 cup.

> ***If wishing to brown the ingredients:***
> *Heat a good dash of oil in a large frying-pan and brown the chicken pieces and bacon well.*

Into the pre-warmed slow cooker put the chicken, bacon and mushrooms. Mix the tomato paste and red wine together, pour into the slow cooker and cover with the lid.

Cook on low for 6–7 hours or on high for 3–4 hours.

Stir in the thyme if using and serve the chicken pieces with your favourite seasonal vegetables or accompaniments.

- 1 x quantity of rich pinot chicken with mushrooms, cold
- 1 x quantity of ginger crust pastry
- beaten egg or milk to glaze

pinot chicken & ginger crust tart

serves 6
preparation time **30 minutes**
cooking time **25–30 minutes**

Turn the oven on to 200 °C. Place the rack into the centre of the oven. Lightly grease a 23–24-cm pie or quiche dish.

Pull the meat from the chicken, discarding the bones. Mix the chicken into the mushroom sauce.

Roll the ginger crust pastry out on a lightly floured bench until it is about 5–6 cm larger than the prepared pie or quiche dish.

Roll the pastry over the dish, allowing the excess pastry to overhang. Pile the cold chicken filling into the centre.

Lift the pastry edges up and over on top of the chicken pie filling. The pastry edges will have to be ruffled together to fit. The centre of the tart will be uncovered so do not worry.

Brush the pastry with the beaten egg or milk to glaze.

Bake the tart in the preheated oven for 25–30 minutes until the pastry is golden and the filling is hot. Serve hot, garnished with fresh herbs.

stuffing

- 3 cups fresh breadcrumbs, white or brown
- ½ cup pine nuts, toasted
- 6–8 semi-dried or sun-dried tomatoes, sliced
- 4 tablespoons oil or butter, melted
- 2 tablespoons chopped fresh rosemary
- ½ teaspoon minced garlic

casserole

- 1.5–1.6-kilogram whole chicken
- 1 onion, peeled and finely sliced
- 250–350 grams button mushrooms, halved
- 1 teaspoon minced garlic
- 4 large juicy tomatoes, quartered
- 1 cup marsala wine or chicken stock
- ¼ cup brandy

chicken marengo with a twist

serves 5–6
preparation time without browning **20 minutes**
preparation time with browning **30 minutes**
cooking time **low 5–7 hours, high 3–4 hours**

Chicken Marengo is a classic French dish that takes its name from the Battle of Marengo – the site of one of Napoleon's victories. The story goes that the dish was thrown together by his chef, using only the ingredients available to him. But, given tomatoes were unknown at this time, there's an element of debate about the original ingredients. I do like the touch of brandy added just before serving, it gives the dish an appealing, slightly alcoholic flavour – one wonders if Napoleon, known for his love of brandy, had an input into this recipe?

Turn the slow cooker on to low to pre-warm while gathering and preparing the ingredients.

In a bowl, toss together the breadcrumbs, pine nuts, semi-dried or sun-dried tomatoes, oil or butter, rosemary and garlic.

Rinse the chicken and pat dry, especially the cavity of the chicken.

Use the stuffing to fill the cavity and crop or neck end of the chicken. Tie the legs together and tuck the wing tips under the chicken to hold the stuffing in the crop or neck end. This will also ensure the chicken keeps good shape when cooked.

If wishing to brown the ingredients:
Heat a good dash of oil in a large frying-pan and brown the chicken as well as possible all over. Cook the onion, mushrooms and garlic until softened and lightly browned.

Into the pre-warmed slow cooker put the chicken and scatter around the onion, mushrooms, garlic and tomatoes. Pour over the wine or stock and cover with the lid.

Cook on low for 5–7 hours or on high for 3–4 hours, or until the chicken is well cooked and tender. Pour in the brandy before serving.

Serve the chicken with plenty of pasta and your favourite seasonal vegetables.

variations

- Pull the meat from the cooked chicken, discarding the bones and skin, and return the chicken to the sauce. Toss with a cooked chunky-style pasta. Add a few chopped stalks of parsley, rocket or a tablespoon of fresh rosemary leaves.
- Use 5–6 chicken leg and thigh portions in place of the whole chicken.

allyson's tip

- When tomatoes are out of season, use a 400-gram can of chopped tomatoes or whole peeled tomatoes in juice.

lamb

allyson's tips

- If cooking a whole leg of lamb at 2.25–2.5 kilograms, use 1½ times the marinade quantity.
- If you do not have chickpea flour, use rice flour or half the measure of wheat or standard flour.
- In place of using the whole spices, use 1½ tablespoons curry powder plus the paprika.

- 1.25–1.5-kilogram short-cut leg of lamb
- 3 tablespoons chickpea flour, toasted
- 2 tablespoons cumin seeds, toasted
- 1 tablespoon black peppercorns, toasted
- 8 whole green cardamom pods, toasted
- 1 cinnamon stick, crushed
- 4 dried red chillies
- 1 tablespoon paprika
- 1½ teaspoons ground nutmeg
- ½ teaspoon ground mace
- 1 cup plain unsweetened Greek-style yoghurt
- ½ cup oil
- 1½ cups chicken stock or water
- 2 onions, peeled and very finely sliced

slow-cooked north indian leg of lamb

serves 6
preparation time the day before **30 minutes**
marinating time **preferably overnight, 4 hours minimum**
preparation time on the day **20 minutes**
cooking time **low 4–5 hours, high 2–3 hours, plus extra 30 minutes**

B

The cuisine map of India is like a well-stitched tapestry – with herbs and spices and flavourings blending from one region to another, sometimes around the edge, sometimes more deeply. It is one of the most amazing places to visit. I find India assaults all your senses and all at the same time. This dish is adapted from a recipe from one of my favourite food writers, Madhur Jaffrey.

Trim the lamb of the knuckle if it is still attached. Cut deep gashes into the fleshiest part of the leg meat.

Into a spice or coffee mill put the flour, cumin seeds, peppercorns, cardamom pods, cinnamon stick, chillies, paprika, nutmeg and mace, and grind to make a fine powder. Mix the ground spices with the yoghurt and massage firmly into the lamb, pressing the mixture into the gashes to ensure the flavour penetrates the meat.

Place the lamb in a deep bowl, cover with plastic wrap and refrigerate, preferably overnight or for at least 4 hours.

When ready to cook, turn the slow cooker on to low to pre-warm while browning the lamb.

Heat about three-quarters of the oil in a large heavy-based frying-pan and brown the leg of lamb in the hot oil. The yoghurt will stick to the pan, but scrape off this sediment and spread onto the lamb.

Once the lamb is well browned, transfer to the pre-warmed slow cooker. Add the stock or water to the pan, stir to lift off any sediment and transfer to the slow cooker.

Add the remaining oil to the pan and cook the onions over a moderately high heat until well browned. Add to the slow cooker and cover with the lid.

Cook on low for 4–5 hours or on high for 2–3 hours, or until the lamb is tender. Transfer the lamb from the slow cooker to a warmed serving platter and cover. Turn the slow cooker to high if it has been on low and cook without the lid for 30 minutes, stirring occasionally.

Use a shallow spoon to lift off any oil that floats to the top and pour the sauce over the lamb to serve. Garnish with fresh herbs or toasted almonds if wished.

- 2 medium-sized purple eggplants
- 1.5 kilograms boneless lean lamb for casseroling
- ¼ cup olive oil
- 1–2 onions, peeled and finely chopped
- 1 teaspoon minced garlic
- 2 x 400-gram cans diced tomatoes in juice
- 2 tablespoons tomato paste
- 1 cup beef stock or water
- 2 tablespoons chopped fresh parsley
- 2 teaspoons sugar
- ½ teaspoon cinnamon
- ½–1 cup olives, either black or green
- ½ cup semi-dried tomatoes, optional
- 2–3 tablespoons chopped fresh oregano
- 1 tablespoon chopped fresh thyme

moussaka lamb braise

serves 5–6
preparation time without browning **20 minutes**
preparation time with browning **30 minutes**
cooking time **low 7–9 hours, high 4–6 hours**

Take the flavours of a classic Greek dish and create this casual, well-flavoured braise.

Turn the slow cooker on to low to pre-warm while gathering and preparing the ingredients.

Cut the eggplants lengthwise into quarters and cut crosswise in 1–2-cm slices.

Cut the lamb into chunky 3-cm pieces and season well with salt and pepper.

If wishing to brown the ingredients:
Brush the eggplant slices with olive oil and pan-fry in a hot frying-pan until well browned on both sides, then set aside. Brown the lamb pieces in a dash of oil in a hot frying-pan. Make sure the lamb is well browned. Set aside. Add the onion and garlic to the pan and cook gently in a dash of oil for 8–10 minutes until softened.

Into the pre-warmed slow cooker put the eggplants, lamb, onion, garlic, canned tomatoes, tomato paste, stock or water, parsley, sugar and cinnamon. Stir to mix evenly and cover with the lid.

Cook on low for 7–9 hours or on high for 4–6 hours, or until the meat is tender.

Stir in the olives and semi-dried tomatoes if using along with the oregano and thyme into the braise and season with salt and pepper. Serve with freshly cooked pasta or feta and mint topped bread.

variations

- Use beef or chicken in place of lamb.
- Add a well-drained can of chickpeas in the last hour of cooking.
- Stir through a couple of handfuls of spinach or rocket in the last 20 minutes of cooking time.
- Serve the braise under a filo pastry top for a scrumptious pie. See filo ruffle on page 16.

feta & mint topped bread

200 grams feta, crumbled
¼ cup grated pecorino or Parmesan
2–3 tablespoons chopped fresh mint
grated rind ½–1 lemon
4 small bread rolls, like ficelle

serves 4–8
preparation time **10 minutes**
cooking time **10 minutes**

Toss together the feta, cheese, mint and lemon rind. Warm the bread rolls in an oven at 180 °C for 10 minutes. Top each roll with equal amounts of the cheese mix and place under a grill until the cheese has softened.

allyson's tips

- When fresh tomatoes are out of season, use a 400-gram can of chopped tomatoes.
- The spices in the casserole are pretty up-front. If you are not accustomed to sweetly spiced meats, cut the amount of spices in half.

- 1 kilogram boneless lean lamb for casseroling
- 1 medium-sized eggplant
- 2 eating apples, peeled
- 2 onions, peeled and diced
- 3–4 juicy tomatoes, quartered
- 2 green capsicums, thickly sliced
- ½ cup dried apricots, chopped
- ½ cup pitted prunes, chopped
- 4–6 whole allspice berries or 1 teaspoon ground allspice
- 1 cinnamon stick or ½ teaspoon ground cinnamon
- 4–6 whole cloves or ½ teaspoon ground cloves
- 1 teaspoon each salt and pepper
- 1 cup beef stock or water
- ½ cup lemon juice

spicy lamb with dried fruits

serves 8
preparation time without browning **20 minutes**
preparation time with browning **30 minutes**
cooking time **low 6–8 hours, high 3–5 hours**

B

Redolent with the sweet spices used in classic Persian dishes, serve this lamb for a special night with pots of thick Greek-style yoghurt to accompany and piles of couscous.

Turn the slow cooker on to low to pre-warm while gathering and preparing the ingredients.

Cut the lamb and eggplant into 2.5–3-cm pieces. Cut the apples into quarters or sixths and cut away the core.

> ***If wishing to brown the ingredients:***
> *Heat a decent dash of oil in a large frying-pan. When hot, brown the lamb well on all sides. This is best done in batches so the lamb does not stew. Brown the onions well.*

Into the pre-warmed slow cooker put the lamb, eggplant, apples, onions, tomatoes, capsicums, apricots, prunes, allspice berries or ground allspice, cinnamon stick or ground cinnamon, whole cloves or ground cloves, salt and pepper.

Add the stock or water and lemon juice, and gently lift the ingredients with a large spoon to mix as well as possible. Cover with the lid.

Cook on low for 6–8 hours or on high for 3–5 hours.

Serve garnished with plenty of parsley and a few pistachio or almond nuts with warm soft breads for soaking up the spiced juices.

variation

- Use beef in place of lamb.
- Use a pre-made Moroccan spice blend in place of all the spices, allowing about 2 tablespoons. Flavours will vary from brand to brand.

allyson's tip

- If using hind shanks, the cooking time will be longer for the lamb so allow an extra hour's cooking time over those given here.

- 6 lamb knuckles, trimmed
- 2 large onions, peeled and finely chopped
- 2 stalks celery, trimmed and finely chopped
- 2 cups dried figs, halved
- 12–20 black olives
- 2–4 tablespoons capers, rinsed
- 6 cloves garlic, crushed, peeled and sliced or 4 teaspoons minced garlic
- 2 tablespoons chopped fresh rosemary leaves
- 1 teaspoon ground black pepper
- 750-millilitre bottle merlot
- ½ cup beef stock
- ¼ cup tomato paste

braised lamb knuckles in merlot with figs

serves 6
preparation time without browning **20 minutes**
preparation time with browning **30 minutes**
Cooking time **low 7–8 hours, high 4–5 hours**

If you cook these lamb knuckles on low, there will be no need to marinate the lamb to achieve a rich, gutsy sauce. If you plan to cook the knuckles on high, then it would be best to marinate the meat in all the ingredients (except stock and tomato paste) overnight, prior to cooking.

Turn the slow cooker on to low to pre-warm while gathering and preparing the ingredients.

If wishing to brown the lamb:
Brown the lamb knuckles in a good dash of oil in a hot frying-pan, turning the knuckles to ensure they are evenly browned.

Into the pre-warmed slow cooker put the lamb, onions, celery, figs, olives, capers, garlic, rosemary and pepper. Mix together the wine, stock and tomato paste and pour into the slow cooker. Cover with the lid.

Cook on low for 7–8 hours or on high for 4–5 hours. Serve with creamy mashed potatoes, flavoured with a little grated Parmesan.

Note: The resulting sauce is not very thick. Should you wish to have thicker sauce, lift out the knuckles and transfer the sauce to a saucepan. Simmer without a lid until reduced to your preferred thickness. Or, alternatively, stir in 4–6 tablespoons beurre manié (page 19) when the knuckles are cooked, cover and cook on high for a further 30 minutes until the sauce is thick.

variations

- Use 2 kilograms lean beef for casseroling in place of the lamb knuckles.
- Add 3–4 slices diced bacon.
- Add 250 grams button mushrooms, whole or halved.

6 lamb shanks, trimmed
2 onions, peeled and thickly sliced
6–8 cloves garlic, crushed, peeled and sliced
1 tablespoon paprika
1 tablespoon flour
1 cup chicken stock or water
½ cup sweeter-style sherry

paprika lamb shanks with rosemary glazed pears

serves 6
preparation time without browning **30 minutes**
preparation time with browning **40 minutes**
cooking time **low 7–9 hours, high 4–6 hours**

B

Lamb shanks are a timeless favourite. Simmered in a slow cooker, their flavour is meltingly delicious. Shanks are traditionally from the hind-quarter. They are larger and meatier than those from the fore-quarter.

Turn the slow cooker on to low to pre-warm while gathering and preparing the ingredients.

If wishing to brown the lamb:
Brown the lamb shanks well in a dash of oil in a hot frying-pan over a high heat. This can take some time as lamb shanks have quite an uneven shape.

Into the pre-warmed slow cooker put the lamb shanks, onions and garlic.

Mix the paprika, flour, stock or water and sherry together to make a smooth sauce. Pour over the lamb shanks and cover with the lid.

Cook on low for 7–9 hours or on high for 4–6 hours, or until the lamb shanks are tender.

Serve the shanks with the rosemary glazed pears and risotto or mashed potato.

variations
- For a smoky flavour, use smoked paprika.
- Add 4–8 rashers diced bacon and brown with the lamb shanks.
- Add 1–2 spicy chorizo sausages, sliced or diced. Brown first to release the oil and use the oil for browning the lamb shanks.

rosemary glazed pears

2–3 firm, ripe pears
25 grams butter
2 tablespoons fresh rosemary
2 tablespoons brown sugar

serves 6
preparation time **10 minutes**
cooking time **10 minutes**

Cut the pears into sixths and core if wished. Brown the pears evenly in the butter in a moderately hot frying-pan on all sides. Add the rosemary and sugar and cook for 5–8 minutes, turning regularly until the pears are glazed and tenderly cooked.

variation

- Use sage in place of rosemary.

1 kilogram boneless lamb necks, well trimmed
½ cup olive oil, extra virgin oil is nice here
1 tablespoon paprika
1 tablespoon ground cumin
1 tablespoon ground coriander
1 tablespoon ground turmeric
1 teaspoon salt
1 teaspoon coarsely ground black pepper
½ teaspoon saffron threads, optional
1–2 medium-sized red onions, peeled and thickly sliced
2 bacon steaks or 6–7 rindless bacon rashers, sliced finely
3 red capsicums, quartered, seeds and core removed
6 cloves garlic, crushed, peeled and sliced
½ cup sun-dried tomatoes in oil, well drained
1 cup tomato purée
1 cup stock or dry sherry
400-gram can chickpeas in brine, well drained

andalucian lamb necks

serves 10
preparation time without browning **30 minutes**
preparation time with browning **40 minutes**
marinating time **preferably overnight, 1 hour minimum**
cooking time **low 5–7 hours, high 3–4 hours, plus extra 15–20 minutes**

This stunning braise with its heady Spanish flavours makes good use of lamb necks, which are almost a forgotten cut. They are chubby pieces of well-marbled meat that, once well-trimmed, cook to tender perfection. This casserole's flavour improves significantly if prepared a day or two before and reheated to serve.

Place the lamb in a large dish or bowl, pour over the olive oil and sprinkle over the paprika, cumin, coriander, turmeric, salt and pepper and saffron if using. Toss well to coat, cover and refrigerate overnight to marinate. Alternatively, cover and leave at room temperature for 1 hour.

Turn the slow cooker on to low to pre-warm while gathering and preparing the ingredients.

If wishing to brown the ingredients:
Brown the lamb necks in a dash of oil in a hot frying-pan. Be careful not to burn the spices, but the lamb needs to be well browned. Set aside. Add the onion and bacon and brown in any residue oil.

Into the pre-warmed slow cooker put the lamb, bacon, capsicums, garlic, sun-dried tomatoes, tomato purée and stock or sherry. Cover with the lid.

Cook on low for 5–7 hours or on high for 3–4 hours, or until the lamb necks are tender. Stir in the chickpeas, cover with the lid and cook on high for 15–20 minutes, or until the chickpeas are hot.

Serve in deep bowls with an artichoke heart if wished. Garnish with fresh parsley leaves. A potato tortilla makes a wonderful accompaniment – do try it!

1½ cups olive oil, virgin olive oil is best here
4 very large floury potatoes, peeled and thinly sliced
1 very large onion, peeled and thinly sliced
8 eggs, well beaten
2 teaspoons minced garlic
½ cup grated fresh Parmesan or Cheddar-style cheese

potato tortilla

serves 8
preparation time **30 minutes**
cooking time **50 minutes**

The perfect accompaniment to winter casseroles, or served on its own with your favourite chutney for brunch or on a tapas platter.

Preheat the oven to 180 °C. Lightly grease a standard (not springform or loose-bottomed) 23-cm cake tin.

Heat the olive oil in a large heavy-based frying-pan and cook the potatoes and onions for about 7–10 minutes. They should not brown, but rather simmer in the olive oil. Transfer to a colander and allow them to drain well.

Beat the eggs and garlic together and season well with salt and pepper.

Pour about one-third of the egg mixture into the cake tin and arrange half of the potato and onion slices in the egg mixture. Repeat with the remaining egg mixture and potato and onion slices, finishing with the egg. Press all down together firmly so that the potatoes and onions are well submerged in the egg mixture. Sprinkle the cheese on top.

Bake in the preheated oven for 40 minutes or until golden brown and the egg mixture has firmly set. Cut into wedges and serve warm.

- 1 kilogram lean lamb mince
- 1–2 onions, peeled and finely diced
- 2 teaspoons minced garlic
- ¾ cup pine nuts, toasted
- ¾ cup pistachio nuts, optional
- 1 cup raisins or currants
- 2–3 teaspoons Moroccan or baharat spice mix (see page 181)
- 2 teaspoons ground coriander
- 2 tablespoons flour
- 1 cup beef stock
- 1–2 x 400-gram cans diced tomatoes in juice

moroccan lamb mince

serves 8
preparation time without browning **20 minutes**
preparation time with browning **30 minutes**
cooking time **low 3–5 hours, high 2–3 hours**

Depending on your needs, cooking a savoury mince mixture in a slow cooker can be quite convenient though the cooking time is not long at all. There's little chance of the mixture burning and the slow cooking allows the flavours to really develop.

Turn the slow cooker on to low to pre-warm while gathering and preparing the ingredients.

> ***If wishing to brown the ingredients:***
> *Brown the mince and onion in a heavy-based frying-pan, breaking up the mince with the back of a spoon as it browns. This will be best done in batches.*

Into the pre-warmed slow cooker put the mince, onion, garlic, pine nuts, pistachio nuts if using, raisins or currants, spice mix and coriander.

In a jug, stir together the flour and stock to make a smooth mix. Add the tomatoes and mix well.

Pour into the mince mixture and stir to mix evenly. Cover with the lid.

Cook on low for 3–5 hours or on high for 2–3 hours. Season with salt.

The texture of the final product will be quite different depending on whether the mince was pan-fried, with the un-browned mince being very smooth in texture.

Serve the mince with couscous, rice or potatoes and your favourite vegetables, or alternatively use the mince to make a flashed-up shepherd's pie topped with mashed orange-flesh kumara, or make the Moroccan lamb filo pies.

variations

- Use beef in place of lamb.
- Use Moroccan-flavoured tomatoes.
- Add ¼ cup chopped fresh coriander at the end of cooking time.
- Use almonds to replace the pine nuts or pistachio nuts.

½ x quantity of Moroccan lamb mince (page 179), cold
24 sheets filo pastry
100 grams butter, melted

moroccan lamb filo pies

makes 12
preparation time **30 minutes**
cooking time **15–18 minutes**

Preheat the oven to 200 °C. Lightly grease a baking tray or line with baking paper.

Have the mince made and cold.

Take one sheet of filo pastry and brush lightly with melted butter. Place a second sheet of filo on top. Brush lightly with butter and fold in half lengthwise.

Place about ¼ cup mixture at the top of the filo strip and flatten the mixture a little. Fold the filo strip over to make a triangle. Continue to fold down the length of the filo pastry to enclose the filling.

Brush the top with butter and place on the prepared tray. Repeat with the remaining ingredients. Sprinkle the pies with a little flaky salt if wished.

Bake in the preheated oven for 15–18 minutes or until the pastries are golden. Serve with yoghurt mint dip if wished.

allyson's tip

- Cut the meat from the neck chops if wished and discard the bones or use the bones to make stock. I like to cook the dish on the bone as they add flavour. Alternatively, use 750 grams lean lamb cut into 3–4cm-sized pieces.

1 kilogram lamb neck chops, well trimmed
50 grams butter, softened
1 kilogram waxy potatoes, washed and thinly sliced
5–6 carrots, peeled and thinly sliced
2 onions, peeled and thinly sliced
3 stalks celery, sliced
1–2 leeks, trimmed, washed and finely sliced
2 teaspoons dried mixed herbs
4 cups light-flavoured beef stock or water

lancashire lamb hot pot

serves 8
preparation time without browning **20 minutes**
preparation time with browning **30 minutes**
cooking time **low 7–8 hours, high 4–5 hours**

B

This working man's family meal originated in northern England during a time when families would bake their own bread in a farmhouse brick oven. Once the bread was cooked, the stews were put in and left to simmer slowly until day's end. In those days the meat was mutton or hogget, and the dish contained oysters. Today we use lamb and, well, the oysters I think would be best served another time, but for a touch of times past, scatter 10–12 fresh oysters under the potato top before serving.

Turn the slow cooker on to low to pre-warm while gathering and preparing the ingredients.

If wishing to brown the ingredients:
Brown the lamb in a dash of oil or knob of butter in a hot frying-pan. Do not crowd the pan, as the lamb will stew.

Spread half the butter over base of the pre-warmed slow cooker. Layer half the potatoes evenly over the base of the pot.

Layer the lamb, carrots, onions, celery and leeks on top of the potatoes. Sprinkle over the dried mixed herbs.

Layer the remaining potato slices on top, ensuring that the top layer is nicely arranged. Season liberally with salt and pepper.

Pour in the stock or water and place a piece of baking paper on top. This will prevent the potatoes from discolouring. Cover with the lid.

Cook on low for 7–8 hours or on high for 4–5 hours, or until the meat and vegetables are tender. Preheat the grill to 220 °C.

Remove the paper. Brush the top potato layer liberally with the remaining butter. Lift the crockery insert from the slow cooker and place under the preheated grill until the potatoes are golden.

Serve with vegetables – peas are a classic partner.

variations

- Use 2 teaspoons chopped fresh rosemary in place of the dried herbs.
- Omit the herbs and serve with classic mint sauce.
- Add a packet of soup mix, such as onion, French onion or spring vegetable, to boost the flavour.
- Add 250 grams sliced mushrooms.

allyson's tips

- In Bali, ½ teaspoon fish paste would be roasted and added to give it a very authentic flavour. If using, you need to wrap it in foil and toast in a frying-pan for about 1 minute as fish paste needs to be pre-cooked. If you like this pungent paste, add it at the beginning of cooking time.
- Use brown or muscovado sugar in place of palm sugar.

- 1 kilogram boneless lean lamb or hogget for casseroling
- 2 onions, peeled and diced
- 1 tablespoon minced garlic
- ¼ cup grated palm sugar
- 1 x quantity of basa genep spice paste
- 1½ cups water or light beef stock
- 3–4 bunches of fresh spinach

balinese spiced lamb casserole

serves 6
preparation time without browning **20 minutes**
preparation time with browning **30 minutes**
cooking time **low 5–7 hours, high 3–4 hours, plus extra 30 minutes**

A unique taste that will float you off to the fragrant spice island of Bali. There, they would normally use pork and it would not be browned before cooking. This lamb version works well with the spices.

Turn the slow cooker on to low to pre-warm while gathering and preparing the ingredients.

Cut the lamb into 3-cm chunks.

> ***If wishing to brown the lamb:***
> *Brown the lamb in batches in a dash of hot oil in a frying-pan.*

Into the pre-warmed slow cooker put the lamb, onions, garlic, palm sugar, basa genep spice paste and water or stock. Stir to mix and cover with the lid.

Cook on low for 5–7 hours, or on high for 3–4 hours.

Remove the coarse stems from the spinach and rinse under cold water. Stir the leaves into the lamb. Cover and cook for a further 30 minutes on high, or until the spinach has wilted and the casserole is hot.

Serve the lamb with rice or breads.

- 1 teaspoon whole black peppercorns
- 1 teaspoon coriander seeds
- ½ teaspoon sesame seeds
- 6 whole cloves garlic, crushed and peeled
- 3 tablespoons grated fresh turmeric, or 1 tablespoon ground dried turmeric
- 2 tablespoons minced ginger
- 1 tablespoon dried laos (galangal)
- 2 large red chillies, deseeded
- 1 shallot, peeled
- 2–3 candle or macadamia nuts
- ¼ teaspoon ground nutmeg
- about ¼ cup water

basa genep spice paste

makes ½ cup
preparation time **15 minutes**
cooking time **5 minutes**

This spice paste is a sacred combination of ground spices and flavourings, which creates the unique flavour of Balinese food. It's quite different from any other Asian spice paste.

Toast the peppercorns and coriander seeds over a moderate heat in a dry frying-pan until they smell fragrant and the coriander seeds become lightly browned. Add the sesame seeds and cook only until lightly golden. Remove the spices and seeds from the pan to arrest any further cooking. Cool.

In a pestle and mortar or mini food processor, put the toasted spices and seeds, garlic, turmeric, ginger, laos, chillies, shallot, candle or macadamia nuts, nutmeg and sufficient water to make a thick paste.

Keep in an airtight container in the fridge. Use within 1 week or, alternatively, freeze in tablespoonfuls.

tomato soup baked lamb shanks

- 2 x 37-gram packets tomato soup powder
- 2 cups beef stock
- 6 lamb shanks, trimmed
- 2 onions, peeled and sliced or diced
- 2 carrots, peeled and chopped
- 1–2 tablespoons fresh rosemary or 1 teaspoon dried rosemary

serves 4–6
preparation time without browning **15 minutes**
preparation time with browning **25 minutes**
cooking time **low 6–7 hours, high 4–5 hours**

Jazz up this family favourite by taking the meat off the bone and serving the boneless casserole under an easy savoury bread and cheese crumble.

Turn the slow cooker on to low to pre-warm while gathering and preparing the ingredients.

Mix together the soup powder and stock, stirring until the soup powder has completely dissolved. A whisk is ideal to use here.

If wishing to brown the lamb:
Heat a dash of oil in a frying-pan and, when hot, brown the lamb shanks well.

Into the pre-warmed slow cooker put the lamb, onions and carrots. Pour over the beef stock mixture and scatter over the rosemary. Season well with pepper and cover with the lid.

Cook on low for 6–7 hours or on high for 4–5 hours, or until the meat is meltingly tender and falling off the bone.

Serve the lamb shanks with plenty of mashed potato and seasonal vegetables.

lamb shanks with savoury crumble

- 1 x quantity of tomato soup baked lamb shanks, cooled
- 2 cups fresh breadcrumbs
- 50 grams butter
- 1 cup lightly grated Parmesan or Cheddar-style cheese
- 1 tablespoon finely chopped fresh rosemary

serves 4–6
preparation time **20 minutes**
cooking time **25 minutes**

Preheat the oven to 200 °C.

Pull the meat from the lamb shanks and discard the bones. Pull or cut the meat into bite-sized pieces and return to the sauce.

Transfer the lamb mixture to an 8–9-cup capacity casserole dish.

Mix together the breadcrumbs, butter, cheese and rosemary. Scatter the crumb mixture on top of the lamb and vegetables.

Bake in the preheated oven for 20–25 minutes, or until the casserole is hot and the crumble lightly golden.

variations

- Use a tomato and vegetable soup mix.
- Add 1 teaspoon yeast extract (Vegemite, Promite or Marmite).
- Vary the herbs. Thyme, chives, oregano and basil all work well with tomato and lamb.

allyson's tips

- When buying lamb shanks, have the bone trimmed or cut down. The finished dish will look more appealing.
- 4 slices of toast bread crumbed will give 2 cups of crumbs. Do not use dry breadcrumbs in this recipe.

- 1 kilogram boneless lean lamb or hogget for casseroling
- 1 large onion, peeled and finely diced
- 8 cloves garlic, crushed, peeled and diced
- 1 tablespoon minced fresh ginger
- 8 whole cardamom pods, crushed
- 8 whole peppercorns
- 8 whole cloves
- 1 small cinnamon stick
- 2 bay leaves
- 1½ tablespoons paprika
- 2 teaspoons ground cumin
- 1 teaspoon ground coriander
- 1 teaspoon salt
- ½ teaspoon ground turmeric
- ½ teaspoon chilli powder
- ½ teaspoon fennel seeds
- 1½ cups beef stock
- ¼–½ cup plain yoghurt, optional

rogan josh

serves 8
preparation time without browning **20 minutes**
preparation time with browning **30 minutes**
cooking time **low 6–8 hours, high 3–4 hours**

B

Rogan Josh is compulsory on every Indian restaurant's menu. It is easily recognisable due to the rich red colour from the paprika and chillies. It is highly aromatic and if you do not have time to prepare this dish with the spices, grab your favourite Rogan Josh curry paste and use. Slow cooking this dish creates an exceptional tasting curry.

Turn the slow cooker on to low to pre-warm while gathering and preparing the ingredients.

Cut the lamb into 3-cm chunks, trimming off any excess fat.

> ***If wishing to brown the lamb:***
> *Brown the lamb in a dash of oil in a hot frying-pan until well browned. This is best done in batches.*

Into the pre-warmed slow cooker put the lamb, onion, garlic, ginger, cardamom pods, peppercorns, cloves, cinnamon stick, bay leaves, paprika, cumin, coriander, salt, turmeric, chilli powder and fennel seeds.

Add the stock and stir to mix the ingredients as well as possible. Cover with the lid.

Cook on low for 6–8 hours or on high for 3–4 hours, or until the meat is tender.

Stir in the yoghurt if using and season with salt and pepper. Do not allow the curry to boil once the yoghurt has been added as it will cause the curry to curdle.

Serve the Rogan Josh with saffron rice (page 190), poppadoms or fresh naan bread.

variations

- If you do not have all the spices, buy your favourite Rogan Josh curry paste or cook-in-style sauce and use with the lamb, onion, garlic and stock only.

allyson's tips

- Classically the meat for a Rogan Josh is never browned, however, I believe it results in a nicer flavour as we are not keen on the 'boiled' flavour these days.
- Refrigerating the casserole for 1 or 2 days before eating will allow time for the flavours to marry further, giving a most delicious result.

2 cups long-grain rice
3 cups light chicken stock or water
½–1 teaspoon saffron threads
1 teaspoon salt

saffron rice

serves 6
preparation time **10 minutes**
cooking time **15 minutes**

To create a truly delightful saffron rice, use basmati rice in this recipe as it is so fluffy when cooked. Wash the rice well until the water is clear to remove any starch and drain well before cooking. If you do not have basmati, jasmine or standard long-grain rice will work just as well.

Wash the rice if wished and drain well.

Heat a good dash of oil or a knob of butter in a medium-sized saucepan and add the rice. Cook over a moderate heat for 2–3 minutes, stirring constantly until many of the opaque rice grains turn white.

Stir in the stock or water, saffron and salt and bring to the boil. Turn the heat down to the lowest setting and cover.

Cook on the lowest possible setting for 10 minutes and then turn off the heat, but do not lift the lid. Stand for 5 minutes before fluffing with a fork. Season with additional salt if wished.

variations

- Fluff in 2 tablespoons finely chopped fresh dill or 1 tablespoon dried dill.
- Toast ½ cup flaked or sliced almonds in a pan over a moderate heat until golden and stir through the rice before serving.

- 1 bulb garlic
- 2 large red capsicums
- 1 x 20-gram packet dried red chillies
- 1 tablespoon caraway seeds, toasted
- ½ tablespoon coriander seeds, toasted
- ½ tablespoon cumin seeds, toasted
- ½ teaspoon salt
- ¼ cup oil, olive is nice here

roast garlic red harissa

makes 2 cups
preparation time **20 minutes**
cooking time **1 hour**

Preheat the oven to 180 °C.

Place the garlic bulb in a square of foil and drizzle with a little olive oil. Wrap to enclose and bake in the preheated oven for 1 hour or until a skewer can easily be inserted. Some bulbs will take more or less time to cook. It's important the bulb is well cooked. Remove from the oven and allow to cool.

Turn the oven to grill, about 200 °C.

Cut the capsicums into thirds, this way you can easily cut around the core and miss the seeds. Place the pieces shiny-side up on a foil-lined tray and grill the capsicums until blackened. Cool, then peel.

Pour boiling hot water over the chillies and leave to soak for 10 minutes. Drain well.

Cut the garlic bulb in half crosswise and squeeze the pulp from both sides into a mini food processor. Add the chargrilled capsicums, chillies, caraway, coriander and cumin seeds, salt and oil. Process to make a thick smooth paste.

Transfer to dry sterilised jars, seal and keep refrigerated. Use within 1 month.

1.25–1.5-kilogram boned shoulder of lamb
2 tablespoons roast garlic red harissa (page 191)
¼ cup olive oil
2 red capsicums, cored and quartered
2 bulbs fennel, quartered lengthwise
8 baby onions, peeled
2 teaspoons minced garlic
1½ cups chicken stock or water
300-gram can chickpeas in brine, well drained
½–1 cup black olives, marinated olives are nice here
2 tablespoons coarsely chopped fennel fronds

lamb with harissa

serves 8
preparation time without browning **35–40 minutes**
preparation time with browning **40–45 minutes**
cooking time **low 5–7 hours, high 3–4 hours, plus extra 20–30 minutes**

Red hot chilli, warm caraway and refreshing fennel spice up this exotic lamb recipe that's best served with piles of couscous drenched with olive oil and seasoned with lemon and salt. Alternatively, mash potatoes with olive oil and season with salt and pepper.

Turn the slow cooker on to low to pre-warm while gathering and preparing the ingredients.

Place the lamb skin-side down on a chopping board and spread the harissa over the centre of the meat. Roll the boned shoulder up and tie with string to securely enclose the harissa. Alternatively, use skewers to hold together.

If wishing to brown the lamb:
Heat the oil in a frying-pan and, when hot, brown the lamb very well on all sides.

Into the pre-warmed slow cooker scatter the capsicums, fennel and onions. Sit the lamb shoulder on top. Pour in oil (if lamb was browned, add it from the frying-pan).

Mix the garlic with the stock or water and pour around the lamb. Cover with the lid.

Cook on low for 5–7 hours or on high for 3–4 hours.

Carefully lift the lamb from the slow cooker and place on a deep serving platter. Cover and keep warm.

Stir in the chickpeas, black olives and fennel fronds and season the mix with salt and pepper. Cover with the lid and cook on high for 20–30 minutes until the mixture is piping hot.

Serve the lamb sliced with a generous serving of the braised vegetables, juice and fresh green vegetables such as grilled courgettes.

Have extra harissa on hand to serve with the lamb for those who would like an extra spoonful of the spicy paste.

allyson's tip

- To serve the lamb cold, lift the lamb from the sauce and refrigerate in a lidded container. Transfer the sauce to a separate container and chill overnight. Lift off and discard any fat that has settled on the top. Warm the vegetables and sauce and mix well with grilled eggplant slices and tomato wedges. Remove the lamb from the fridge one hour before carving to ensure that it is not too cold as you will not be able to appreciate the flavour. Serve with the sauce, which should be at room temperature.

250 grams frozen or fresh spinach
2 spring onions, trimmed and finely chopped
¼ cup well-packed chopped fresh parsley
½ teaspoon dried dill leaves or 1 tablespoon chopped fresh dill
100 grams feta, crumbled
¼ cup grated Parmesan
½ –¾ cup pine nuts, toasted
1 boned full leg of lamb
1–2 onions, peeled and finely chopped
1–2 teaspoons minced garlic
1 cup green olives
1 cup dry white wine
½ cup olive oil, extra virgin olive oil is nice here
400-gram can borlotti beans, butter beans or chickpeas, well-drained and rinsed
½ cup chopped fresh parsley
grated rind one lemon

greek lamb with spinach, pine nuts & feta

serves 10
preparation time without browning **30 minutes**
preparation time with browning **40 minutes**
cooking time **low 5–7 hours, high 3–4 hours, plus extra 30 minutes**

Inspired by the flavours of a spanakopita – spinach, feta, herbs and pine nuts in a filo pastry – this lamb is delectable and ideal for a special occasion such as Easter or Christmas. Do allow the resting time as suggested to ensure it is tender to cut and the slices remain whole when carved.

Turn the slow cooker on to low to pre-warm while gathering and preparing the ingredients.

Defrost the spinach if frozen and place between two dinner plates. Squeeze the plates over a sink and allow excess moisture to fall away. Press as firmly as you can so the spinach is as dry as possible. If using fresh spinach, wash the leaves, remove the stalks and cook the leaves in a saucepan with only the water that clings to the leaves, until wilted. Drain and chop finely.

Mix the spinach together with the spring onion, parsley, dill, feta, Parmesan and pine nuts. Season well with pepper.

Using skewers, secure the opening at the knuckle-end of the boned leg of lamb. Pack the filling into the cavity where the bone has been removed. Use skewers and/or string to secure the opening at the top of the leg of lamb to ensure the filling is well-enclosed.

If wishing to brown the lamb:
Brown the lamb as well as possible in a dash of oil in a hot frying-pan. Transfer to the slow cooker.

Scatter in the onion, garlic and olives, and then pour in the wine and olive oil. Season with salt and pepper and cover with the lid.

Cook on low for 5–7 hours or on high for 3–4 hours.

Carefully remove the lamb from the slow cooker. Scatter in the beans or chickpeas, parsley and lemon rind and stir to mix. Cover and cook on high for a further 30 minutes while the lamb is resting.

Serve the lamb sliced with spoonfuls of the sauce and vegetables and accompany with grilled, sliced eggplant and baked vine tomatoes, if wished.

1 cup dried haricot or baby lima beans
1 leek, trimmed
1 short-cut leg of lamb
½ cup puy, brown or green lentils
1–2 stalks celery, finely diced
1 large carrot, peeled and finely diced
1 lean bacon steak, finely diced or 3–4 lean slices bacon, diced
1 cup chicken stock or water
1 large bouquet garni
2 tablespoons chopped fresh parsley
2 tablespoons chopped fresh thyme

lamb, bacon & lentil braise

serves 4–6
soaking time **overnight**
preparation time without browning **20 minutes**
preparation time with browning **30 minutes**
cooking time **low 6–8 hours, high 4–5 hours**

This lamb dish is best cooked on low. The lamb and beans soak up the aromatic flavours of the braising liquid until both are meltingly tender. A short-cut leg of lamb has been trimmed to remove the shank and rump end. It will fit into a mid-sized 4.5-litre slow cooker with ease.

Soak the haricot or lima beans in plenty of water overnight. Allow 3 times the amount of water to beans. Drain well.

Turn the slow cooker on to low to pre-warm while gathering and preparing the ingredients.

Cut the leek in half lengthwise and wash under a tap to remove any grit that has become trapped in the layers. Trim and dice finely.

> ***If wishing to brown the lamb:***
> *Heat a dash of oil in a large frying-pan and, when hot, brown the lamb as well as possible on all sides.*

Scatter the beans, leek, lentils, celery, carrot and bacon into the pre-warmed slow cooker. Stir in the chicken stock or water and add the bouquet garni.

Sit the lamb on top of the vegetables, lentils and bacon. Season the lamb well with salt and pepper and cover with the lid.

Cook on low for 6–8 hours or on high for 4–5 hours.

Lift the lamb from the slow cooker and place on a warmed serving platter. Cover and set aside to rest. This will ensure the meat is tender when carved.

Stir in the parsley and thyme and season well with salt and pepper. Remove the bouquet garni before serving.

Serve the lamb sliced and accompanied with your favourite seasonal greens.

variations

- Use pancetta in place of bacon steaks.
- Use half white wine or vermouth and half chicken stock.
- Stir 1 tablespoonful of prepared mustard into the beans and stock before serving. Try a tarragon mustard – it is green, not yellow, and has an intense tarragon/aniseedy flavour.

allyson's tip

- If you do not have buttermilk, use 1 cup unsweetened plain yoghurt and 1 cup milk. Alternatively, use 1½–2 cups milk, soured with 1 tablespoon lemon juice. Allow to stand for 10 minutes before using.

8 shoulder lamb chops
2–3 large onions, peeled
3 large potatoes, peeled
2 large parsnips, peeled
1–2 large swedes, peeled
2 large carrots, peeled
1 bay leaf, optional
4 cups water or light chicken stock
¼ cup Worcestershire sauce
½ cup chopped fresh parsley

irish stew

serves 8
preparation time **20 minutes**
cooking time **low 8–9 hours, high 4–5 hours**

As a kid, this was a favourite in our home. It came served with well-buttered, toasted crusty bread slices, plenty of chopped parsley and was seasoned with good splashes of piquant Worcestershire sauce. My mum never browned the lamb for her Irish stew, but feel free to.

Turn the slow cooker on to low to pre-warm while gathering and preparing the ingredients.

Trim the excess fat from the lamb chops. Season the chops well with salt and pepper.

Dice the onions finely. Cut the potatoes, parsnips, swedes and carrots into large chunky pieces.

Layer the lamb and vegetables in the pre-warmed slow cooker. Add the bay leaf, if using. Pour the water or chicken stock into the slow cooker and cover with the lid.

Cook on low for 8–9 hours or on high for 4–5 hours.

Drizzle in the Worcestershire sauce and scatter over the parsley before serving with warm buttered Irish soda bread.

3½ cups flour
2 teaspoons baking soda
2 teaspoons cream of tartar
½ teaspoon salt
50 grams butter, chilled and diced
1½–2 cups buttermilk

irish soda bread

makes 1 large loaf
preparation time **10 minutes**
cooking time **40 minutes**

Soda breads are easy to make and the result is ideal to mop up the juices of a casserole like Irish stew.

Preheat the oven to 200 °C. Lightly grease a baking tray or line with baking paper.

Sift the flour, baking soda, cream of tartar and salt into a large bowl. Rub in the butter and make a well in the centre. Using a wooden spoon, add sufficient buttermilk to mix to a soft, scone-like dough.

Turn out onto a lightly floured bench and knead very gently to just bring together.

Shape the bread into a 20–22-cm round and place on the prepared baking tray. Dust the top with a little extra flour if wished and cut a shallow cross in the centre.

Bake in the preheated oven for 40 minutes or until cooked. To test when the soda bread is cooked, tap it underneath and the bread should sound hollow.

Transfer to a cake rack to cool, but serve freshly baked and warm.

variation

- Divide the mixture into individual portions and bake for 15–20 minutes.

1.5 kilograms boneless lean lamb or hogget for casseroling

vindaloo paste

2 teaspoons cumin seeds
2 dried red chillies
1 teaspoon black peppercorns
1 teaspoon cardamom seeds
1 cinnamon stick
2 teaspoons mustard seeds
1 teaspoon fenugreek seeds
¼ cup wine vinegar
1 teaspoon brown sugar
½ teaspoon salt

2 onions, peeled and sliced
1 tablespoon minced ginger
1 tablespoon minced garlic
1 teaspoon ground turmeric
2 cups beef stock

lamb vindaloo

serves 8
preparation time **30 minutes**
cooking time **low 8–9 hours, high 4–5 hours**

This gutsy vindaloo is not too fiery, so feel free to add more chillies if you like hot stuff.

Turn the slow cooker on to low to pre-warm while gathering and preparing the ingredients.

Cut the lamb into 3-cm-sized pieces and set aside.

To prepare the vindaloo paste, grind the cumin seeds, chillies, peppercorns, cardamom seeds, cinnamon stick, mustard seeds and fenugreek seeds in a coffee mill or spice grinder until fine.

Mix the ground spices with the vinegar, sugar and salt.

Heat a good dash of oil in a frying-pan and cook the onions over a moderately high heat until they are well browned and crisp, but not burnt. Allow about 15 minutes.

Place the onions in a food processor with the spice paste and process until fine.

Into the pre-warmed slow cooker put the spicy onion purée with the ginger, garlic, turmeric and stock, and stir well.

Place the lamb into the slow cooker and stir to mix with spice paste as evenly as possible. Cover with the lid.

Cook on low for 8–9 hours or on high for 4–5 hours.

Serve with rice spiked with nigella seeds, and crispy poppadoms.

variation

- Use beef in place of lamb.
- Use 1 x 400-gram can chopped tomatoes in place of 1 cup beef to add a sweeter flavour.

allyson's tips

- Nigella seeds are a relative to the decorative plant love-in-a-mist. The little black seeds have a nutty, peppery flavour that works well with starchy foods such as rice, bread and potatoes.
- For low-fat poppadoms, cook them in the microwave. Cook 2–3 at a time, allowing approximately 1 minute on high power (100%) until crispy.

1 kilogram boneless lean lamb for casseroling
4 tablespoons chermoula spice mix (see page 204)
pared rind and juice one orange
¼ cup olive oil, virgin olive oil is nice here
3 parsnips, peeled
8–10 baby onions or large shallots, peeled
2 tablespoons quince paste
½ cup raisins, optional
2 tablespoons flour
1 cup chicken or beef stock
1 teaspoon minced garlic
2 oranges
½ cup black olives, optional

chermoula braised lamb with orange

serves 8
preparation time without browning **20 minutes**
preparation time with browning **30 minutes**
marinating time **preferably overnight, 20 minutes minimum**
cooking time **low 6–8 hours, high 3–5 hours**

B

Morocco is the home of chermoula spice mix. It is a sweet and not-too-hot blend of spices that partners particularly well with lamb, whether the meat is to be slow cooked or chargrilled. Chermoula mixes are available in boutique food stores, but making your own is simple and the flavours tend to be fresher as a result.

Cut the lamb into large 4-cm-sized pieces and place in a resealable bag. Sprinkle in the chermoula spice mix, orange rind and juice and olive oil. Seal the bag and massage to mix well, ensuring all the lamb pieces are coated. Refrigerate overnight if possible. Otherwise, leave at room temperature for 20 minutes to marinate.

Turn the slow cooker on to low to pre-warm while gathering and preparing the remaining ingredients. Cut the parsnips into chunky pieces. If the baby onions are large, then cut in half.

If wishing to brown the lamb:
Heat a good dash of oil in a frying-pan and, when hot, brown the lamb in batches, making sure it is well browned but the spices are not being burnt.

Into the slow cooker put the lamb, any reserved marinade, parsnips, onions or shallots, quince paste and raisins if using. In a jug, mix together the flour, stock and garlic and, when smooth and lump free, pour over the meat and vegetables. Stir to mix the ingredients in the liquid as well as possible. Cover with the lid.

Cook on low for 6–8 hours or on high for 3–5 hours, or until the lamb and vegetables are tender. Grate the rind from the second measure of oranges and use for the couscous. Use a small, sharp knife to trim away the bitter white pith. Cut the oranges into thin slices. Add the orange slices, and olives if using, to the braise and stir gently to mix. Serve garnished with mint leaves if wished and accompanied with the cinnamon & orange couscous (page 204) and your favourite vegetables.

variation

- Blanch 250 grams of broad beans in boiling water for 1 minute. Refresh in cold water, drain and peel to reveal peridot-jewel-like beans and stir in to the chermoula braise before serving.

(P

Front: ch

2 cups dried instant couscous
1 cinnamon stick or ¼ teaspoon ground cinnamon
3 cups boiling water
¼ cup olive oil
1 teaspoon salt
grated rind 2 oranges
1–2 cups loosely packed rocket and/or parsley leaves

cinnamon & orange couscous

serves 8
preparation time **10 minutes**
cooking time **2 minutes**

Place the couscous in a large microwave-proof bowl with the cinnamon. Pour in the boiling water and stir to mix. Stand for 10 minutes or until the couscous has absorbed all the water. Fluff to loosen the grains and sprinkle over the olive oil.

Cover with plastic wrap, microwave on high power for 2 minutes and then fluff again. Season with salt and stir in the orange rind and rocket or parsley leaves. The cinnamon stick can be removed before serving if wished.

¼ cup onion flakes
2 teaspoons paprika
1 teaspoon turmeric
1½ tablespoons dried parsley
1 tablespoon ground cumin
1 teaspoon dried orange peel, optional
1 teaspoon minced garlic
¼ teaspoon each cayenne pepper, black pepper and salt

chermoula spice mix

makes ½ cup
preparation time **5–10 minutes**

Mix together the onion flakes, paprika, turmeric, parsley, cumin, orange peel if using, garlic, cayenne and black pepper and salt. Toss to mix. Keep refrigerated in a sealed container and use within 2 weeks.

1 kilogram boenless lean lamb for casseroling
2 onions, peeled and finely diced
250 grams mushrooms, diced
1 teaspoon minced garlic
3 tablespoons flour
½ cup light beef stock
1 cup dry white or red wine
125 grams chicken liver pâté

alsace lamb

serves 6–8
preparation time without browning **30 minutes**
preparation time with browning **40 minutes**
cooking time **low 5–7 hours, high 3–4 hours**

A simple casserole enriched with gutsy red wine and finished with chicken liver pâté – an unusual combination that results in a truly delicious casserole.

Turn the slow cooker on to low to pre-warm while gathering and preparing the ingredients.

Cut the lamb into 2-cm-sized pieces and season well with salt and pepper.

> ***If wishing to brown the ingredients:***
> *Heat a good dash of oil in a frying-pan and brown the lamb and onion well. This is best done in batches.*

Into the pre-warmed slow cooker put the lamb, onions, mushrooms and garlic. Mix together the flour, stock and wine and stir into the lamb. Cover with the lid.

Cook on low for 5–7 hours or on high for 3–4 hours, or until the lamb is very tender. Add the pâté and stir until the pâté melts. Season with salt and pepper if wished.

Serve with seasonal vegetables.

1 x quantity of Alsace lamb (see page 205), chilled
400-gram block frozen puff pastry, defrosted
beaten egg or milk to glaze

alsace lamb pie

serves 6–8
preparation time **20 minutes**
cooking time **35–40 minutes**

Preheat the oven to 220 °C and place the rack in the middle.

Pile the Alsace lamb into an 8-cup-capacity pie dish and place a pie funnel into the centre of the dish. Set aside.

Roll the pastry out on a lightly floured bench to 3-mm thickness. Brush the lip of the pie dish with water. Cut sufficient 1-cm-wide strips of pastry to press onto the lip of the pie dish. Brush the pastry strip with beaten egg or milk.

Roll the remaining pastry over the rolling pin, unroll over the pie and press the two pastry edges together. Trim the pastry edges neatly.

Brush the top of the pie with the beaten egg or milk to glaze well. Cut a cross in the centre, where the pie funnel is, to allow the funnel to pierce its way easily through the pastry.

Trim the pastry and use any remaining trimmings to decorate the pie if wished. Brush these with egg glaze. Use a large cook's knife to 'knock-up' the edge of the pastry – this will help the puff pastry rise beautifully. Hold the knife horizontally and tap the cut edge of the pastry several times with the sharp edge of the knife. Do this all the way round the pie.

Bake in the preheated oven for 20 minutes, then lower the temperature to 200 °C for a further 15–20 minutes or until the pastry is well cooked and the lamb hot.

Serve with mashed parsnips and potato mixed together and seasonal vegetables.

variations

- Use a short crust pastry.
- Use beef in place of lamb.
- Make into individual pies. Line the base of 6 small metal pie dishes with short crust pastry. Fill with the Alsace lamb and cover with puff pastry. Bake as above, though the cooking time will be about 10 minutes less.

1 full leg of lamb
4–6 cloves garlic, crushed and peeled
½ cup fresh oregano or marjoram leaves
¼ cup fresh rosemary leaves
12–18 sun-dried tomato halves in oil, well drained
2 teaspoons sugar
¾ cup white or rosé wine

to finish, optional

4 large juicy tomatoes, quartered
400-gram can chickpeas, well drained, optional
1 cup black olives
4 artichoke hearts, quartered
¼ cup fresh oregano leaves

mediterranean leg of lamb

serves 10
preparation time without browning **20 minutes**
preparation time with browning **30 minutes**
cooking time **low 7–8 hours, high 4–5 hours**

B

The original version of this recipe is one of my husband's favourites. It was done with a boned, butterflied leg of lamb and cooked on the barbecue, turned slowly to ensure an even, well-browned outside and tender pink inside so that, when carved, the lamb is sensational. This slow-cooker version is equally scrumptious.

Turn the slow cooker on to low to pre-warm while gathering and preparing the ingredients.

Use a sharp, long, thin-bladed knife to make 12–18 deep slits all over the lamb.

Slice each garlic clove in three. Wrap a slice of garlic and a few leaves of oregano or marjoram and rosemary in a sun-dried tomato half and push into one of the deep cuts. Repeat with remaining ingredients.

> ***If wishing to brown the lamb:***
> *Heat a dash of oil in a frying-pan and brown the lamb well.*

Into the pre-warmed slow cooker put the lamb. Sprinkle over the sugar and pour the wine around the lamb. Cover with the lid.

Cook on low for 7–8 hours or on high for 4–5 hours, or until the lamb is well cooked.

The lamb can be enjoyed as is at this time with the juices that have collected from the cooking, or finished with the remaining ingredients. If wishing to add the finishing ingredients, remove the lamb to a warm plate, cover and leave to rest. Add the tomatoes, chickpeas if using, olives, artichoke hearts and oregano. Cover and cook on high for 20–30 minutes. Season with salt and pepper.

Transfer the lamb to a large meat platter and cover. Allow to rest for 20 minutes before carving. Sprinkle with flaky salt if wished.

allyson's tips

- Allow sufficient resting time to ensure the lamb is juicy and moist when carved. Use a thin-bladed, very sharp carving knife to cut thin slices, as thick slices (of any roast meat) can seem tougher than they are.
- After carving the leg of lamb, the bone can be used to make soup. Add to a stockpot of water with onion, carrot, celery and one packet of dried flavoured soup mix. Any meat remaining on the bones will fall off into the soup.

allyson's tips

- Lamb shoulder chops can be easily cut in half lengthwise. This makes handling the chops easier and allows more choice for the serving sizes.
- Cardamom has a warm, pleasant camphor and eucalyptus note, which complements curries very well. It is also a delight added to boiled or pilaf rice for both sweet and savoury rice dishes. Crush 2–3 pods per 2 cups of rice for a rice with panache.

8 lamb shoulder chops
2 large onions, peeled and thickly sliced
400-gram can diced tomatoes in juice
½ cup of your favourite korma curry paste
8 cardamom pods, crushed
2 tablespoons chopped fresh coriander
½ cup water
1 bay leaf
1 cup cream
¼–½ cup unsweetened plain yoghurt

lamb korma curry

serves 6–8
preparation time without browning **20 minutes**
preparation time with browning **30 minutes**
cooking time **low 5–7 hours, high 3–4 hours**

B

Some years ago, I had the pleasure of travelling through southern India on a media tour with Meena Patak, once owner of the celebrated Patak food company. It was an opportunity to experience an India that did not feature in travel magazines. We went off the beaten track to spend time making poppadoms, literally by hand, picking and drying spices, learning the art of Ayurvedic massage and cooking and supping the very alcoholic and dangerous drink, toddy, in the rice paddy fields with the locals. We really experienced the total colourful gloriousness that is India. Korma curry was a hot favourite on that tour, and this recipe is truly delicious.

Turn the slow cooker on to low to pre-warm while gathering and preparing the ingredients.

Trim the lamb chops of any excess fat and season well with salt and pepper.

> ***If wishing to brown the lamb:***
> *Heat a dash of oil in the frying-pan and, when very hot, brown the lamb chops on both sides. Do not overcrowd the pan or the chops will stew rather than brown.*

Into the pre-warmed slow cooker layer the lamb shoulder chops and onions. In a jug, mix together the tomatoes, curry paste, cardamom pods, coriander and water. Pour over the chops and turn to coat. Sit the bay leaf on top and cover with the lid.

Cook on low for 5–7 hours or on high for 3–4 hours, or until the lamb is tender.

Lift the lamb from the slow cooker. Stir the cream and yoghurt into the spiced tomato sauce. Return the lamb chops to the slow cooker and turn to coat in the sauce.

Serve with pilaf or boiled rice.

variations

- Use 8 chicken leg and thigh portions in place of lamb.
- Beef can also be used – allow about 1.5 kilograms boneless meat, cut into chunky pieces.

did you know?

✤ Honey comes in three flavour categories:

- **Sheer Honeys** – Vipers Bugloss, Nodding Thistle, Blue Borage, South Island Liquid, Clover (creamed or runny), Tawari, Lavender
- **Mellow Honeys** – Manuka, Rata, Pohutukawa, North Island Clover (creamed and runny)
- **Seasoning Honeys** – Rewa Rewa, Wild Thyme, Honeydew, Kamahi.

- 3–4 parsnips, peeled
- 3–4 carrots, peeled
- 500 grams small waxy potatoes, scrubbed
- 3–4 tablespoons medium- to strong-flavoured honey
- 2 tablespoons oil
- ½ teaspoon ground cinnamon
- 1.5–1.6-kilogram boned and rolled shoulder of lamb
- 1 cup beef stock, plus extra to finish
- 3 tablespoons instant gravy powder

honeyed shoulder of lamb

serves 6
preparation time without browning **15 minutes**
preparation time with browning **20 minutes**
cooking time **low 6–8 hours, high 4–5 hours**

B

Lamb has an affinity with honey and both partner well with cinnamon. Cooking with honey in the slow cooker allows the unique flavours of the particular honey being used to penetrate through the lamb and vegetables without the risk of honey burning due to direct heat. If you're not fond of sweet spices with lamb, delete the cinnamon and replace with 1 teaspoon dried thyme or rosemary.

Turn the slow cooker on to low to pre-warm while gathering and preparing the ingredients.

Cut the parsnips, carrots and potatoes into chunky pieces. If the parsnip core is tough, cut it out.

Toss the parsnips, carrots and potatoes with the honey, oil and cinnamon.

If wishing to brown the lamb:
Heat a dash of oil in a large heavy-based frying-pan and, when hot, brown the lamb as well as possible on all sides.

Place the lamb into the pre-warmed slow cooker and scatter the honey-coated vegetables over and around the lamb.

Pour in the stock and cover with the lid.

Cook on low for 6–8 hours or on high for 4–5 hours, or until the lamb and vegetables are tender.

Carefully lift the lamb and vegetables from the slow cooker and arrange on a warm meat platter.

Make the braising liquid in the slow cooker up to 2 cups with beef stock and place into a saucepan with the gravy powder. Stir over a moderate heat until thickened.

Serve the lamb sliced with the vegetables and gravy.

minted pea & new potato medley

500 grams new potatoes, well-scrubbed and halved
150–200 grams snow peas
150–200 grams sugar snap peas
400 grams fresh asparagus
75 grams butter, softened
2 tablespoons finely chopped mint

serves 8
preparation time **15 minutes**
cooking time **2–3 minutes**

Cook the potatoes in boiling salted water until tender. Trim the snow and sugar snap peas and asparagus. Drain and toss with potatoes, butter and mint.

- 4 rindless rashers bacon, finely diced
- 2 shallots, peeled and very finely diced or ¼ onion
- ¼ cup finely chopped fresh mint
- 1.6–1.7-kilogram boned shoulder of lamb
- ½ cup pinot gris or other white wine
- chicken stock or light beef stock, about 1 cup, if necessary
- 2–3 tablespoons instant gravy powder

mint & bacon stuffed lamb

serves 8
preparation time without browning **30 minutes**
preparation time with browning **40 minutes**
cooking time **low 6–8 hours, high 4–5 hours**

B

When I was an apprentice chef, this was a recipe we made regularly as it gave us practice at boning the lamb, stuffing and securing evenly with string. The simple stuffing permeates its way through the lamb as it cooks. The bacon, which will colour the lamb meat pink, gives a light smoky flavour which is softened by the sweet shallots and fresh garden mint – lamb's classic partner.

Turn the slow cooker on to low to pre-warm while gathering and preparing the ingredients.

Heat a dash of oil in a frying-pan and cook the bacon and shallots or onion until lightly golden. Cool and mix with the mint.

Spread the mixture on the inside of the shoulder of lamb. Roll up and secure with string or bamboo skewers, which may need trimming to get the lamb into the slow cooker.

If wishing to brown the lamb:
Heat a dash of oil in a frying-pan and brown the lamb well on all sides. It needs to be well browned for good flavour.

Into the pre-warmed slow cooker put the lamb and wine and cover with the lid.

Cook on low for 6–8 hours or on high for 4–5 hours.

Make the braising liquid remaining in the slow cooker up to 2 cups with stock and place in a saucepan.

Whisk in the instant gravy powder and stir over a medium heat until lightly thickened. Season with salt and pepper.

Serve the lamb thinly sliced with a minted pea & new potato medley.

- 1.5 kilograms boneless lean lamb for casseroling
- 1 leek, trimmed and washed, optional
- 1 onion, peeled and finely diced
- 2 carrots, peeled and finely diced
- 2 large parsnips, peeled and finely diced
- 535-gram can favourite cook-in-style sauce
- 400-gram can diced tomatoes in juice, tomato purée or tomato soup
- ½ cup water
- 1 tablespoon flour

potato topping

- 1.5 kilograms floury potatoes, peeled
- ½ cup milk
- 50 grams butter
- 1 cup grated Parmesan cheese

slow-cooker shepherd's pie

serves 8–10
preparation time without browning **15 minutes**
preparation time with browning **25 minutes**
cooking time **low 5–7 hours, high 3–4 hours**

B

Load this shepherd's pie up with vegetables so that it is a one-dish meal. The parsnips give this humble dish a sweet, earthy flavour.

Turn the slow cooker on to low to pre-warm while gathering and preparing the ingredients.

Cut the lamb and leek if using into small 1-cm dice.

If wishing to brown the lamb:
Heat a dash of oil in a frying-pan and brown the lamb pieces well. They should be evenly browned.

Into the pre-warmed slow cooker put the lamb, leek, onion, carrots and parsnips.

In a jug, mix together the cook-in-style sauce, canned tomato product, water and flour and stir until no flour lumps remain.

Pour into the slow cooker and stir to mix evenly. Cover with the lid.

Cook on low for 5–7 hours or on high for 3–4 hours.

For an easy presentation, pile the warm mashed potatoes directly on top and serve from the slow cooker. Alternatively, transfer the casserole to an ovenproof dish or six individual dishes, pile on the warm mashed potatoes and sprinkle with the cheese.

Bake at 190 °C for 10–15 minutes or until piping hot and the cheese has melted and is golden.

potato topping
Cut the potatoes into even-sized pieces and cook in boiling salted water until tender. Drain. Mash well and stir in the milk and butter. Season with salt and white pepper if wished, and top with the Parmesan.

- 1–1.25 kilograms lamb shoulder chops
- 2 onions, peeled and thinly sliced
- 2 tablespoons flour
- 1 cup beef stock
- ¼–½ cup port wine jelly, warmed
- 1 tablespoon finely chopped fresh thyme, optional
- 1 teaspoon cracked black pepper

lamb shoulder chops in port wine jelly gravy

serves 6–8
preparation time without browning **15 minutes**
preparation time with browning **25 minutes**
cooking time **low 5–7 hours, high 3–4 hours**

A quick 'n' tasty mid-week family meal.

Turn the slow cooker on to low to pre-warm while gathering and preparing the ingredients.

Trim any excess fat from the lamb chops. Season well with salt and pepper.

> ***If wishing to brown the lamb:***
> *Heat a dash of oil in a large frying-pan and, when hot, cook the lamb until well-browned.*

Into the pre-warmed slow cooker layer the lamb and onions.

Mix together the flour, stock, jelly, thyme if using and pepper to make a smooth sauce. Pour over the lamb and onions and cover with the lid.

Cook on low for 5–7 hours or on high for 3–4 hours, or until the lamb is tender.

Pile into a serving dish and accompany with your favourite greens and mashed kumara – spiked with honey and grated orange rind is delicious. Garnish with fresh thyme if wished.

variations

- Use blackcurrant or redcurrant jelly in place of port wine jelly.
- Use sliced cross-cut beef blade steaks in place of lamb shoulder chops.
- In place of flour, use a favourite packet of soup mix, like onion, or use instant gravy powder.
- Use red onions or leeks in place of onions, or add more vegetables like sliced carrots, parsnips, swedes and so on.

pork

12 pork schnitzels
24 sage leaves
12 small slices prosciutto
1 cup Marsala
1 onion, peeled and finely chopped
1 teaspoon minced garlic
½ cup cream or mascarpone
1 cup grated mozzarella

pork saltimbocca style

serves 8–10
preparation time without browning **20 minutes**
preparation time with browning **30–35 minutes**
cooking time **low 5–6 hours, high 3–4 hours**

Literally translated, *saltimbocca* means 'jump in the mouth'. This famous Italian dish is usually prepared from veal escalopes with sage and prosciutto and pan-fried. The flavours work well with pork and the slow-cook twist on this rather special dish is perfect to have with friends. It can be made in advance and reheated later as it will retain its flavour and texture well.

Turn the slow cooker on to low to pre-warm while gathering and preparing the ingredients.

Place a piece of plastic wrap on a chopping board and sprinkle with water. Place a schnitzel on top, sprinkle with water and cover with a layer of plastic wrap.

Hit firmly with a mallet or rolling pin to ensure the pork schnitzels are an even thickness; about 3 mm. Do not hit them until they are too thin or they will tear. Repeat with the remaining schnitzels.

Place the schnitzels on a chopping board. On one half, place 2 sage leaves and a piece of prosciutto. Season well with pepper. Fold over to enclose the sage and prosciutto and secure with a toothpick.

If wishing to brown the ingredients:
Heat a good dash of oil or a knob of butter in a heavy-based frying-pan and, when hot, brown the pork parcels on both sides. Set aside and add the Marsala to the pan. Stir to lift any sediment from the pan.

Into the pre-warmed slow cooker put the pork parcels, Marsala, onion and garlic and cover with the lid.

Cook on low for 5–6 hours or on high for 3–4 hours, or until the pork is tender.

Remove the pork from the slow cooker and stir in the cream or mascarpone. Season with salt and pepper and serve sprinkled with the mozzarella.

Alternatively, transfer the pork to a heatproof dish. Mix the juices in the slow cooker with the cream or mascarpone and pour over the pork. Scatter over the mozzarella cheese and fan grill under a moderately high heat until the cheese has melted and become golden.

variation

- Use chicken breast in place of pork. Flatten with the mallet or rolling pin until the breast is about twice its original size.

allyson's tips

- When flattening any cut of meat, it is always wise to place it between two dampened pieces of plastic to avoid tearing the meat, which can easily happen if it sticks to a dry chopping board.
- Don't forget to remove the toothpick before serving.
- Marsala is a fortified wine that originates from the town of the same name in Sicily. While not the same, Madeira can be substituted.

allyson's tip

- Chorizo sausages originate from Spain. Prepared from minced pork, they are well marbled with pork fat and flavoured with sweet or hot paprika or red capsicum pulp, hence the characteristic red colour. Additional seasonings include garlic, pepper and herbs. They can be bought fresh, which need cooking, or cured and dried, which can be eaten thinly sliced (delicious with a glass of chilled sherry on a tapas platter) or cooked and enjoyed hot.

- 2 red capsicums
- 750-gram lean piece pork belly, skin removed
- 3 thick smoked chorizo sausages
- 4 thin or 2 thick pork sausages
- 2 bacon steaks or 4 rashers bacon, diced
- 1 onion, peeled and sliced
- 1 tablespoon minced garlic
- 1 tablespoon paprika
- ½ teaspoon saffron threads, optional
- 400-gram can tomato purée
- 6 large juicy tomatoes, roughly chopped

mixed pork ragout

serves 6
preparation time without browning **20 minutes**
preparation time with browning **30 minutes**
cooking time **low 4–5 hours, high 3–4 hours**

This hearty flavoured pork dish is best cooked on low to allow the flavours to 'mellow in' together.

Turn the grill on to 220 °C. Line a baking tray with foil. Turn the slow cooker on to low to pre-warm while gathering and preparing the ingredients.

Cut the capsicums in halves or thirds and place cut-side down on the prepared tray. Brush lightly with oil if wished. Grill the capsicums under the preheated grill until they are well blackened all over. Wrap loosely in the foil and allow to cool before peeling away the charred skin. Cut into 1-cm-wide strips.

Cut the pork belly into 3–4-cm-sized pieces. Cut the smoked chorizo sausage on an angle into 1-cm-thick slices. Twist the pork sausages in half to make them smaller.

If wishing to brown the ingredients:
Heat a good dash of oil in a large heavy-based frying-pan and brown the pork belly, chorizo and pork sausages and bacon over a moderately high heat until well browned on all sides. This will be best done in batches to avoid the pan from becoming overcrowded and the meat stewing rather than browning. Set aside and brown the onion in any remaining oil until golden brown, but not burnt.

Into the pre-warmed slow cooker put the pork, sausages, bacon, onion, garlic, paprika, saffron if using, tomato purée and fresh tomatoes and cover with the lid.

Cook on low for 4–5 hours or on high for 3–4 hours, or until the pork is tender. Serve over a bowl of creamy gnocchi or mashed potatoes and garnish with plenty of fresh herbs, like parsley, oregano or rosemary (as pictured).

allyson's tips

- Keep juniper berries in an airtight container away from heat and light. Use only berries that are juicy when squashed and crush just before using as, if left too long, their essential oils will evaporate.
- When wanting baby onions to stay whole or not fall into leaves if cut in half for cooking, leave the core end intact when peeling.

juniper pork with mushrooms & sage

serves 6–8
preparation time without browning **30 minutes**
preparation time with browning **40 minutes**
cooking time **low 5–7 hours, high 3–4 hours, plus extra 30 minutes**

- 1 kilogram lean pork for casseroling
- 4–5 stalks celery, washed and trimmed
- 8–10 baby onions, peeled
- 4 rashers bacon, diced
- 12 baby potatoes, washed and quartered
- 100 grams fresh shiitake mushrooms, sliced
- 150 grams button mushrooms, sliced
- ¼ cup dried porcini mushrooms, optional
- 1 cup Madeira or a rich-tasting port
- 1 cup chicken stock
- 1 tablespoon juniper berries, crushed
- 1 tablespoon chopped fresh sage
- 1 teaspoon minced garlic
- 2–3 tablespoons beurre manié (see page 19)

Crunch a handful of softly dried ebony-mauve juniper berries, and you'll be hit by the aromas of gin. After all, it is the Dutch name for this berry, *jenever,* that was adapted to give the alcohol its name. Its underlying piney resinous scent brings a freshness to pork and aids with the digestion of rich meats. It partners well with sage and mushrooms in this delicious pork casserole.

Turn the slow cooker on to low to pre-warm while gathering and preparing the ingredients.

Trim any fat from the pork and cut into 3-cm-sized pieces. Cut the celery into 3–4-cm lengths. Halve the onions if large.

If wishing to brown the ingredients:
Heat a good dash of oil or knob of clarified butter in a frying-pan and brown the pork pieces over a high heat. Do this in batches to avoid the meat from stewing. Brown the celery, onions and bacon if wished.

Into the pre-warmed slow cooker put the pork, celery, onions, bacon, potatoes, shiitake mushrooms, button mushrooms and porcini mushrooms if using.

In a jug, mix together the Madeira or port, stock, juniper berries, sage and garlic with a good seasoning of salt and pepper. Pour over the pork and stir to mix as well as possible. Cover with the lid.

Cook on low for 5–7 hours or on high for 3–4 hours, or until the pork is tender. Stir in 2–3 tablespoons beurre manié, cover and cook a further 30 minutes on high until the sauce has thickened.

Serve with your favourite seasonal vegetables or as a pie.

1 x quantity of juniper pork with mushrooms & sage (page 227), cold
1 x quantity of cream cheese & sage pastry (page 229), well chilled
beaten egg or milk to glaze

juniper pork pie with cream cheese & sage pastry

serves 8
preparation time **15 minutes**
cooking time **35–45 minutes**

Nestle the juniper-infused pork braise under a buttery-rich pastry crust for a special meal with friends.

Preheat the oven to 220 °C and place the oven rack in the centre.

Transfer cold pork braise into an 8–10-cup-capacity pie dish. Push a pie funnel into the centre. Brush the rim of the pie dish with a little water.

On a lightly floured bench, roll out the cream cheese & sage pastry until it is about 3 cm wider than the top of the pie dish. Cut sufficient 1.5-cm-wide pastry strips to go around the edge of the dish. Press the strips onto the dampened pie-dish edge. Brush the pastry strip with a little beaten egg or milk.

Roll the remaining pastry over the rolling pin and then unroll over the pie. Press the pastry edges together well. Trim the edges and use any scraps to decorate the top of the pie if wished. Brush with beaten egg or milk to glaze and place the pie dish on a baking tray – to catch any spills.

Place into the pre-warmed oven and immediately turn the temperature down to 190 °C for 35–45 minutes or until the pastry is golden-brown and the filling is hot.

2 cups flour
150 grams butter, chilled and diced
125 grams traditional cream cheese, chilled and diced
2 tablespoons finely chopped fresh sage or 1 teaspoon dried sage
1 egg yolk
2 tablespoons water

cream cheese & sage pastry

makes 550 grams, sufficient for the top of a 30-cm-wide pie dish
preparation time **10 minutes**

Rich, smooth and slightly herbaceous, this pastry will have you asking for seconds.

Sift the flour into a wide mixing bowl. Use your fingers to rub in the butter and cream cheese until the mixture looks like coarse crumbs. Do not use the palm of your hands as they are too hot and will melt the butter and cream cheese, making the pastry greasy. Stir though the sage.

Make a well in the centre. Add the egg yolk and water and cut in with the blade of a knife. Turn out onto a lightly floured bench, bring together and knead lightly. Wrap in greased paper or plastic wrap and refrigerate for 30 minutes before using.

food processor method
Put the flour and sage into a food processor fitted with the metal blade. Add the butter and cream cheese and pulse until the mix looks like crumbs. Pulse in the egg yolk and water until the mix forms small, moist balls of dough. Do not process to form a ball as the pastry will be tough. Turn out onto the board and proceed as above.

allyson's tip

- Rest the pork for 15–20 minutes before carving to ensure the meat retains all its juices when carved, rather than having them spill onto the board. Also, it ensures the meat carves easily.

- 1 cup fresh white breadcrumbs
- ½ cup finely chopped pecans
- ½ cup dried cranberries
- 3–4 pieces crystallised ginger or papaya, diced, optional
- 75 grams butter, softened
- grated rind one orange
- 1 teaspoon ground allspice or mixed spice
- 1.5-kilogram piece belly of pork, well-scored
- 1 onion, sliced (can be unpeeled)
- 1 orange, sliced
- 4–6 whole cloves garlic, crushed only
- 1 cup chicken stock or water

gravy

- 2 tablespoons instant light-flavoured gravy powder
- 1 cup chicken stock
- 1 cup dried cranberries

cranberry-seasoned rolled pork belly

serves 8
preparation time **30 minutes**
cooking time **low 6–7 hours, high 4–5 hours**

Pork belly has recently become very popular. Cooked slowly in a slow cooker on a bed of oranges and onions and served with a dried cranberry-studded gravy, this pot-style roast is easy to prepare and truly delicious.

Turn the slow cooker on to low to pre-warm while gathering and preparing the ingredients.

Mix together the breadcrumbs, pecans, cranberries, ginger or papaya, butter, orange rind and allspice or mixed spice.

Place the pork skin-side down on a board and spread the filling lengthwise down the centre.

Roll the pork up from the shorter edge to enclose the filling. Secure with string or skewers.

Place the onion, orange and crushed garlic into the base of the pre-warmed slow cooker. Sit the pork on top, pour in the stock and cover with the lid.

Cook on low for 6–7 hours or on high for 4–5 hours. To test when the pork is cooked, pierce the meat with a meat fork. If the juices run clear, the pork is cooked. Alternatively, cook to 71 °C on a meat thermometer.

Remove the pork from the slow cooker and place on a warm serving platter. Cover and keep warm.

Strain the remaining cooking juice from the slow cooker into a saucepan, being careful to avoid any fat from going into the saucepan. Mix the gravy powder and stock together and stir into the saucepan. Cook over a moderate heat until the gravy has thickened. Add the cranberries and simmer for 5 minutes. Season with salt and pepper.

Serve the pork sliced with a good serving of the cranberry gravy and your favourite vegetables.

variation

- Use white wine in the gravy in place of the chicken stock.

allyson's tips

- When we think of Thai curries, so often we think of only green and red curry pastes, but there are others that can be enjoyed:
  - **Yellow curry paste** prepared simply with chillies, laos (see page 113), lemon grass, garlic and shrimp paste.
  - **Panaeng curry paste** is heady with more spices than green or red curry pastes.
  - **Chiang Mai curry paste** is a sweet, gutsy curry paste with turmeric and plenty of laos.

- 1 kilogram lean pork for casseroling
- 2 large kumara, peeled
- 2 large carrots, peeled
- 1 onion, peeled and finely diced
- ¼–½ cup Thai red curry paste
- ¼ cup tomato paste
- 6 fresh or dried kaffir lime leaves
- 400-millilitre can coconut cream or milk
- 1–2 juicy ripe tomatoes, quartered, optional
- 250 grams sugar snap or snow peas, blanched
- 1 cup fresh basil leaves
- 2–3 tablespoons chopped fresh coriander

thai kumara & pork curry

serves 6
preparation time without browning **20 minutes**
preparation time with browning **30 minutes**
cooking time **low 5–7 hours, high 3–4 hours, plus extra 15 minutes**

B

Choose an authentic, good-quality Thai curry paste for this dish and, if you have the time, cook on low so the flavours of all the spices in the curry paste have time to evolve.

Turn the slow cooker on to low to pre-warm while gathering and preparing the ingredients.

Cut the pork, kumara and carrots into chunky 3-cm pieces.

If wishing to brown the pork and onion:
Heat a dash of oil in a large heavy-based frying-pan and brown the pork pieces over a high heat. Brown the onion lightly, adding a dash more oil if wished.

Into the pre-warmed slow cooker put the pork, kumara, carrots, onion, curry paste, tomato paste, kaffir lime leaves and coconut cream or milk. Stir to mix the ingredients evenly and cover with the lid.

Cook on low for 5–7 hours or on high for 3–4 hours. Season with pepper and a dash of fish sauce if wished. Add the tomatoes if using, sugar snap or snow peas, basil and coriander and cover with the lid. Cook on high for 15 minutes before serving with boiled, delicately scented jasmine rice.

variations

- Use chicken or beef in place of pork.
- Vary the vegetables using potatoes or pumpkin for a change.
- Add 1 or 2 chunkily chopped red, green or yellow capsicums with the pork.

- 1½ cups dried baby lima beans
- 750 grams pork mince
- 1 teaspoon minced garlic
- 1½ tablespoons chopped fresh thyme or 1 teaspoon dried thyme
- 1–2 teaspoons fresh rosemary or ½ teaspoon dried rosemary
- 2–3 thick slices pancetta or bacon steaks, diced
- 2 stalks celery, diced
- 2 carrots, peeled and diced
- 1 onion, peeled and chopped
- 8 cups chicken stock
- ½ savoy cabbage, shredded
- 2 tablespoons chopped fresh sage or 1 teaspoon dried sage
- 1 tablespoon chopped fresh rosemary or thyme or ½ teaspoon dried rosemary or thyme

italian pork meatball & bean hot pot

serves 6–8
soaking time **overnight**
preparation time without browning **20 minutes**
preparation time with browning **30 minutes**
cooking time **low 5–7 hours, high 3–4 hours, plus extra 30–45 minutes**

This hearty, country-style one-pot meal is full of great flavours that your family and friends will all enjoy.

Soak the baby lima beans in cold water overnight. You will require 3–4 times the amount of water to beans. Drain, rinse and drain well again.

Mix together the mince, garlic, thyme and rosemary and season with salt and pepper. With wet hands, shape into 30–40 meatballs. Set aside.

Turn the slow cooker on to low to pre-warm while gathering and preparing the ingredients.

Place the beans into a large saucepan, cover with clean cold water and bring to the boil. Boil rapidly for 30 minutes. Drain well and scatter into the pre-warmed slow cooker.

If wishing to brown the ingredients:
Heat a good dash of oil in a frying-pan and brown the pork meatballs and pancetta or bacon well on all sides.

Add the meatballs to the slow cooker with the pancetta or bacon, celery, carrots, onion and stock. Use a large spoon to mix the ingredients together as well as possible. Cover with the lid.

Cook on low for 5–7 hours or on high for 3–4 hours, or until the beans are tender. Add the cabbage, sage and rosemary or thyme. Stir, cover and cook a further 30–45 minutes on high or until the cabbage has wilted. Serve in deep bowls and garnish with herbs if wished.

allyson's tip

- All cabbage needs to be cooked until just crisp tender, otherwise it looks grey and tastes horrid. Savoy cabbage is a variety of green cabbage with thick, crinkled leaves. It is milder in flavour and the leaves are a bit more tender than the standard green cabbage and therefore require less cooking. Standard green cabbage can be used here if wished. Look for cabbages that are unblemished and have no wilted leaves. Savoy cabbages will not keep as well as standard cabbages so buy and use within a few days.

allyson's tip

- If planning to brown the pork, do not use a plastic-style string to tie the pork to keep in shape, as it will melt when placed into the hot frying-pan. As the pork will spit wildly when browning, keep your lower arms covered to avoid getting burnt.

1.5-kilogram pork Scotch fillet
1 cup gutsy-flavoured red wine
2 tablespoons wine vinegar
2 carrots, peeled and sliced
1 onion, peeled and sliced
10 juniper berries, crushed
2 bay leaves, crushed
1–2 teaspoons chopped fresh tarragon or ½ teaspoon dried tarragon
½ teaspoon ground ginger
¼ teaspoon ground cloves
¼ teaspoon ground allspice or 4 whole allspice, crushed
grated rind one lemon
½ cup sour cream or cream, optional

german pork

serves 8–10
marinating time **overnight**
preparation time without browning **20 minutes**
preparation time with browning **30 minutes**
cooking time **low 5–7 hours, high 3–4 hours**

This pork is also great cold, served thinly sliced in sandwiches with layers of salad greens, mustard and mayonnaise.

Tie the pork Scotch fillet at 2.5–3-cm intervals to ensure it keeps a good shape while cooking.

Place the pork in a deep dish, lidded container or a resealable plastic bag with the wine, vinegar, carrots, onion, juniper berries, bay leaves, tarragon, ginger, cloves, allspice and lemon rind. Turn to coat evenly and cover or seal. Refrigerate overnight.

Turn the slow cooker on to low to pre-warm while preparing the pork for cooking.

Remove the pork from the marinade and strain the marinade, reserving both the liquid and the vegetables and spices.

If wishing to brown the ingredients:
Pat the pork dry on an absorbent paper towel. Heat a good dash of oil in a frying-pan and, when very hot, add the pork and brown well on all sides. The pan will spit wildly, but if the pork does not spit, then it will be stewing, so you need it to be hot! Set aside. Brown the carrots, onion and spices. Add the marinade and bring to the boil.

Into the pre-warmed slow cooker put the pork, vegetables, spices and reserved marinade and cover.

Cook on low for 5–7 hours or on high for 3–4 hours, or until the meat is tender. Carefully remove the pork from the slow cooker and set aside.

If making a sauce to accompany the pork, strain the cooking liquid from the vegetables into a saucepan and simmer until reduced by half. Stir in the cream and season with salt and pepper and a dash of prepared mustard if wished.

Serve with potato gnocchi and steamed carrots tossed with butter and chopped fresh tarragon.

variations

- Use a sweeter-style white wine like Riesling or Gewürztraminer in place of red wine.
- Look for a German mustard, it is darker than French or English and has a pungent sweet/sour taste.
- Use orange rind in place of lemon rind.

pickled pork

serves 6–8
preparation time **15 minutes**
cooking time **low 4–5 hours, high 3–4 hours**
resting time **2 hours**

2 apples, unpeeled and sliced
1 onion, peeled and sliced
½ teaspoon ground cinnamon
1.25-kilogram piece pickled pork
4 tablespoons honey
1½ cups apple juice or water

Think of pickled pork as being to pork what corned beef is to beef. It is an economical cut that's ideal to have on hand in the fridge to make sandwiches or to enjoy cold with hot mashed potatoes and salad.

Turn the slow cooker on to low to pre-warm while gathering and preparing the ingredients.

Layer the apple and onion slices in the base of the slow cooker and sprinkle over the cinnamon.

Place the pickled pork on top and spoon the honey over.

Pour the apple juice or water into the slow cooker and cover with the lid.

Cook on low for 4–5 hours or on high for 3–4 hours, turning the pork over halfway through the cooking time if possible.

Turn the slow cooker off and allow the pork to cool in the slow cooker for 2 hours before removing to a plate. Cover and cool for 30 minutes before refrigerating. Serve cold, thinly sliced.

tropical pickled pork salad

serves 6
preparation time **20 minutes**

600–700 grams cold cooked pickled pork
1 red or orange capsicum, sliced
1 green capsicum, sliced
½ fresh pineapple, cut into chunks
1 frilly-style lettuce, washed and torn into chunks
1 cup macadamia nuts, toasted
2–3 spring onions, sliced

piquant lemon 'n' chilli mayo
1 cup of your favourite mayonnaise
2 tablespoons finely chopped gherkins
2–3 tablespoons sweet chilli sauce
1–2 tablespoons finely chopped fresh chives
grated rind and juice 1 lemon

Cut the pickled pork into chunky 2–3-cm sized pieces and place in a bowl with the capsicums, pineapple, lettuce, macadamia nuts and spring onions.

Toss with the piquant lemon 'n' chilli mayo and serve soon after dressing.

piquant lemon 'n' chilli mayo
Stir together the mayonnaise, gherkins, chilli sauce, chives and lemon rind and juice.

allyson's tip

- The pickled pork can be served hot with a favourite sauce such as mustard (see page 53).

allyson's tips

- Having the pork scored will make carving easier.
- Mirin is often referred to as a rice wine. It is brewed from rice rather than fermented and is used for cooking and not drinking, to impart a unique flavour to glazes and sauces. Sherry can be substituted.

- 2 kilograms boned shoulder of pork, skin scored
- ¾ cup chicken stock or water
- ½ cup black bean and garlic sauce
- ¼ cup mirin
- 5-cm piece fresh ginger, peeled and sliced
- 3 whole star anise
- 2 teaspoons cornflour
- 1 tablespoon sherry or water
- 400-gram can whole baby corn, well drained
- 227-gram can water chestnuts, well drained
- 227-gram can bamboo shoots, well drained
- 4 bok choy, halved lengthwise

black bean & garlic pork braise

serves 10–12
preparation time **15 minutes**
cooking time **low 8–9 hours, high 4–5 hours, plus extra 30 minutes**

A boned well-marbled pork shoulder will cook to perfection in a slow cooker and will tolerate being left longer than planned. Any leftover cold meat has a delicious flavour, imparted from the braising sauce.

Turn the slow cooker on to low to pre-warm while gathering and preparing the ingredients.

Tie the pork together to ensure it cooks evenly and keeps a good shape while cooking.

Mix together the stock or water, black bean and garlic sauce and mirin and pour into the pre-warmed slow cooker. Sit the pork on top, scatter in the ginger and star anise and cover with the lid.

Cook on low for 8–9 hours or on high for 4–5 hours, or until the pork is tender.

If you have a meat thermometer, pork is cooked when the thermometer reaches 71 °C.

Remove the pork from the slow cooker, place on a warm plate and cover with foil. Allow the pork to rest before carving and while finishing the dish. Turn the slow cooker to high.

Mix the cornflour with the sherry or water and stir into the cooking liquid in the slow cooker.

Add the baby corn, chestnuts, bamboo shoots and bok choy and stir well. Cover and cook for a further 30 minutes.

Cut the pork into generous slices and serve over your favourite Asian noodles with a serving of the black bean sauce and vegetables. Garnish with peanuts if wished, before serving.

- 1.25-kilogram boneless lean pork for casseroling
- 1 leek, trimmed
- 2–3 carrots, peeled and sliced
- 2–3 stalks celery, peeled and sliced
- 1 red capsicum, diced
- 1 green capsicum, diced
- 1 tablespoon minced garlic
- 1 tablespoon minced ginger
- 440-gram can crushed pineapple
- ¼ cup brown sugar
- 1 cup water or chicken stock
- ¼ cup cider or white wine vinegar
- 2 tablespoons cornflour

pineapple sweet & sour pork braise

serves 8–10
preparation time without browning **20 minutes**
preparation time with browning **30 minutes**
cooking time **low 5–7 hours, high 3–4 hours, plus extra 30 minutes**

B

A slow-cooking twist on a stir-fry classic.

Turn the slow cooker on to low to pre-warm while gathering and preparing the ingredients.

Cut the pork into chunky 3-cm sized pieces. Cut the leek into thick slices and wash to remove any grit caught between the layers. Drain well.

If wishing to brown the pork:
Brown the pork pieces well in a dash of oil in a hot frying-pan. This will be best done in several batches.

Into the pre-warmed slow cooker put the pork, leek, carrots, celery, red and green capsicum, garlic, ginger, pineapple and juice, sugar, water or stock and vinegar. Stir to mix evenly and cover with the lid.

Cook on low for 5–7 hours or on high for 3–4 hours.

Mix the cornflour with a little water to make a smooth paste, about the consistency of pouring cream, and stir into the pork. Cover and cook a further 30 minutes on high.

Serve the pork braise with steamed rice, garnished with cashews if wished.

variations

- Add a small can of well-drained pineapple chunks before serving.
- Stir in 4–5 finely chopped spring onions before serving.
- Add ¼ cup tomato paste with the vegetables.
- Add ½ cup sliced dried apricots.
- Use boneless chicken thigh portions in place of pork. Cut the chicken thigh portions into thirds. Browning will add flavour, so it is recommended.

RUE
DE
SEINE

2 cups green or brown lentils
3–4 smallish fennel bulbs, quartered
2 carrots, peeled and sliced
2 red apples, peeled and thickly sliced
1 onion, peeled and diced
1 teaspoon dried sage
3 cups chicken stock
2 tablespoons golden syrup
1–1.25-kilogram piece boiling bacon

boiling bacon with lentils & apples

serves 6
preparation time **20 minutes**
cooking time **low 5–7 hours, high 3–4 hours**

An uncomplicated dish, rich in flavour from the slow cooking of boiling bacon, with pantry staple ingredients like apples, golden syrup and dried herbs.

Turn the slow cooker on to low to pre-warm while gathering and preparing the ingredients.

Put the lentils, fennel, carrots, apples, onion, sage, stock and golden syrup into the pre-warmed slow cooker and stir to mix the ingredients evenly.

Sit the bacon on top and cover with the lid.

Cook on low for 5–7 hours or on high for 3–4 hours, or until the lentils are tender.

Serve the bacon thickly sliced with a hearty serving of the lentils and vegetables, garnished with parsley if wished.

variations

- Use dried rosemary, thyme or oregano in place of sage.
- Add 1–2 sliced chorizo-style sausages.
- Add the pared rind of an orange with 1 teaspoon chopped green peppercorns.
- For a touch of spice, add 1 teaspoon curry powder.
- Use pears in place of apples.

1-kilogram piece pork belly, skin on and well-scored
1 teaspoon ground cinnamon
1 teaspoon curry powder or Indian-style curry paste
½ teaspoon ground cardamom or ginger
½ teaspoon ground nutmeg or mace
grated rind one orange
¼ cup oil
2 onions, peeled and finely sliced
1 red-skinned apple, peeled and thinly sliced
1½ cups chopped dried dates
1 cup raisins
1 teaspoon minced garlic
1 cup port or sweet-style sherry
1 cup chicken or light beef stock

slow pot-roasted pork belly

serves 6
preparation time without browning **30 minutes**
preparation time with browning **45 minutes**
cooking time **low 5–6 hours, high 3–4 hours, plus extra 25–30 minutes**
chilling time **overnight**

This slow-roast pork dish requires you to begin preparation about 3 days in advance. First the pork needs to be marinated overnight, slow cooked and allowed to cool. Then it is chilled for a night before roasting in a hot oven to crispen up the pork crackling and reheat the meat until meltingly tender. It is truly worth the effort for a special occasion.

Place the pork into a large sealable plastic bag or into a large dish. Sprinkle over the cinnamon, curry powder or paste, cardamom or ginger, nutmeg or mace, orange rind and oil, and massage into the pork. Seal or cover with plastic wrap and refrigerate overnight.

Turn the slow cooker on to low to pre-warm while gathering and preparing the ingredients.

If wishing to brown the ingredients:
Heat a frying-pan and, when hot, brown the pork well on both sides. Brown the onions if wished, adding a dash more oil if necessary.

Into the slow cooker put the onions, apple, dates, raisins and garlic and sit the pork skin-side up. Pour in the port or sherry and stock and cover with the lid.

Cook on low for 5–6 hours or on high for 3–4 hours, or until the pork is tender. Turn the slow cooker off and leave the pork to cool in the slow cooker for a further 2 hours.

Place the crock (crockery insert) into the fridge to chill overnight.

Continued overleaf

slow pot-roasted pork belly *(continued)*

About 2 hours before serving, place the crock back into the slow cooker and turn onto high. Remove the pork and place on a foil-lined tray skin-side up. Keep covered while the onion mixture is reheating. It will take about 1½ hours to reheat. Alternatively, this can be done on the stove in a frying-pan in a much shorter time.

Preheat the oven to 200 °C fan bake, or 220 °C bake. About 40 minutes before serving, place the pork into the oven and cook for 25–30 minutes or until very hot. The crackling will have become crisp and the meat should be very tender.

Serve the pork sliced on the hot apple and onion mixture and accompanied with your favourite greens.

variations

- Use pears in place of apple.
- Use currants in place of raisins.
- Add ¼ cup glacée mixed peel if wished.
- Use red or white wine or vermouth in place of port.

3½ cups chicken stock
1 cup instant polenta
¼ cup cream
½ cup grated fresh Parmesan
1 tablespoon fresh rosemary leaves
or ½ teaspoon dried rosemary

parmesan & rosemary polenta

serves 4–5
preparation time **5 minutes**
cooking time **5–8 minutes**

In a heavy-based saucepan bring the stock to the boil. Gradually pour the polenta into the stock, stirring continuously until the polenta has been absorbed and the mixture is thick and bubbling.

Continue to stir over a moderate heat for a further 2 minutes to ensure the polenta is well cooked. Remove from the heat and stir in the cream, Parmesan and rosemary.

Season well with salt and pepper. Serve while warm.

Alternatively, spread the polenta onto a baking-paper-lined 20 x 30-cm slice tin and level off. Refrigerate until chilled. Cut into wedges or squares, and pan-fry in oil or butter until golden.

1 kilogram boneless lean pork for casseroling
8–10 thick-cut slices pancetta
400-gram can diced tomatoes
1 cup chicken stock
1 tablespoon minced garlic
1 tablespoon fresh rosemary leaves or ½ teaspoon dried rosemary

garlic & tomato pork braise

serves 8
preparation time without browning **15 minutes**
preparation time with browning **25–30 minutes**
cooking time **low 5–7 hours, high 3–4 hours**

Take a few simple ingredients, slow cook them gently and create this stunning-tasting dish!

Turn the slow cooker on to low to pre-warm while gathering and preparing the ingredients.

Cut the pork into 3–4-cm pieces. Dice the pancetta.

If wishing to brown the ingredients:
Heat a good dash of oil in a frying-pan and brown the pork pieces over a high heat until well browned. This is best done in batches. Brown the pancetta with the last batch of pork.

Place the pork and pancetta, with any remaining oil from the pan (the pancetta will have given the oil a gutsy flavour), into the pre-warmed slow cooker.

Mix together the tomatoes, stock, garlic and rosemary and pour into the slow cooker.

Cover and cook on low for 5–7 hours or on high for 3–4 hours, or until the pork is meltingly tender.

Serve with Parmesan & rosemary polenta (page 249) and your favourite seasonal vegetables.

variations

- Add ½ cup black olives.
- Add ¼ –½ cup semi-dried tomatoes.
- Use sage in place of rosemary.
- Add a diced onion.
- Use bacon rashers or steaks in place of pancetta.

allyson's tips

- If browning, do not overcrowd the pan as the pork will stew rather than brown.
- Deglaze the pan with a little stock to lift all the sediment off the base of the frying-pan. It will add a little extra flavour to the braise.
- Pancetta is streaky bacon cut from belly pork and cured with salt, pepper and other spices. It is sweeter and spicier than smoked bacons.

10–12 thick pork sausages
1–2 onions, peeled and thickly sliced
6 cloves garlic, crushed, peeled and sliced
2 red or yellow capsicums, thickly sliced
1 cup puy or brown lentils
½ –1 cup black olives
1½ cups tomato purée
½ cup white wine
¼ cup olive oil
2 tablespoons chopped fresh sage or thyme
2 teaspoons green peppercorns in brine, rinsed, optional

pork sausage & lentil braise

serves 6–8
preparation time without browning **15 minutes**
preparation time with browning **20 minutes**
cooking time **low 5–6 hours, high 3–4 hours**

B

Thick pork sausages make a great autumn dish when braised with the complementary flavours of olives, green peppercorns, wine, capsicum and winter herbs like sage or thyme. These herbs help soften the wind-causing nature of the onion and lentils, and cut through the richness of the pork sausages.

Turn the slow cooker on to low to pre-warm while gathering and preparing the ingredients.

If wishing to brown the ingredients:
Place the pork sausages into a cold or just-warm frying-pan with a dash of oil and gradually heat the pan to brown the sausages. Doing it this way will avoid the sausages splitting. Set aside while lightly cooking the onion and garlic until they have softened and become golden brown, without burning the garlic.

Into the pre-warmed slow cooker put the sausages, onion, garlic, capsicums, lentils and black olives.

Mix together the tomato purée, wine, olive oil, sage and peppercorns if using, and pour over the sausages. Stir to mix the ingredients as evenly as possible and cover with the lid.

Cook on low for 5–6 hours or on high for 3–4 hours, or until the lentils are soft and the sausages are cooked. Season if wished with salt and pepper and add extra fresh herbs if wished.

Serve in large bowls with plenty of crusty bread to mop up the cooking juices.

variations

- Use thick beef or lamb sausages in place of pork.
- Use a flavoured tomato purée.
- Use a can of chopped tomatoes in place of the purée.
- Vary the wine – try sherry, vermouth or even a deep-flavoured red wine.

1 cup navy beans
1 onion, peeled and sliced
1 cup chicken stock
¼ cup golden or maple syrup
¼ cup whisky, preferably Bourbon
2 teaspoons prepared mustard
1–1.25-kilogram piece boiling bacon
500–750 grams yams, washed
1 tablespoon cinnamon sugar
400-gram can peach halves, well drained

peach & boiling bacon hot pot

serves 6
soaking time **overnight**
preparation time **30 minutes**
cooking time **low 5–7 hours, high 3–4 hours, plus extra 20 minutes**

A scrumptious combination of sweet, savoury and fruity flavours.

Place the navy beans in a large bowl and cover with 3–4 times the amount of water and leave overnight.

Turn the slow cooker on to low to pre-warm while gathering and preparing the ingredients.

Drain the beans well and place in a saucepan, cover with fresh water and boil for 20 minutes. Drain well.

Scatter the beans into the pre-warmed slow cooker with the onion, stock, golden or maple syrup, whisky and mustard and stir to mix evenly. Sit the bacon on top and scatter the yams around the side. Sprinkle with half the cinnamon sugar and cover with the lid.

Cook on low for 5–7 hours or on high for 3–4 hours, or until the beans and yams are tender.

Heat a dash of butter in a frying-pan and brown the peaches, sprinkling with the remaining cinnamon sugar as they brown. Add these to the slow cooker, cover and cook for a further 20 minutes on high.

Serve the bacon sliced with a hearty portion of the beans, yams and peaches.

variation

- Use baby lima beans in place of navy beans.
- Add 1 tablespoon minced ginger.
- Stir 1–2 tablespoons balsamic vinegar into the beans and yams before serving for a sweet and sour finish.
- Use chunkily cut peeled kumara or pumpkin in place of the yams.

allyson's tip

- When measuring heavy syrups, such as honey, golden or maple syrup, heat the measuring spoon in a jug of hot water. The syrup will fall easily off the spoon. Don't forget to level the syrup off once in the spoon to ensure the correct measure.

did you know?

- Bourbon whisky hails from America and is prepared primarily from corn. Its warm flavour marries well with pork and sweet spices like cinnamon.

8 pork loin chops, skin removed
150 grams salami, sliced thinly
2 x 140-gram tubs tomato pizza paste
400-gram can chopped tomatoes in juice
½ cup chicken or light beef stock or water
1 tablespoon minced garlic, optional

optional additions
3 artichoke hearts, quartered
½ cup black olives
¼ cup sun-dried tomato halves in oil, well drained
2–3 tablespoons oregano or marjoram leaves

pork chops in pizza sauce

serves 6–8
preparation time without browning **10 minutes**
preparation time with browning **20 minutes**
cooking time **low 5–7 hours, high 3–4 hours**

B

The bold, pizza-inspired flavours of tomatoes, garlic and oregano turn these pork chops into a great-tasting family meal.

Turn the slow cooker on to low to pre-warm while gathering and preparing the ingredients.

> ***If wishing to brown the pork:***
> *Heat a dash of oil in a frying-pan and brown the pork chops on both sides over a high heat.*

Into the pre-warmed slow cooker layer the pork chops and salami. In a jug, mix together the pizza paste, tomatoes, stock or water and garlic if using, and pour over the pork and salami. Cover with the lid.

Cook on low for 5–7 hours or on high for 3–4 hours. Stir in the optional ingredients if using: artichoke hearts, black olives, sun-dried tomatoes and oregano or marjoram. Serve with oven-baked, hot garlic pizza bread.

variation
- Use 10–12 boneless chicken thigh portions or 8–10 lamb shoulder chops in place of the pork.

allyson's tip

- Jalapeño peppers are plump, small, thick-skinned, green peppers that are available fresh or bottled in brine. They are moderate in their heat rating.

horseradish mashed spuds

1.5 kilograms floury potatoes, peeled and diced
½ cup warm milk
25–50 grams butter
2 tablespoons horseradish sauce
2 tablespoons chopped fresh thyme leaves

serves 8
preparation time **10 minutes**
cooking time **10 minutes**

Cook potatoes in boiling salted water until tender. Drain well. Mash with the milk, butter, horseradish sauce and thyme until smooth, adding more milk if required. Season if wished.

- 3 tablespoons minced jalapeño peppers
- 2 teaspoons minced garlic
- 1 teaspoon sugar
- 1 teaspoon paprika
- ½ teaspoon ground white pepper
- ½ teaspoon ground black pepper
- ¼ teaspoon ground cayenne pepper
- ½ teaspoon dried thyme
- 2–2.5-kilogram boned shoulder of pork
- 400-gram can diced tomatoes in juice
- 2 onions, peeled
- 2 green capsicums
- 6 medium-sized juicy ripe tomatoes
- 1 teaspoon chopped fresh thyme
- 2–3 tablespoons light-flavoured instant gravy powder

cajun pork pot roast with horseradish mashed spuds

serves 8
preparation time **30 minutes**
cooking time **low 6–8 hours, high 4–5 hours, plus extra 30 minutes**
resting time **30 minutes**

This hot and spicy pork pot roast was inspired by the flavours of New Orleans, where the three peppers, black, white and red, are always used in harmony with fresh thyme and all work so well with pork. The horseradish-infused mashed potatoes make a sensational partner.

Turn the slow cooker on to low to pre-warm while gathering and preparing the ingredients.

Mix together the jalapeño peppers, garlic, sugar, paprika, white and black pepper, cayenne and thyme.

Place the pork skin-side down on a chopping board and spread the jalepeño pepper mix over the meat. Roll up and secure with string or skewers.

Put the canned tomatoes into the slow cooker and sit the pork on top. Chop the onions and capsicums into large chunks and scatter around the pork. Cover with the lid.

Cook on low for 6–8 hours or on high for 4–5 hours, or until the pork is cooked. Remove the pork from the slow cooker and set aside to rest for 30 minutes.

Cut the fresh tomatoes into thin wedges and add to the slow cooker with the thyme and gravy powder. Stir to mix evenly and cover with the lid. Cook on high for a further 30 minutes until the sauce is hot and thickened.

Serve the pork sliced over the horseradish mashed spuds with a generous serving of the sauce.

1 cup dried borlotti beans
1 cup dried baby lima beans
3–4 carrots, peeled and sliced
2 red onions, peeled and diced
2–3 teaspoons minced garlic
1–2 teaspoons dried basil
1 teaspoon dried mixed herbs
1 litre tomato juice
1 cup chicken or vegetable stock or water
2 bacon hocks
½ cup chopped fresh parsley or basil

tomato braised bacon hocks

serves 6–8
soaking time **overnight**
preparation time **20 minutes**
cooking time **low 12–13 hours, high 8–9 hours**

Bacon hocks, off-cuts from the bacon curing process, are often sold at a much cheaper price than ham hocks. They impart a deep, smoky, bacony flavour to any dish and under the leather-like skin there's plenty of meat, making them a good buy.

Soak the borlotti and lima beans in plenty of cold water overnight. You will need 3–4 times the amount of water to beans.

Turn the slow cooker on to low to pre-warm while gathering and preparing the ingredients.

Drain the beans and transfer to the pre-warmed slow cooker. Add the carrots, red onions, garlic, basil, mixed herbs, tomato juice and stock or water. Stir well to mix evenly. Place the bacon hocks on top and cover with the lid.

Cook on low for 12–13 hours or on high for 8–9 hours. It will take this long to soften the beans as the acidity of the tomato juice will slow the cooking time of the beans considerably.

Lift the bacon hocks from the slow cooker and allow to cool. Remove and discard the skin. Pull the meat from the bones and break into chunky pieces. Return to the slow cooker. Season with pepper if wished.

Serve the braise garnished with the chopped parsley or basil.

variations

- Vary the beans in this dish to create different textures and flavours.
- Use a ham bone – especially useful for using up the leftover ham bone from Christmas or other celebrations.

- 1 cup dried haricot beans
- 4 stalks celery, trimmed and finely chopped
- 1 onion, peeled and chopped
- 3 teaspoons minced garlic
- 1 tablespoon prepared mustard
- 1-kilogram piece salted pork belly
- 1 bouquet garni
- 2 tablespoons golden syrup
- 2 cups chicken stock
- 8 chicken wing portions
- 6 thick pork sausages

french country pork braise

serves 6–8
soaking time **overnight**
preparation time **20 minutes**
cooking time **low 7–9 hours, high 4½–6 hours**

The ultimate slow-cooked pork dish – perfect for winter nights.

Soak the beans in plenty of cold water overnight. Allow 3–4 cups of water.

Turn the slow cooker on to low to pre-warm while gathering and preparing the ingredients.

Drain the beans and place in a saucepan with sufficient clean cold water to cover and bring to the boil. Boil rapidly for 20 minutes. Drain well.

Scatter the beans into the pre-warmed slow cooker. Stir through the celery, onion, garlic and mustard.

Sit the pork on the beans, fat-side uppermost. Add the bouquet garni, golden syrup and stock and cover with the lid.

Cook on low for 5–6 hours or on high for 3–4 hours.

Cut the chicken wings in half, cut off and discard the wing tip portion. Brown the chicken and sausages in a dash of oil in a frying-pan. The sausages can be cut into halves or thirds if wished.

Place the chicken and sausages around the outside of the pork belly and cover with the lid.

Cook for a further 2–3 hours on low or 1½–2 hours on high.

Serve the casserole by slicing the pork and placing in deep plates or shallow bowls with a generous serving of beans and cooking juices, chicken wings and sausages. Scatter with chopped fresh parsley or thyme before serving if wished.

- 8–12 lean pork belly slices, skin removed
- ¼ cup olive oil, lemon-infused olive oil is nice here
- grated rind one lemon
- 2 tablespoons chopped fresh thyme
- 3–4 medium-sized fennel bulbs
- 2 leeks, trimmed and halved
- 2 x 400-gram cans butter beans, well-drained
- ½ cup vermouth
- ½ cup chicken stock

pork with fresh thyme & fennel

serves 4
preparation time **25 minutes**
cooking time **low 5–6 hours, high 3–4 hours**

Add a touch of French country chic to your mid-week entertaining with this simple and inexpensive dish of pork slices, which are stretched out by the addition of pre-cooked canned butter beans.

Turn the slow cooker on to low to pre-warm while gathering and preparing the ingredients.

Toss the pork slices in the olive oil, lemon rind and half the thyme. Cover and set aside to marinate for 15 minutes.

Slice the fennel bulbs in half then cut lengthwise into long, thin slices. Cut the leeks into thick slices.

> ***If wishing to brown the ingredients:***
> *Brown the pork slices on both sides in a moderately hot frying-pan. Brown the fennel and leek, adding more oil if required.*

Into the pre-warmed slow cooker put the pork, sliced fennel, leeks, butter beans, vermouth, stock and remaining thyme. Season with salt and pepper and cover with the lid.

Cook on low for 5–6 hours or on high for 3–4 hours. Serve with mashed potato seasoned with fresh thyme and plenty of steamed green beans.

variations

- Use chicken thigh portions in place of pork.
- Add an extra ½ cup of chicken stock and 1 cup chopped prunes.

2–3 apples, washed
1 tablespoon whole cloves
½ cup golden syrup
1 cup water or apple juice
3–3.5-kilogram raw half leg of ham on the bone

slow-cooked ham

serves 18
preparation time **10 minutes**
cooking time **low 10–12 hours, high 6–7 hours**

The slower cooking ability of a slow cooker is perfect for cooking a raw ham. It will be best if you cook to temperature as this will prevent the ham from overcooking. You will need a large 6-litre-plus slow cooker for a 3–3.5-kilogram raw ham on the bone.

Turn the slow cooker on to low to pre-warm while gathering and preparing the ingredients.

Slice the apples thinly, there is no need to peel or core.

Place the apples in the base of the pre-warmed slow cooker. Scatter over the cloves and pour over the golden syrup and water or apple juice.

Sit the ham on top. If using a meat thermometer, insert it into the thickest part of the meat, ensuring it does not touch the bone, as this will give a false higher reading. Cover with the lid.

Cook on low for 10–12 hours or on high for 6–7 hours, or until the thermometer reads 71 °C.

Carefully remove the ham from the slow cooker to a large plate. Cover with foil and set aside to cool for 1–2 hours before refrigerating.

If wishing to glaze, remove the skin and glaze as wished. Bake at 180 °C for 40 minutes or until the fat layer is golden. Decorate as wished.

1 kilogram lean pork for casseroling
10–12 baby onions, peeled
8–10 whole cloves garlic, crushed and peeled
6–8 dried pear halves
1 tablespoon coriander seeds, toasted and crushed
2 teaspoons cumin seeds, toasted
few threads saffron, optional
few whole peppercorns
1 cup medium-dry sherry
1 cup chicken stock
1 cup pear or apple juice
½ x 500-gram bag frozen broad beans
½ preserved lemon, sliced, optional (see tip)
½ cup toasted almonds

pork with pears & sherry

serves 6–8
preparation time without browning **15 minutes**
preparation time with browning **25 minutes**
cooking time **low 5–7 hours, high 3–4 hours**

B

Bring a touch of Morocco to the table with this dish.

Turn the slow cooker on to low to pre-warm while gathering and preparing the ingredients.

Cut the pork into large 3–4-cm sized pieces. Halve the baby onions, if wished.

If wishing to brown the ingredients:
Brown the pork in a good dash of oil in a large heavy-based frying-pan. This is best done in 2–3 batches to avoid the meat from stewing. Gently pan-fry the onions and garlic cloves until lightly brown; add more oil if required.

Into the pre-warmed slow cooker put the pork, onions, garlic, pears, coriander seeds, cumin seeds, saffron if using, peppercorns, sherry, stock and juice. Stir to mix as well as possible and cover.

Cook on low for 5–7 hours or on high for 3–4 hours.

Place the broad beans in a heatproof jug or dish and pour boiling water over to cover them generously. Stand for one minute, drain and refresh in cold water. Peel if wished.

Add the beans to the slow cooker with the preserved lemon if using, and almonds, and serve with mashed potatoes or couscous.

variations

- Replace dried pears with fresh pears. Use 2–3 pears, peeled, cored and quartered and browned if wished.
- Use 1 kilogram boneless chicken thigh portions in place of pork pieces. Cut the chicken thighs in half.

allyson's tip

- When using preserved lemons, scoop out and discard the mushy centre pulp. Wash the rind well as this is the part you use.

- 2 cups dried haricot or small lima beans
- ½ cup olive oil, virgin olive oil is nice here
- 200 grams salami, thinly sliced
- 2 red onions, peeled and cut into eighths
- 2 green capsicums, diced
- 1 tablespoon minced garlic
- ½–1 teaspoon loosely packed saffron threads
- 1 teaspoon dried oregano
- 1 bay leaf
- 6 cups vegetable stock or water
- 1 cup dry sherry

spanish tapa beans

serves 6
soaking time **12 hours or overnight**
preparation time without browning **20 minutes**
preparation time with browning **30 minutes**
cooking time **low 9–10 hours, high 4–5 hours**

Sherry has been much maligned as a grandmother's drink, bought by the flagon and kept in the hall cupboard only to find the light of day at Christmas in the trifle! But a delicious dry fine sherry, well chilled, gives you a small but significant taste of Spain, and such exquisite vino deserves a good nibble to accompany it at any time of the year, like these beans.

Cover the beans with 3 times the amount of water to beans. Cover and set aside for 12 hours or overnight. Drain well.

Turn the slow cooker on to low to pre-warm while gathering and preparing the ingredients.

> ***If wishing to brown the ingredients:***
> *Heat a dash of the oil in a heavy-based frying-pan and, when hot, pan-fry the salami until the fat runs and the slices become slightly crispy around the edges. Set aside.*

Add the onions and capsicums to the pan with the residue fat from the cooking of the salami and cook the vegetables until browned.

Into the pre-warmed slow cooker put the well-drained beans, olive oil, salami, onions, capsicums, garlic, saffron, oregano, bay leaf, stock and sherry. Stir well to mix the ingredients evenly and cover with the lid.

Cook on low for 9–10 hours or on high for 4–5 hours, or until the beans are tender.

Serve in tapa or other individual shallow dishes with plenty of warm bread to soak up the juice.

variations

- Add a cup of halved, stuffed green olives.
- Add extra flavour with a bouquet garni.
- Add 1–2 teaspoons smoked paprika with the saffron.
- In place of salami, use 200 grams thinly sliced bacon or pork belly.
- Vary the beans – try borlotti or cannellini beans.
- Stir in 12–20 semi- or sun-dried tomato halves before serving.

allyson's tips

- Bay leaves have a sweeter, softer taste if they are used dried. Look for bright green dried bay leaves, these will be good quality. Dusty pale, khaki-coloured dry bay leaves are past their best.
- Keep dried herbs in airtight containers away from light to ensure they keep at their best. Dried herbs need to be replaced after 12 months and if left opened in the packet, replace earlier as the herb will have lost much of the essential flavour.

vegetarian

- 2 tablespoons tamarind pulp
- 2½ cups warm water or vegetable stock
- 1 kilogram large mushrooms
- 2 onions, peeled and finely diced
- 2–3 stalks celery, sliced
- 400-gram can diced tomatoes in juice
- 1 cup brown lentils
- 2 tablespoons tikka masala curry paste or similar
- 1 tablespoon curry powder, optional
- 1 tablespoon minced garlic
- 1 teaspoon ground cumin
- 1 teaspoon ground ginger
- 1 cup cashew nuts, toasted but unsalted

mushroom & cashew nut curry

serves 8
preparation time **20 minutes**
cooking time **low 7–8 hours, high 3–4 hours**

Use both curry paste and powder to give this mushroom curry layers of flavours. While the cashew nuts add a wonderful texture, they can be omitted or replaced with toasted almonds or chopped Brazil nuts.

Turn the slow cooker on to low to pre-warm while gathering and preparing the ingredients.

Leave the tamarind to soak in the water or stock for 10 minutes. Squeeze the softened pulp in your hand and strain the mix to remove any seeds and fibrous matter.

Into the pre-warmed slow cooker put the tamarind water, mushrooms, onions, celery, tomatoes, lentils, curry paste, curry powder if using, garlic, cumin and ginger. Stir to mix as well as possible and cover with the lid.

Cook on low for 7–8 hours or on high for 3–4 hours, or until the lentils and vegetables are tender.

Stir in the cashew nuts and serve with plenty of steamed rice. Garnish with coriander or parsley if wished.

variations

- Use Indian-flavoured canned tomatoes.
- Add 2–3 chopped fresh tomatoes in the last hour or two of cooking.
- Vary the flavour by using different curry pastes.
- Add cream or yoghurt just before serving to add a creamy richness. About 1 cup of either, or half a cup of both. If adding yoghurt, do not boil as this will cause the curry to curdle.

2 medium-sized eggplants
2 medium-sized onions, peeled and finely chopped
½ cup brown lentils
3–4 tablespoons toasted sesame seeds
2 tablespoons vegetable stock powder
1 tablespoon mustard seeds
2 teaspoons cumin seeds
2 teaspoons minced garlic
2 teaspoons curry powder
2 teaspoons ground turmeric
1½ teaspoons salt
4 cups water
2 cups frozen peas

peanut & coriander sprinkle
1 cup raw, skinned peanuts (untoasted)
¼ red onion, finely diced
¼ teaspoon ground cumin
2 tablespoons chopped fresh coriander

eggplant curry with peanut & coriander sprinkle

serves 6
preparation time without browning **20 minutes**
preparation time with browning **30 minutes**
cooking time **low 5–6 hours, high 3–4 hours, plus extra 30 minutes**

B

Browning the eggplant and onion and cooking this dish on a low heat will ensure this curry has more depth of flavour. Like so many curries, it's even more delicious the next day. Add a diced red or green chilli for an extra kick if wished.

Turn the slow cooker on to low to pre-warm while gathering and preparing the ingredients.

Cut the eggplants into 3–4-cm-wide slices. Brush each side with a little oil and cut in half.

> ***If wishing to brown the ingredients:***
> *In a heavy-based frying-pan or ridged grill pan, pan-fry the eggplant slices over a high heat to brown well. Set aside and brown the onions in the pan, adding a dash more oil if required.*

Into the pre-warmed slow cooker put the eggplants, onions, lentils, sesame seeds, stock powder, mustard and cumin seeds, garlic, curry powder, turmeric and salt.

Pour in the water and stir to mix as well as possible. Cover with the lid.

Cook on low for 5–6 hours or on high for 3–4 hours. If possible, stir once during the cooking time. Once the eggplant is tender, stir in the peas, cover and cook a further 30 minutes on high.

Serve the curry with rice and a smattering of the peanut & coriander sprinkle.

peanut & coriander sprinkle
Heat a good dash of oil in a frying-pan and cook the peanuts over a moderate heat until lightly golden. Add the red onion and toss quickly over the heat before adding the cumin. Remove from the heat and toss through the coriander. Season with salt and pile into a serving dish.

variations

- Try various curry pastes from different countries and regions.
- Add 500 grams sliced mushrooms and 1 tablespoon crushed coriander seeds with the eggplant slices to the slow cooker.
- Use 1 cup red lentils in place of brown lentils.
- Omit 1 cup water and add 1 x 400-gram can diced tomatoes.

allyson's tips

- If a curry is too hot and your mouth is on fire, place a large spoonful of plain yoghurt into your mouth and let it melt all over the surface of your mouth and tongue. The casein in the milk will help to cool the blow of the chilli. Don't grab a chilled glass of water, that will make your mouth feel even hotter!
- If you feel a curry is not well balanced in terms of flavour, add ground coriander – it is a wonderful spice for helping to marry other spices together.

- 2 cups navy or black-eyed beans
- 1 large onion, peeled and finely diced
- 500 grams large mushrooms, thickly sliced
- 5–7-cm piece fresh ginger, peeled
- 1–2 teaspoons minced fresh garlic
- 240-gram jar char siu sauce
- 3 cups water or vegetable stock
- ½ cup medium dry sherry
- 2 tablespoons dark soy sauce
- 4 bok choy
- 100–150 grams shiitake mushrooms

char siu beans with mushrooms

serves 6
soaking time **overnight**
preparation time **15 minutes**
cooking time **low 7–8 hours, high 3–4 hours**

A jar of prepared Chinese barbecue sauce (char siu) transforms these beans into a sensational meal.

Soak the beans in plenty of cold water overnight. Allow 3–4 times the amount of water to beans.

Turn the slow cooker on to low to pre-warm while gathering and preparing the ingredients.

Drain the beans well and scatter into the pre-warmed slow cooker. Stir through the onion, mushrooms, ginger and garlic.

In a jug, mix together the char siu sauce, water or stock, sherry and soy sauce. Stir into the slow cooker and cover with the lid.

Cook on low for 7–8 hours or on high for 3–4 hours, or until the beans are tender, stirring once or twice during cooking if possible.

When the beans are soft, cut the bok choy in half lengthwise and stir into the beans. Cover and continue cooking while pan-frying the shiitake mushrooms.

Cut large shiitake mushrooms in half and pan-fry the mushrooms in a dash of oil until softened and lightly browned. Stir into the beans. Remove the ginger before serving the beans. Have sweet chilli sauce on the side and garnish as wished. I use crunchy tamarind-coated, roasted sunflower seeds.

variations

- Use any preferred combination of dried beans; larger beans will require more water and the cooking time will need extending.
- When pan-frying the shiitake mushrooms, finish by drizzling with a little sesame oil.

did you know?

- Portobello mushrooms are large Swiss brown mushrooms also known as Cremini or Italian Brown. They are related to the white mushroom but not the same variety. Button mushrooms (white mushrooms) when grown up are called large flat mushrooms. Both hold their shape well in slow-cooker cooking, though their flavour varies a little and Portobellos seem to remain firmer when slow cooked.

allyson's tip

- For extra flavour, brush the eggplant slices with oil and pan-fry until well browned on each side.

1 large or 2 small eggplants
1 large onion, peeled and roughly chopped
2 red capsicums, diced
1 tablespoon minced garlic
1 tablespoon minced ginger
1 teaspoon minced chilli
1–2 tablespoons berbere spice mix
1 cup brown lentils
400-gram can chopped tomatoes in juice
3 cups vegetable stock or water
3–4 bunches fresh spinach

berbere spice mix
1½ tablespoons each cumin and coriander seeds
1½ teaspoons fenugreek seeds
1 teaspoon each whole allspice berries, peppercorns, cloves and cardamom seeds
2–3 teaspoons chilli powder
1 teaspoon ground nutmeg
½ teaspoon ground cinnamon

north african vegetable & lentil stew

serves 6–8
preparation time without browning **10 minutes**
preparation time with browning **20 minutes**
cooking time **low 6–8 hours, high 3–4 hours, plus extra 30 minutes**

I like to serve this dish with a sharp-tasting pickled fruit on the side like sweet-spiced and pickled pears or figs. Failing this, pan-fry pear slices in a little butter until golden, drizzle with a little balsamic vinegar and serve with the stew. The berbere spice mix is essential for an authentic flavour. It is most commonly used in the cooking of Ethiopia.

Turn the slow cooker on to low to pre-warm while gathering and preparing the ingredients.

Cut the eggplant into 1-cm thick slices and cut each slice in half.

If wishing to brown the ingredients:
Heat a good dash of oil in a frying-pan and cook the onion and capsicums over a moderate heat until well-browned. Stir in the garlic, ginger, chilli and spice mix and cook for a further 1–2 minutes until the ingredients are very fragrant.

Into the pre-warmed slow cooker put the eggplant, onion, capsicums, garlic, ginger, chilli, spice mix, lentils, tomatoes and stock or water. Stir as well as possible and cover with the lid.

Cook on low for 6–8 hours or on high for 3–4 hours, or until the lentils are soft. Stir once during this time if possible.

Tear the coarse stems from the spinach and rinse the leaves, shaking off any excess water. Add the leaves to the stew, stir in, cover and cook for a further 30 minutes on high.

Season well with salt and pepper and serve the lentils with sweet-spiced pickled figs or similar and garnish with coarsely chopped parsley leaves.

berbere spice mix
Toast the whole spices in a dry hot frying-pan for 2 minutes or until lightly toasted and fragrant. Transfer to a spice grinder and cool. Add the chilli, nutmeg and cinnamon and grind until fine. Store in an airtight container.

allyson's tips

- 2 cups of brown lentils are just under 500 grams, so if buying the lentils in a 500-gram bag, use all of them.
- Any leftovers will freeze well, though they may require a little extra stock when reheating.
- To shorten the cooking time, soak the lentils overnight in plenty of cold water. Drain well.
- Cumin and lemon seasoning is a spice blend of ground cumin, garlic powder and lemon rind. Look for it in the spice section of the supermarket. If you do not have it, use ground cumin and lemon rind and add extra garlic.

- 2 cups green or brown lentils
- 3–4 firm ripe pears
- 1 tablespoon minced garlic
- 4 cups vegetable stock or water
- 2 x 400-gram cans Moroccan-flavoured tomatoes
- 2 tablespoons cumin and lemon seasoning
- 1 bay leaf
- 1 cinnamon stick
- 1 preserved lemon, halved
- 12 fresh dates, stoned and halved

arabesque lentil & tomato braise with mint labne

Serves 10
Preparation time **20 minutes**
Cooking time **low 9–11 hours, high 4½–5 hours**

Labne is a fresh yoghurt cheese that is often made scented with mint. The creaminess of the cheese is a perfect partner to serve with these spiced lentils. Spread toasted pita bread with the cheese and then scoop up the lentils and munch – it's delicious!

Turn the slow cooker on to low to pre-warm while gathering and preparing the ingredients.

Wash the lentils and drain well. Cut the pears into quarters (peel and core only if wished).

Into the pre-warmed slow cooker put the lentils, pears, garlic, stock or water, tomatoes, cumin and lemon seasoning, bay leaf and cinnamon stick. Stir well to mix the ingredients as evenly as possible, and cover with the lid.

Cook on low for 9–11 hours or on high for 4½–5 hours, or until the lentils are tender.

Wash the lemon well. Scoop out and discard the soft pulpy flesh. Slice the peel finely and stir into the lentils with the dates. Season with salt before serving with toasted pita bread and mint labne (page 282).

variations

- Use dried beans such as baby lima or navy beans in place of lentils. Don't forget to soak them overnight and adjust the cooking time as required. Add extra stock or water if required.
- Add 4–5 quartered artichoke hearts before serving.

500 grams unsweetened plain yoghurt
1 teaspoon dried mint

mint labne

makes 1½ cups
preparation time **10 minutes**
standing time **overnight**

For best results, use a thick Greek-style yoghurt to get a firm, well-flavoured yoghurt cheese.

Stir the yoghurt and mint together. Place a clean Chux cloth or muslin square into a sieve and place it over a basin.

Spoon the yoghurt mixture into the cloth. Bring the ends together and tie the cheese into a tight ball, securing with string. Tie knots in the end of the cloth so you can hang the bag from a wooden spoon over a deep bowl.

Place in the fridge to drain overnight. The next day, season the mix in the bag with salt to taste. Keep refrigerated in an airtight container and use within one week.

- ½ cup olive oil, virgin olive oil is nice here
- 1 onion, peeled and roughly chopped
- 1 tablespoon minced garlic
- 1.5 kilograms juicy, red tomatoes, roughly chopped
- 3 large red capsicums, deseeded and chopped
- 1 tablespoon balsamic vinegar
- 2 teaspoons sugar
- 1 teaspoon salt
- 2 chargrilled red capsicums, peeled and sliced
- 1 cup well-packed fresh basil leaves

red capsicum & tomato pasta sauce

makes 8–9 cups
preparation time without browning **10 minutes**
preparation time with browning **20 minutes**
cooking time **low 6–7 hours, high 3–4 hours**

Turn the slow cooker on to low to pre-warm while gathering and preparing the ingredients.

> ***If wishing to brown the ingredients:***
> *Heat the oil in a frying-pan. Add the onion and cook over a moderate heat for 6–8 minutes or until softened. Add the garlic and cook for a further minute.*

Into the pre-warmed slow cooker put the oil, onion, garlic, tomatoes, capsicums, balsamic vinegar, sugar and salt. Stir well to mix and cover with the lid.

Cook on low for 6–7 hours or on high for 3–4 hours.

Sieve the mixture through a mouli or in a food processor or blender. Return the sieved sauce to the warm slow cooker and stir in the chargrilled red capsicums and basil.

Serve tossed through pasta.

Keep the pasta sauce in an airtight container and use within 3 days, or alternatively freeze and use within 6–12 months.

- ½ cup olive oil, virgin olive oil is nice here
- 2 large onions, peeled and finely diced
- 8–10 cloves garlic, crushed, peeled and sliced
- 3 kilograms large juicy ripe tomatoes, chopped
- ½ cup tomato paste
- 1 teaspoon dried oregano
- ½ teaspoon dried basil

tomato & garlic pasta sauce

makes 13 cups
preparation time without browning **15 minutes**
preparation time with browning **20 minutes**
cooking time **low 6–7 hours, high 3–4 hours**

Slow cooking all the ingredients for a classic tomato pasta sauce produces a richly flavoured sauce that can form the basis of many dishes.

Turn the slow cooker on to low to pre-warm while gathering and preparing the ingredients.

> ***If wishing to brown the ingredients:***
> *Heat the oil in a frying-pan. Add the onions and cook over a moderate heat for about 8–10 minutes until the onions are softened and become lightly brown. Stir regularly. Add the garlic and cook a further minute or until the mixture is fragrant.*

Into the pre-warmed slow cooker put the oil, onions, garlic, tomatoes, tomato paste, oregano and basil. Stir to mix as well as possible and cover with the lid.

Cook on low for 6–7 hours or on high for 3–4 hours.

Sieve the mixture through a mouli or push through a sieve to remove seeds and skins. Alternatively, purée in a food processor or blender. Season with salt and pepper and serve as wished. If wishing to keep, freeze the mixture in 1 or 2 cupful lots, label with a name and date and use within 6–12 months.

variations

pancetta or bacon
Cook 4–6 finely diced slices of bacon or thick-cut pancetta in a frying pan until crispy. Stir into the puréed sauce with any oil from the pan for extra flavour if wished.

rocket
Once the sauce has been sieved, return to the slow cooker, add 2–3 cups of well-packed rocket leaves, cover and cook a further 20–30 minutes on high or until the sauce is hot enough again to serve.

anchovy
Add 2–3 tablespoons finely minced anchovies to the sieved sauce.

roasted garlic
Add the pulp of 2 roasted garlic bulbs to the cooked tomatoes before processing them through the mouli.

fresh herb
Add 1 cup of mixed finely chopped fresh herbs such as parsley, chives, thyme, oregano or marjoram.

- 2 cups dried red kidney beans
- 2 onions, peeled and finely diced
- 2 green capsicums, diced
- 400-gram can diced tomatoes in juice
- 2 long green chillies, diced (deseeded only if wished)
- 2 chipotle peppers, optional
- 2 tablespoons Mexican seasoning mix
- 1 tablespoon minced garlic
- 2½ cups water
- 1 x quantity of radish & tomato salad (see opposite)

mexican frijoles

serves 8
soaking time **overnight**
preparation time **20 minutes**
cooking time **low 7–9 hours, high 4–5 hours**

This rustic bean recipe is best served well seasoned and accompanied with a salad like this crunchy sweet/hot fresh radish & tomato salad, and a basket full of fresh warm tortillas.

Soak the beans in plenty of cold water overnight. Allow 3–4 times the amount of water to beans.

Turn the slow cooker on to low to pre-warm while gathering and preparing the ingredients.

Drain the beans well, place into a large saucepan and cover with fresh water. Bring to the boil and boil rapidly, uncovered, for 20 minutes. Drain well.

Place the beans into the pre-warmed slow cooker with the onions, capsicums, tomatoes, chillies, chipotle peppers if using, Mexican seasoning mix and garlic. Stir in the water and mix the ingredients evenly. Cover with the lid.

Cook on low for 7–9 hours or on high for 4–5 hours, or until tender.

Use a potato masher to mash the beans roughly and season well with salt and pepper.

Serve the frijoles with the radish & tomato salad and warm fresh tortillas if wished.

variations

- Stir in ½ cup evaporated milk before serving.
- Use Mexican-flavoured canned tomatoes.

radish & tomato salad

8–10 fresh, crisp radishes, washed and trimmed
4 juicy tomatoes, sliced or diced
1 red onion, peeled and finely sliced
¼ cup chopped fresh oregano

dressing
¾ cup vinaigrette
2 tablespoons honey

serves 8
preparation time **10 minutes**

Slice the radishes finely. Toss together with the tomatoes, onion, oregano, vinaigrette and honey.

- 1 kilogram waxy potatoes, washed
- 1 red capsicum
- 1 green capsicum
- 1½ cups blanched peanuts, roasted and finely chopped
- 2 long green chillies, sliced, deseeded if wished
- 1 tablespoon minced ginger
- 1 teaspoon minced garlic
- ½ cup korma curry paste
- 400-millilitre can coconut milk
- 1 cup water
- 1 tablespoon grated palm sugar or brown sugar
- 1 teaspoon salt
- 200 grams green beans or small head broccoli
- 4 hard-boiled eggs, peeled and quartered
- 2 tablespoons chopped fresh coriander

potato & roasted peanut hot pot

serves 6
preparation time **30 minutes**
cooking time **low 5–6 hours, high 3–4 hours, plus extra 30 minutes**

This recipe is based on one of Indonesia's most well-known dishes – gado-gado. It's a meal prepared from cooked vegetables served with a spicy peanut sauce and is delicious. Take the ingredients and cook them slowly into a hearty vegetable dish, packed with plenty of flavour. For an authentic touch, serve piles of krupuk or prawn crackers on the side.

Turn the slow cooker on to low to pre-warm while gathering and preparing the ingredients.

Peel the potatoes if wished and cut into large chunks. Cut the capsicums into large 3-cm pieces.

Into the pre-warmed slow cooker put the potatoes, capsicums, peanuts, chillies, ginger and garlic.

In a jug, stir together the curry paste, coconut milk, water, sugar and salt and pour into the slow cooker. Stir to mix evenly and cover with the lid.

Cook on low for 5–6 hours or on high for 3–4 hours, or until all the vegetables are tender.

Top and tail the beans and cut in half or cut the broccoli into florets and stir into the slow cooker. Cover with the lid and cook on high for an additional 30 minutes. Alternatively, blanch the vegetables and add to the slow cooker; there will be no requirement for extra cooking time.

Stir in the eggs and coriander and season with extra salt if required.

variations

- Cut half a cauliflower into florets and add to the hot pot with the beans or broccoli.
- Add 2 peeled and sliced carrots with the potatoes and an additional ½ cup water.
- Place a handful of bean sprouts in the base of every bowl before ladling in the vegetables and sauce.

allyson's tip

- Waxy potatoes are ideal for slow cooking as they remain whole and have a firm texture when cooked. Look for Nadine, Draga, Frisia or Red King Edward. Alternatively, use a general-purpose potato such as Rua, Desiree, Karaka, Moonlight or Mavis Anchor.

2 onions, peeled
1 green capsicum
1 red capsicum, optional
1 large eggplant
1 kilogram courgettes
1 kilogram ripe, juicy tomatoes
¾ cup olive oil, virgin olive oil is nice here
8 cloves garlic, peeled and sliced
½ cup tomato paste
1 cup loosely packed fresh basil leaves

ratatouille

serves 7–8
preparation time **15 minutes**
cooking time **low 6–7 hours, high 3–4 hours**

This classic dish hit fame around the 1970s as eggplants became available and people grew the rather 'new' vegetable, the courgette, which flourished in their gardens. The abundant crops meant people searched for a new way to present them – beyond stuffing and boiling! Ratatouille originated in and around Nice, in southern France, and its name translated means 'a coarse stew'. No doubt its popularity was assisted by the celebrity chefs of the time, Robert Carrier and Graham Kerr, who popularised cooking from the Mediterranean on the earliest food shows, though black and white television did not really do justice to the wonderful melange of colours of a good ratatouille. If time permits, brown the eggplant and courgettes too as that will enhance the colour and flavour.

Turn the slow cooker on to low to pre-warm while gathering and preparing the ingredients.

Chop the onions into smallish diced pieces, but not too fine. Cut the capsicums into 2–3-cm-sized pieces. Cut the eggplant into large chunks, the courgettes into thick slices and the tomatoes into chunky wedges.

Heat half the oil in a large frying-pan and, when hot, cook the onions and garlic over a moderately high heat until well browned but certainly not burnt. Stir regularly. Transfer to the pre-warmed slow cooker.

Add the remaining oil to the pan and cook the tomato paste in the oil, stirring constantly until it turns a deep brown/red colour. Add half of the tomatoes and toss with the tomato paste. This will help lift any brown sediment easily from the base of the frying-pan to be added to the slow cooker as it is full of flavour.

Into the slow cooker add all the tomatoes and tomato paste, courgettes, capsicums and eggplant. Mix all the ingredients together as well as you can and cover with the lid.

Cook on low for 6–7 hours or on high for 3–4 hours.

Stir in the basil leaves and season with salt and pepper. Serve hot, or allow the ratatouille to cool and serve just warm. Either way, serve drizzled with extra olive oil, fresh basil leaves and a little shaved Parmesan if wished.

variations

- Serve the ratatouille in pastry cases as an entrée or as a light lunch option (see rich short pastry, page 292).
- For a non-vegetarian option, pan-fry 3–4 roughly chopped bacon steaks with the onions, or even chopped, thickly cut pancetta slices.
- Add ½ cup brown or green lentils and 1 cup water.
- Stir in 1 cup toasted pine nuts and 1 cup whole black juicy olives before serving with grated Parmesan or pecorino cheese on top.
- Add well-drained anchovies to taste and a tablespoon or two of capers before serving. Finish with crumbled feta or grilled halloumi cheese on top as a garnish.
- Add 250 grams blanched green beans after cooking and fold through chunks of mozzarella before serving with piles of basil and dill.

1½ cups flour
½ teaspoon salt
150 grams butter, chilled and diced
2 egg yolks
1–2 tablespoons chilled water

rich short pastry

sufficient to make 4–5-cm x 8–10-cm tartlet cases
preparation time **10 minutes**
chilling time **1 hour**

Ideal for savoury tartlets. For a less rich version, omit the egg yolks and use 3–4 tablespoons iced water.

Sift the flour and salt into a bowl. Use your fingertips to rub in the butter until the flour resembles fine crumbs.

Using a knife, cut in the egg yolks and sufficient water until the pastry begins to form large clumps, which when gathered in the hand and pressed should stay together. Turn the dough and bring together. Wrap in greaseproof paper and refrigerate for 1 hour before using.

food processor method
Place the flour, salt and butter into a food processor fitted with the metal blade and process until the mixture resembles fine crumbs.

Pulse in the egg yolks and sufficient water, until the moisture forms small, moist balls of dough. When a small portion is gathered in the hand and pressed it should stay together. Do not process until the mixture forms a ball as the dough will be tough and shrink when cooked.

Turn out and bring together, kneading only lightly. Wrap in greaseproof paper and refrigerate for 1 hour.

to use
Roll the pastry out on a lightly floured bench to 3-mm thickness. Use to line the base and sides of 4–5-cm x 8–10-cm tartlet tins or 10–12 standard-sized muffin tins. For best results, bake blind. Line the pastry-lined tarts with baking paper and fill with baking blind material (see tip). Bake at 190 °C for 15 minutes or until the edges begin to brown. Remove the baking blind material and paper and return to the oven for a further 8–10 minutes or until the cases are browned and well cooked.

allyson's tip

- For baking blind material, use dried pulses, rice or ceramic beads. All can be cooled and re-used.

1 cup red lentils
1 onion, peeled and finely sliced
2 teaspoons minced garlic
½ cup tomato paste
4 large tomatoes, chopped
1 tablespoon chopped fresh rosemary
2 teaspoons dried basil
grated rind 1 lemon
4 cups vegetable stock or water

red lentil pasta sauce

serves 5–6
preparation time without browning **10 minutes**
preparation time with browning **20 minutes**
cooking time **low 4–5 hours, high 2–3 hours**

A great basic recipe to have at hand for vegetarian friends when you're looking for something new to cook. The sauce freezes well and makes a great mid-week meal served over a baked potato or kumara or tossed through your preferred chunky-cut pasta.

Turn the slow cooker on to low to pre-warm while gathering and preparing the ingredients.

Rinse the red lentils thoroughly and drain well.

If wishing to brown the ingredients:
Brown the onion in a good dash of oil in a heavy-based frying-pan over a moderately high heat until lightly browned. Add the garlic and cook a further 1–2 minutes until the mixture is fragrant.

Into the warmed slow cooker put the lentils, onion, garlic, tomato paste, chopped tomatoes, rosemary, basil, lemon rind and stock or water. Stir to mix the ingredients well and cover with the lid.

Cook on low for 4–5 hours or on high for 2–3 hours, or until the lentils are tender. Season with salt and pepper once the lentils are cooked. If wished, mash the lentils with a potato masher for a smoother textured sauce.

For a thinner sauce, stir in extra hot stock or water before serving.

Toss the sauce through your favourite pasta, such as fettuccini, and garnish with olives, diced semi-dried tomatoes and picked fresh parsley leaves or whichever ingredients you prefer.

variations

- Use tomato paste that's pre-flavoured for pizzas; there are a number of brands available on the market.
- To add a little meat, add a few rashers of diced, crispy, cooked and crumbled bacon before serving.

- 2 cups dried chickpeas
- 1 onion, peeled and finely diced
- 10–12 cloves garlic, crushed, peeled and sliced
- 2 x 400-gram cans chopped tomatoes in juice
- 3 cups vegetable stock or water
- ½ cup black olives
- 29-gram can anchovies, well drained, optional
- 2 tablespoons capers, rinsed
- ½ teaspoon dried basil
- ½ teaspoon dried oregano
- ¼–½ cup sun-dried tomato paste or pesto

puttanesca chickpea braise

serves 6–8
soaking time **12–16 hours**
preparation time without browning **15 minutes**
preparation time with browning **20 minutes**
cooking time **low 10–12 hours, high 5–7 hours**

Gutsy ingredients flavour up this robust Mediterranean-inspired dish.

Soak the chickpeas in plenty of cold water overnight or for at least 12 hours. You will require about 3 times the amount of water to chickpeas. Drain well.

Turn the slow cooker on to low to pre-warm while gathering and preparing the ingredients.

> ***If wishing to brown the ingredients:***
> *Brown the onion in a dash of oil until lightly browned. Add the garlic and cook a further 1–2 minutes or until the mixture is fragrant.*

Put the onion, garlic, tomatoes, stock or water, olives, anchovies if using, capers, basil, oregano and the well-drained chickpeas into the pre-warmed slow cooker. Stir to evenly mix the ingredients and cover with the lid.

Cook on low for 10–12 hours or on high for 5–7 hours, or until the chickpeas are tender. They do take a long time to cook, so do not be tempted to keep lifting the lid, as they will take some hours to cook to a gentle bite.

Stir in the sun-dried tomato paste or pesto and season with salt and pepper before serving in deep plates or shallow bowls. Garnish with extra anchovies and rocket or basil leaves if wished. Accompany with heavily infused garlic butter grilled bread for a real taste of the Mediterranean.

variations

- Use other dried beans in place of chickpeas.
- Use flavoured canned tomatoes such as Italian-seasoned.
- Use sun-dried capsicum pesto in place of tomato paste or pesto.
- For a little meat, add 200 grams sliced salami before serving.
- Add 3–4 diced and crisply cooked bacon steaks before serving.
- Stir in 500 grams flaked smoked fish before serving.

allyson's tip

- No time to make pistou? Buy basil pesto from the chiller and look for one that has only a small amount of cheese in the ingredient list.

2 cups dried borlotti beans
3 red capsicums, thickly sliced
2 onions, peeled and diced
1 tablespoon minced garlic
2 tablespoons provençal herb 'n' salt mix (see page 300)
5 cups vegetable stock or water
12–18 baby new potatoes, halved
250 grams green beans, trimmed

pistou
40 large basil leaves
4 cloves garlic, crushed and peeled
¼ cup olive oil, extra virgin olive oil is nice here

provençal bean & red capsicum pot

serves 6
soaking time **12–16 hours**
preparation time **15 minutes**
cooking time **low 10–11 hours, high 6–7 hours**

The provençal herb 'n' salt mix gives this simple dish great character and flavour. Drizzle freshly made basil pistou over each serve and be immediately escorted to the fields of Provence on a summer's day.

Soak the borlotti beans in plenty of water to cover – you'll need about 3 times the amount of water to beans. Cover and set aside overnight or for at least 12 hours.

Turn the slow cooker on to low to pre-warm while gathering and preparing the ingredients.

Drain the borlotti beans and place in the slow cooker. Add the capsicums, onions, garlic, herb mix and stock or water. Stir well and cover with the lid.

Cook on low for 10–11 hours or on high for 6–7 hours. In the last quarter of cooking time, add the potatoes. Cover and keep cooking until the borlotti beans and potatoes are tender.

Blanch the green beans for 2 minutes in boiling water. Drain and stir into the slow cooker. Season with salt and pepper if wished.

Serve drizzled with pistou and sprinkled with flaky salt if wished.

pistou
Put the basil leaves, garlic and oil in a mini food processor and process until smooth. Alternatively, mash the basil and garlic together with a mortar and pestle, adding a little of the olive oil as you mash, until all the oil has been added.

variations

- Add a can of chopped tomatoes in juice.
- Add ¼ cup Pernod with the stock or water.
- Add in 2–3 tablespoons chopped fresh tarragon before serving.
- When small potatoes are out of season, use chunky diced waxy potatoes. (For a list of waxy potatoes, see page 289.)

- 2 tablespoons white or black peppercorns
- 2 tablespoons flaky salt or 1 tablespoon pouring salt
- 2 teaspoons dried basil
- 1 teaspoon dried marjoram
- 1 teaspoon dried thyme
- 1 teaspoon fennel seeds

provençal herb 'n' salt mix

makes about ¼ cup
preparation time **10 minutes**

Traditionally, a Provençal herb mix will include dried lavender buds. I have omitted them here as the long slow cooking highlights the 'camphor' note lavender has. If you wish to use this herb 'n' salt blend to season a whole chicken for roasting, add 1 teaspoon dried lavender. It's available in good food shops where specialty spices are sold.

Crush the peppercorns coarsely in a mortar and pestle, spice grinder or peppermill. Stir the pepper together with the salt, basil, marjoram, thyme and fennel seeds.

Keep in an airtight container. Also good with fish and chicken.

6–8 medium-sized red-skinned apples
2 tablespoons prepared mustard
2 tablespoons brown sugar
2 tablespoons rum, orange juice or water

sweet mustard baked apples

serves 6–8
preparation time **10 minutes**
cooking time **1 hour**

Try these with a roast of pork or, for a change, make the recipe with pears.

Preheat the oven to 190 °C.

Peel the apples to about halfway down or in a circular pattern. Place the apples in a small ovenproof dish – one that they fit snugly into.

Mix together the mustard, sugar and rum, juice or water. Brush the apples with half the mixture.

Bake in the preheated oven for 1 hour or until the apples are tender. Baste with the remaining glaze, halfway through the cooking time.

variations

- Add 1 tablespoon grated fresh ginger.
- Core the apples and fill the hollowed centres with raisins or sultanas.

1½ cups dried cannellini or navy beans
6–7 pork belly slices
4–6 rashers of bacon, diced
2 medium-sized onions, peeled and finely diced
6–8 cloves garlic, crushed, peeled and sliced
3 cups chicken or vegetable stock
400-gram can condensed tomato soup
2 tablespoons Worcestershire sauce
2 tablespoons golden syrup
2 tablespoons dark brown or muscovado sugar
1 tablespoon prepared mustard
1 tablespoon curry powder

boston baked beans

serves 6–8
soaking time **10–12 hours**
preparation time without browning **20 minutes**
preparation time with browning **30 minutes**
cooking time **low 10–12 hours, high 6–8 hours**

Well, this recipe may not strictly be vegetarian, but you can always leave out the pork belly and bacon rashers and it will still taste delicious. The beans only get better if prepared a day in advance and reheated, and the sweetness and lightness of baked apple is a good foil for the chunky, gutsy flavoured beans. This dish is one of my home's all-time favourites.

Cover the cannellini or navy beans with plenty of water, cover and set aside for 10–12 hours. They require covering in 3–4 times the amount of water to beans.

Turn the slow cooker on to low to pre-warm while gathering and preparing the ingredients.

Cut the pork belly slices into 1-cm-wide pieces.

If wishing to brown the ingredients:
Heat a dash of oil in a frying-pan and brown the pork and bacon well. This will be best done in batches. Set the pork and bacon aside. Cook the onions until well browned, but not burnt. Add the garlic and cook, stirring constantly for an extra 1–2 minutes.

Drain the beans well.

Into the pre-warmed slow cooker put the beans, pork, bacon, onions, garlic, stock or water, tomato soup, Worcestershire sauce, golden syrup, sugar, mustard and curry powder. Stir well to mix the ingredients evenly and cover with the lid.

Cook on low for 10–12 hours or on high for 6–8 hours, or until the beans are tender.

Season with salt, pepper and a dash of vinegar to add a little sharpness if wished.

Serve accompanied by sweet mustard baked apples (page 301) if wished.

allyson's tips

- Cooking time will vary greatly depending on the variety of dried bean and how dried they are (see page 12).
- Regulate the heat of the beans by the type of mustard you use. For a real bite try Hot English, or for a mild taste try Dijon or American.

did you know?

- Boston baked beans – the real kind, not the canned variety which bears little to no resemblance – is a traditional New England dish. It is recorded as having been served on the Sabbath day by the Puritan families who settled in the area.

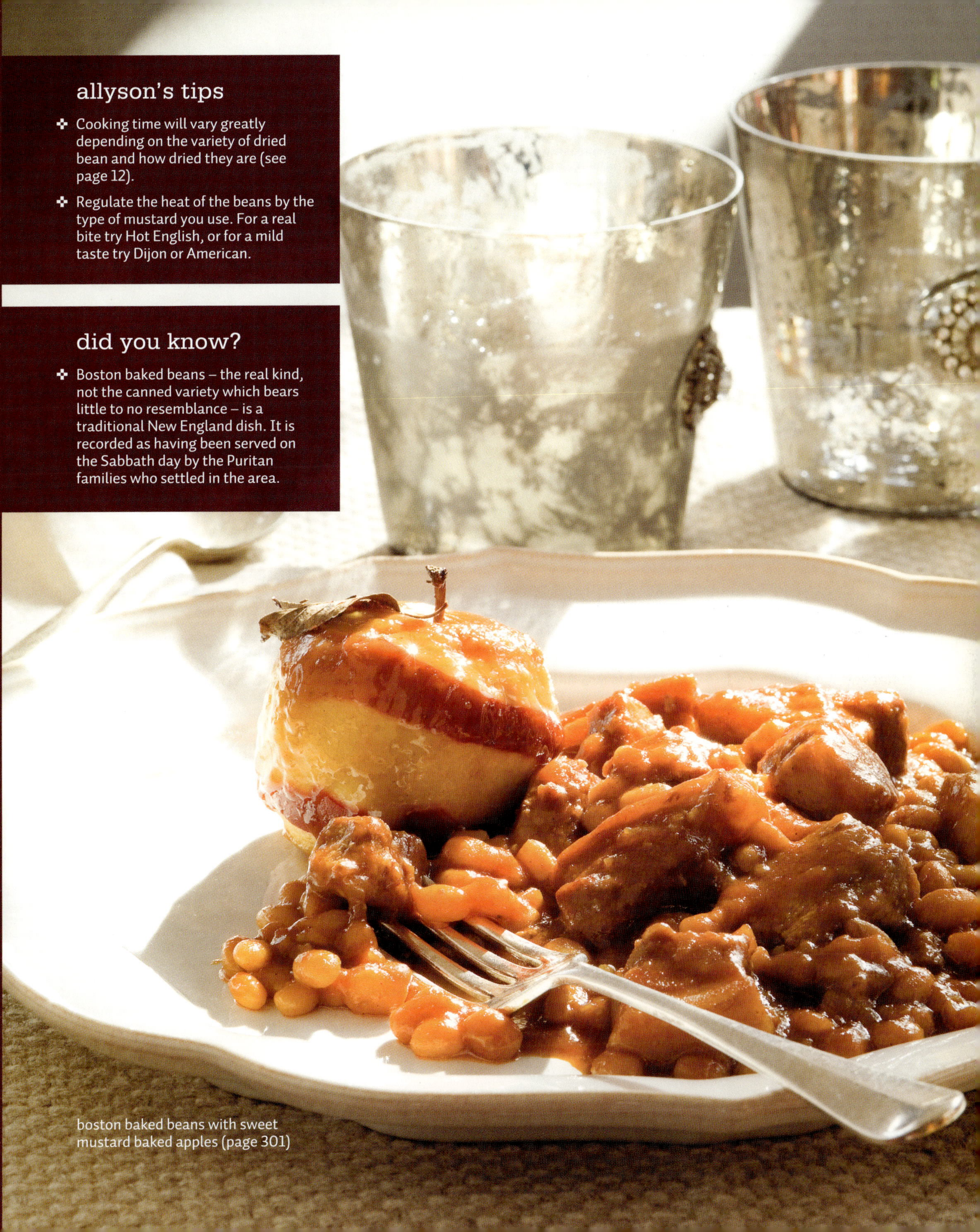

boston baked beans with sweet mustard baked apples (page 301)

allyson's tip

- Chickpeas will benefit from extra-long soaking overnight to ensure they cook in a reasonable time frame, otherwise you will find that the cooking time is extremely long.

2 cups dried chickpeas
1 tablespoon ground cumin
1 tablespoon ground coriander
1 tablespoon paprika
1 teaspoon ground ginger
1 teaspoon ground chilli powder
½ teaspoon caraway seeds
3 fresh long green chillies, de-seed if wished
5 cups vegetable stock or water
400-gram can diced tomatoes in juice
1 kilogram pumpkin, peeled

herb & pistachio nut paste
4 fresh long green chillies
1 cup loosely packed coriander
1 cup well-packed spinach leaves, well-washed
½ cup loosely packed mint
¼ cup shelled pistachio nuts
½–1 teaspoon minced garlic
½ teaspoon coriander seeds, toasted
½ teaspoon cumin seeds, toasted
¼–½ cup olive oil, virgin olive oil is nice here

chickpea tagine

serves 10
soaking time **12–16 hours**
preparation time **20 minutes**
cooking time **low 11–12 hours, high 8–9 hours**

Caraway seeds give this spicy vegetarian tagine a special warm note that partners well with the herb and pistachio nut harissa-style paste that's spooned over just before serving. If you don't have any, don't fret, the tagine is still delicious without them.

Soak the chickpeas in plenty of cold water overnight, preferably for 12–16 hours. You will need 3–4 times the amount of water to chickpeas.

Turn the slow cooker on to low to pre-warm while gathering and preparing the ingredients.

Drain the chickpeas and place in the slow cooker with the cumin, coriander, paprika, ginger, chilli powder, caraway seeds, green chillies, stock or water and tomatoes. Stir to mix evenly and cover with the lid.

Cook on low for 9 hours or on high for 6 hours.

Cut the pumpkin into 3–4-cm-sized pieces and add to the tagine, stirring to mix into the hot chickpeas. Cover with the lid.

Continue to cook for a further 2–3 hours on low or high or until the chickpeas and pumpkin are tender.

Serve the tagine in deep plates with a generous spoonful of herb & pistachio nut paste and garnished with extra pistachio nuts if wished.

herb & pistachio nut paste

Trim the stems off the green chillies and de-seed if wished.

Put the chillies into a mini food processor with the coriander, spinach, mint, pistachio nuts, garlic and coriander and cumin seeds, and process until well chopped.

With the motor running, pour in sufficient oil to make a smooth, soft paste. Season with salt to taste if wished. Keep refrigerated in an airtight container.

allyson's tips

- Large lima beans take a good while to cook. They require long soaking and are best cooked on low where they will hold their shape well and soften from the long slow cooking.
- Paprika was once called Turkish pepper. Spice lovers should look beyond the supermarket standard for different grades of paprika to taste and be able to appreciate this intriguing spice. Hungarian paprika comes in grades including exquisite delicate, delicate, noble sweet and hot.

did you know?

- In Spain, paprika is called pimentón and is often smoked. It tastes very different from Hungarian paprika but try it here for a variation if wished.

1 cup dried large lima beans
420-gram can condensed tomato soup
4 cups vegetable stock or water
1–1½ tablespoons paprika
1 tablespoon minced garlic
¼–½ teaspoon caraway seeds, optional
2 bay leaves
4 medium-sized waxy potatoes, peeled
3–4 carrots, peeled
2 parsnips, peeled
2 large onions, peeled
2 green capsicums, cored
250-gram tub sour cream (not lite)

hungarian bean & vegetable hot pot

serves 4–5
soaking time **12 hours**
preparation time **20 minutes**
cooking time **low 10–12 hours, high 6–8 hours**

The sweet, pungent and even earthy and gutsy flavour of paprika brings a touch of Hungary to this easy-to-make and economical vegetarian dish.

Soak the lima beans in plenty of water for 12 hours. Allow 3–4 times the amount of water to beans.

Turn the slow cooker on to low to pre-warm while gathering and preparing the ingredients.

Drain the beans well and place into the pre-warmed slow cooker.

Stir together the tomato soup with the stock or water, paprika, garlic and caraway seeds if using. Pour over the beans, add the bay leaves and stir to mix evenly. Cover with the lid.

Cook on low for 6 hours or on high for 4 hours.

Cut the potatoes into quarters. Cut the carrots and parsnips into 4-cm chunks. Chop the onions and capsicums roughly.

Scatter in the potatoes, carrots, parsnips, onions and capsicums and stir to mix as evenly as possible. Cover with the lid.

Continue to cook on low for a further 4–6 hours or on high for a further 2-4 hours or until the vegetables and lima beans are tender.

Stir in the sour cream before serving. Have a bowl of extra sour cream and a bowl of toasted caraway seeds to serve alongside for those who would like to add more of each.

variations

- Use half smoked paprika with sweet red paprika for a rich smoky flavour.
- Use pumpkin in place of potato. Try a firm pumpkin such as a crown.
- Use different beans, like small lima beans or dried butter beans.

- 1½ cups urad dal (black lentils)
- ½ cup red kidney beans
- 8 cloves garlic, crushed and peeled
- 10 cardamom pods, crushed
- 1 cinnamon stick, crumbled
- 2–3 blades mace, optional
- 1 tablespoon cumin seeds, toasted
- 1 tablespoon coriander seeds, toasted
- ½–1 teaspoon whole cloves
- 4 cups water
- ¼–1 teaspoon chilli powder
- 1 cup cream
- 150 grams butter

dal makhani

serves 6–8
preparation time **15 minutes**
soaking time **overnight**
cooking time **low 5–6 hours, high 3–4 hours, plus extra 30 minutes**

On my first trip to India, rather taken aback by the culture shock of it all, I sought refuge in the hotel's dining room where I fell in love with this dish. It probably had something to do with the copious amounts of cream and butter, but it is truly scrumptious and makes a great addition to an Indian meal.

Soak the urad dal and kidney beans in separate bowls overnight in plenty of water. Allow 3–4 times the amount of water to beans and dal.

Turn the slow cooker on to low to pre-warm while gathering and preparing the ingredients.

Boil the kidney beans in plenty of fresh water for 20 minutes. Drain well and place with the dal into the pre-warmed slow cooker.

Take a new or clean Chux cloth or piece of muslin and place the garlic, cardamom pods, cinnamon stick, mace if using, cumin and coriander seeds and cloves into the centre and tie securely to enclose the spices. Add to the slow cooker with the water and cover with the lid.

Cook on low for 5–6 hours or on high for 3–4 hours, or until the beans are tender. Check the water level towards the end of cooking as sometimes more may be required. You need the lentils and beans to have just enough to cover by the end of cooking time but no more as the finished sauce will be too thin.

Remove the spice bag and mash the lentils and beans coarsely with a potato masher if wished.

Season with sufficient chilli powder to suit your taste. Stir in the cream and butter and, once the butter has melted, allow the dal makhani to cook on high for a further 30 minutes without the lid, stirring occasionally.

Serve garnished with chopped fresh coriander if wished as part of an Indian meal, or with naan or paratha bread as a meal on its own.

- 1 kilogram waxy potatoes
- 1 kilogram firm-fleshed pumpkin
- 1 onion, peeled and finely sliced
- 2 tablespoons tamarind pulp
- 5–7-cm piece fresh ginger, peeled and grated
- 4 tablespoons Thai red curry paste
- 2 tablespoons grated palm sugar or brown sugar
- 2 teaspoons Thai curry powder (refer to tip below for recipe)
- 1 tablespoon fish sauce
- 2½ cups water
- 400-gram can coconut milk
- 250 grams round green beans, topped and tailed

thai pumpkin & potato coconut curry

serves 6
preparation time **20 minutes**
cooking time **low 5–7 hours, high 3–4 hours, plus extra 20–30 minutes**

This curry has the most delicious sweet flavour from the subtle blend of spices that make up a Thai curry powder. The blend is unique and very different from any Indian curry powder.

Turn the slow cooker on to low to pre-warm while gathering and preparing the ingredients.

Peel the potatoes and pumpkin and cut into large chunky pieces. Place in the slow cooker with the onion.

Mash the tamarind pulp in ½ cup warm water until pulpy. Strain and discard the seeds and fibrous matter.

Mix together the tamarind water, ginger, curry paste, sugar, Thai curry powder, fish sauce, water and coconut milk. Pour into the slow cooker and stir to mix as evenly as possible. Cover with the lid.

Cook on low for 5–7 hours or on high for 3–4 hours. Add the green beans, cover and cook a further 20–30 minutes until the beans are tender.

Serve with slices of fresh or canned mango and spoonfuls of sweet chilli sauce if wished.

variations

- Add diced green and red capsicum in place of the green beans.
- Use long snake beans in place of round beans.
- Replace half the potatoes with red-skinned kumara.
- Finish with a cupful of roasted peanuts or cashews.
- Cut 2–3 single boneless and skinless chicken breasts into large 3-cm-wide pieces and add to the curry halfway through cooking. Stir to mix into the hot ingredients.

2 cups moong dal
5 cups water
½ teaspoon turmeric
1 teaspoon salt
3 dried red chillies
3 whole cloves
1 teaspoon coriander seeds, toasted
½ teaspoon cumin seeds, toasted
½ cinnamon stick
¼ teaspoon cardamom seeds
½ teaspoon black peppercorns
¼ cup oil
1 red onion, peeled and finely chopped
3–4 bunches fresh spinach, washed

simple moong dal

serves 6
preparation time **10 minutes**
cooking time **low 5–6 hours, high 3–4 hours, plus 30 minutes extra**

Dal refers to both the ingredient and the dish made from it. Dal is a split pulse and there are a plethora of varieties including those from beans, peas or lentils. Dal is one of the main dishes of India and ranges from a thin soupy-style dish to a thick porridge-like mix. The choice is yours.

Turn the slow cooker on to low to pre-warm while gathering and preparing the ingredients.

Put the dal, water, turmeric and salt into the pre-warmed slow cooker. Cover and cook on low for 5–6 hours or on high for 3–4 hours, until the dal is mushy.

Into a spice mill or coffee mill put the chillies, cloves, coriander and cumin seeds, cinnamon stick, cardamom seeds and peppercorns and grind until fine.

Heat the oil in a frying-pan and cook the onion over a moderately high heat until well browned. Add in the ground spices and toss quickly in the hot onions until very fragrant. Do not overcook as they will burn and give the dal a bitter flavour. Remove from the heat.

Shake excess water from the spinach and tear the leaves away from any coarse stems. Stir the spinach leaves, onion and spice mix into the dal. Cover and cook for an extra 30 minutes on high.

Serve in bowls with a wedge of lemon or lime to squeeze onto the dal before eating. Serve with poppadoms, or try warmed naan or paratha bread. For a thinner dal, stir in hot water to achieve the consistency preferred.

Rear: simple moong dal
Front: south Indian spiced channa dal
(page 312)

- 2 cups channa dal (yellow split peas)
- 4½ cups water
- 3–4 fresh hot green chillies, sliced (de-seeded if wished)
- 1 teaspoon cumin seeds, toasted
- ¼–½ teaspoon ground turmeric
- 4 shallots, peeled and sliced
- ¼ cup oil
- ½ teaspoon black or yellow mustard seeds
- 10 curry leaves, dried or fresh
- 1 large dried red chilli, crumbled
- 2 cloves garlic, peeled and sliced
- 1 large red tomato, diced
- 1 cup coconut milk

south indian spiced channa dal

serves 4–5
preparation time **10 minutes**
cooking time **low 5–6 hours, high 3–4 hours**

Turn the slow cooker on to low to pre-warm while gathering and preparing the ingredients.

Wash the dal well in a sieve under a running tap. Drain and place into the pre-warmed slow cooker with the water. Stir in the chillies, cumin seeds, turmeric and half the shallots and cover with the lid.

Cook on low for 5–6 hours or on high for 3–4 hours, stirring once if possible during the cooking time. The dal should be mushy – add more water or extend cooking time if required.

Heat the oil in small frying-pan and, when hot, cook the remaining shallots with the mustard seeds until the seeds begin to pop. Once this happens, stir in the curry leaves, chilli, garlic and tomato and stir-fry, tossing quickly for about 1 minute until very fragrant.

Stir the spice mixture into the dal with the coconut milk and season with salt. For a soupier-style dal, stir in extra hot water.

- 1 cup pearl barley
- 2 carrots, peeled and thinly sliced
- 2 stalks celery, sliced
- 1 large onion, peeled and diced
- 1 bulb fennel, trimmed and thinly sliced, optional
- 2 cups frozen corn
- 32-gram packet onion soup mix
- 1 tablespoon vegetable stock powder
- 5 cups water
- 2 bunches spinach or 1 bunch silver beet, washed

barley & winter vegetable braise

serves 6
soaking time **overnight**
preparation time without browning **15 minutes**
preparation time with browning **25 minutes**
cooking time **low 4–5 hours, high 2–3 hours, plus extra 30 minutes**

Barley is a wonderful old-fashioned grain that we have almost forgotten. With its chewy texture and nutty flavour, and being high in fibre and protein, not to mention cheap, barley is well worth reviving and keeping on hand in the pantry.

Soak the barley in plenty of water overnight or for at least 6–8 hours. You will need about 3–4 times the amount of water to barley.

Turn the slow cooker on to low to pre-warm while gathering and preparing the ingredients.

> ***If browning the ingredients:***
> *Heat a good dash of oil in a large frying-pan and, when hot, brown the carrots, celery, onion and fennel if using over a high heat. This is best done in batches.*

Drain the barley and place into the slow cooker. Add the carrots, celery, onion, fennel and corn.

In a jug, mix together the soup mix with the stock powder and water. Stir into the barley and cover with the lid.

Cook on low for 4–5 hours or on high for 2–3 hours, or until the barley is tender.

Strip the tender spinach leaves from the coarse stems and stir the leaves into the barley or if using silver beet, slice finely and stir in. Cover and cook for a further 30 minutes on high. Season well with salt and pepper.

variations

- Mix in 6–8 crumbled, crispy-grilled bacon rashers with the spinach.
- Omit the corn at the beginning and add 400-gram can cream-style corn with the spinach.
- For extra flavour, use 2 packets of onion soup mix.
- Use a different soup mix such as mushroom or chicken.

dessert

- 4 thick slices bread, sour dough is great here
- 2 tablespoons butter, softened
- 2½ cups milk
- 3 eggs
- ¼ cup sugar
- 1–2 teaspoons vanilla essence
- ¼ cup sultanas, optional

bread & butter pudding

serves 6
preparation time **15 minutes**
cooking time **low 5–6 hours, high 3–4 hours**

Bread-based puddings began life some centuries ago somewhat more frugally than the pud we have come to know today. Leftover bread, crumbed, soaked in milk and sweetened, became much more glorious once fat (like butter) and richness (in the form of eggs) were added. Then all it took was for the bread to become leftover croissants or brioche and it is now a gourmet's treat. This is a basic recipe that can easily have your own touch – just be creative.

Turn the slow cooker on to low to pre-warm while gathering and preparing the ingredients. Lightly grease the inside of a 6-cup capacity pudding basin. Place an upturned saucer into the base of the slow cooker.

Trim the crusts from the bread only if they are very hard, and discard. Spread each slice of bread with a little of the butter.

Beat the milk, eggs, sugar and vanilla essence together and strain if wished.

Layer the bread slices, and sultanas if using, into the prepared bowl. Carefully pour over the beaten egg and milk mixture and allow the dessert to stand for 10 minutes for the bread to soak up all the liquid. Sprinkle with a little cinnamon or cinnamon sugar on top if wished. Cover loosely with a piece of greased baking paper.

Sit the pudding basin on top of the saucer in the slow cooker. Pour in sufficient cold water to come halfway up the sides of the pudding basin and cover with the lid.

Cook on low for 5–6 hours or on high for 3–4 hours, or until a knife inserted into the pudding comes out clean. It will be moist, but should be clear. Lift out and serve warm, dusted with icing sugar or extra cinnamon sugar if wished and accompanied with poached seasonal fruit.

variations

- Use 4–6 large stale croissants, torn into chunky pieces or 6–8 thick slices of brioche. As both of these are rich in butter content, you may wish to omit the butter.
- Sprinkle a little spice of your choice onto the bread slices when spreading with butter. Try mixed spice, or cardamom for a change.
- Use half cream and half milk, and 4 eggs for a richer pud.
- Vary the dried fruits, trying currants or raisins.

½ cup lemon juice
4 kilograms apples, peeled
1–1½ cups sugar
1½ teaspoons mixed spice
1 teaspoon ground cinnamon

stewed apples

makes sufficient for 4 family-sized desserts
preparation time **30–40 minutes**
cooking time **low 5–6 hours, high 3–4 hours**

Crisp, sweet or tart, new season's apples, tenderly cooked in layers of spiced sugar, make a great base for a crumble or pie. Pack the slow cooker firmly with the fruit to make it worth the time involved and freeze excess for another time when you need to make a pud in a hurry.

Turn the slow cooker on to low to pre-warm while gathering and preparing the ingredients.

Place the lemon juice in a large bowl.

Quarter the apples and trim out the core. Slice the fruit thinly and place in the bowl, tossing with the lemon juice as you add more apples. This prevents the apples from browning.

Mix the sugar, mixed spice and cinnamon together.

Layer the apples and spiced sugar in the pre-warmed slow cooker finishing with a layer of sugar and cover with the lid.

Cook on low for 5–6 hours or on high for 3–4 hours. Lift the lid and test the apples for doneness – they should be soft.

Transfer to a lidded heatproof container, cover and cool before refrigerating or freezing.

variations

- Use half apples and half pears.
- Vary the spices. Try a mix of cardamom, coriander and ginger.
- Add a few slices of quince paste when layering the apples and sugar.
- Add a drizzle of rosewater when layering the fruit.

100 grams gingernut biscuits, roughly broken
1 cup wholegrain or rolled oats
½ cup flour
½ cup white or brown sugar
½ cup thread, flaked or desiccated coconut
125 grams butter, melted
3–4 cups stewed apples (page 317), hot

gingernut, oat & apple crumble

serves 6
preparation time **20 minutes**
cooking time **30–40 minutes**

Apple crumble in its many guises is probably one of every family's most loved puddings. Crushed-up gingernut biscuits add flavour and crunch.

Preheat the oven to 180 °C.

In a bowl stir together the gingernut biscuits, oats, flour, sugar, coconut and butter.

Put the hot apples into an 8-cup capacity ovenproof dish. Scatter over the crumble mixture.

Bake in the preheated oven for 30–40 minutes. Serve dusted with icing sugar.

variations

- Use another favourite sweet biscuit, un-iced of course.
- Add spices such as ginger, cardamom or mixed spice.

8 firm, ripe pears
juice ½ lemon
70-gram packet macadamia nuts, roasted and chopped
50 grams butter, softened
½ cup brown sugar
1 teaspoon vanilla essence
½ cup whisky or orange juice

whisky baked pears

serves 8
preparation time **15–20 minutes**
cooking time **low 4–4½ hours, high 2–2½ hours**

Baked fruit makes a simple, elegant dessert. Firm but juicy pears are best, but with slow cooking, pears that are a little less than ripe will become meltingly delicious too.

Turn the slow cooker on to low to pre-warm while gathering and preparing the ingredients.

Core the pears and replace a small plug of the core in the base of each pear. Peel the pears if wished, or peel only halfway. Brush the cut surface of the pear with lemon juice to prevent discolouration.

Mix the macadamia nuts with the butter, brown sugar and vanilla essence. Use three-quarters of the mixture to fill the pear cavities.

Place the pears in the pre-warmed slow cooker. Drop the remaining stuffing mix into the slow cooker. Pour in the whisky or orange juice, sprinkle over the sugar and cover with the lid.

Cook on low for 4–4½ hours or on high for 2–2½ hours. Cooking time will depend on the ripeness of the pears.

Serve with your favourite custard or glace orange ice cream, spooning any syrup that has formed in the base of the slow cooker onto each pear.

2 kilograms tamarillos
1–1½ cups sugar
1 cinnamon stick
2 star anise
pared rind 1 orange
about 1–1½ cups water

cinnamon poached tamarillos

makes 2 kilograms poached fruit
preparation time **10 minutes**
cooking time **low 4–5 hours, high 2–3 hours**

Tamarillos poach up beautifully in the slow cooker. Do not overcrowd them and they will keep their shape. Cooking on low will ensure the colour of the skin soaks into the fruit, turning them a jewel-like ruby red.

Turn the slow cooker on to low to pre-warm while gathering and preparing the ingredients.

Using a small knife, cut a cross through the skin on the base of each tamarillo. This will allow the skin to be peeled off easily once cooked.

Pile the tamarillos snugly into the slow cooker. Scatter over the sugar and place in the cinnamon stick, star anise and orange rind.

Pour sufficient water into the slow cooker to come halfway up the level of the fruit and cover with the lid.

Cook on low for 4–5 hours or on high for 2–3 hours.

Carefully remove the tamarillos from the slow cooker and place in a single layer in a lidded container. When cool enough to handle, peel away the thick skin.

Pour over the syrup, cover and cool before chilling.

If wishing to serve warm, peel the fruit and place in a heatproof dish before pouring the syrup over. Serve with whipped cream and cinnamon pecan biscuits (opposite).

250 grams butter, diced
1 cup sugar
2 eggs, beaten
1 teaspoon vanilla essence
2 cups self-raising flour
1–1½ teaspoons ground cinnamon
70-gram packet pecans

cinnamon pecan biscuits

makes 30–36 biscuits
preparation time **15 minutes**
cooking time **10–12 minutes**

These flat and crisp, sweet-spiced biscuits are ideal to serve with poached fruits for a simple, tasty dessert at any time of the year.

Preheat the oven to 200 °C. Lightly grease 2 baking trays or line with baking paper.

Melt the butter in a saucepan over a moderate heat. Stir in the sugar and remove from the heat. Allow to cool for 5 minutes.

Beat in the eggs and vanilla essence a little at a time.

Sift together the flour and cinnamon and stir into the mixture.

Place heaped teaspoonful lots onto the prepared baking trays, leaving room as the biscuits will spread. Place a pecan in the centre of each biscuit.

Bake in the preheated oven for 10–12 minutes until the biscuits have turned a deep brown colour (not burnt). Transfer to a cake rack to cool. Store in an airtight container.

2½ cups water
1 cup medium- or short-grain rice
¼–½ cup sugar
1 tablespoon butter
½ teaspoon ground cinnamon, nutmeg or mixed spice
1½ cups cream (or use ½ cream and ½ milk)

classic creamed rice

serves 6
preparation time **10 minutes**
cooking time **low 4–5 hours, high 2–2½ hours**

Rice in pre-Elizabethan times was so rare it was locked up in the spice cupboards of the wealthy and only eaten on special occasions. By Charles I's reign (1625–49) rice cooked with milk, sugar and cinnamon was regarded as an aphrodisiac, no doubt due to its expense, though it certainly didn't do Charles I any good – he ended his reign ingloriously beheaded!

Turn the slow cooker on to low to pre-warm while gathering and preparing the ingredients.

Place the water, rice, half the sugar, butter and spice into the pre-warmed slow cooker.

Cook on low for 4–5 hours or on high for 2–2½ hours, or until the rice is tender and most of the water has been absorbed.

Using a thin large metal spoon, gently cut in the cream and sufficient remaining sugar to achieve the sweetness level you prefer. Do not over-stir, especially with a thick-edged wooden spoon, as this will turn the creamed rice into mush.

Serve in bowls with poached seasonal fruits.

variations

- Chop 50–100 grams dark chocolate and stir into the rice with the cream. Stand for 5–10 minutes before serving as this will allow the chocolate to melt.
- Use white chocolate in place of dark.
- Replace the spice with the grated rind of a lemon. Add only whole milk or cream to finish as lite-style milk will curdle from the inclusion of the lemon rind.
- For a richer creamed rice, beat 2 egg yolks into the cream before cutting into the rice.
- For kids, pop 2–3 marshmallows into the serving bowls before topping with the creamed rice; the marshmallows will soften quickly.

- 3½ cups mixed dried fruit
- ½ cup Guinness or other dark beer
- ½ cup brandy
- grated rind and juice 1 orange
- grated rind 1 lemon
- 70-gram packet slivered almonds
- 1 apple, peeled and grated
- 1 large carrot, peeled and grated
- 2 tablespoons marmalade
- 2 teaspoons mixed spice
- 1 teaspoon ground nutmeg
- 1 teaspoon ground cinnamon
- 1 cup flour
- 125 grams Shreddo or butter, grated
- 1 cup fresh white breadcrumbs
- 3 eggs, beaten

lucy's christmas pudding

serves 12–16
preparation time **30 minutes**
standing time **overnight**
cooking time **5–7 hours, high only**

This recipe comes from a dear friend and it is truly delicious and worth over-indulging in on Christmas Day.

In one large bowl put the mixed dried fruit, Guinness or dark beer, brandy, orange rind and juice, lemon rind, almonds, apple, carrot, marmalade, mixed spice, nutmeg and cinnamon. Stir well, cover and leave to stand overnight.

Turn the slow cooker on to pre-warm while mixing the pudding ingredients together. Lightly grease an 8-cup capacity pudding bowl.

In a second large bowl, put the flour, Shreddo or butter and breadcrumbs and stir to mix evenly. Make a well in the centre.

Add the fruit and eggs to the dry ingredients and stir just until combined.

Transfer the mixture to the prepared bowl. Cover with two layers of baking paper and secure tightly with string. Cover with a layer of foil and secure with string.

Put an upturned saucer in the base of the pre-warmed slow cooker. Sit the pudding on top of the saucer. Pour about 2 cups of boiling water into the slow cooker. The water needs to come halfway up the sides of the pudding bowl. Cover with the lid.

Cook on high power for 5–7 hours.

Turn the pudding out onto a serving platter. Serve thick slices with a generous spoonful of hard brandy butter sauce (page 328).

250 grams butter, softened
¾–1 cup icing or caster sugar
½ cup brandy

hard brandy butter sauce

serves 10–12
preparation time **15 minutes**

As a young girl, my nana would only ever have hard brandy sauce and runny cream with her Christmas pudding and, while it is incredibly rich, to me, it is still the only way to have this festive treat.

Cream the butter and sugar together well until it is light and fluffy. Slowly beat in the brandy so that it is evenly mixed in and the mixture does not separate; it should be light and fluffy.

Pile into a bowl to serve, or refrigerate for one hour or until the mixture is a little firmer. If served too soft, the brandy butter can seem greasy.

variations

- Use whisky or rum in place of brandy.
- Add the grated rind of an orange.

1½ cups self-raising flour
1–2 teaspoons ground ginger
50 grams butter, diced
¼ cup sugar
1 cup milk
1 large banana, peeled and thickly sliced

rum sauce
1¾ cups boiling water
½ cup golden syrup
¼ cup dark rum
1 teaspoon vanilla essence

banana & rum saucy pud

serves 6
preparation time **10 minutes**
cooking time **2–2½ hours, high only**

I lost track of how many times I tried to make golden syrup dumpling in the slow cookers while testing all the recipes for this book. In some slow cookers they would work, in others not. So in the end I have combined the ingredients with rum and bananas to make a rather over-the-top, family-style self-saucing pud that would be great in winter or enjoyed at the bach.

Turn the slow cooker on to low to pre-warm while gathering and preparing the ingredients.

Sift the flour and ginger into a bowl and rub in the butter until the mixture resembles fine breadcrumbs. Stir in the sugar and make a well in the centre.

Pour in the milk and mix gently to make a thick batter. Spoon about half the batter into the pre-warmed slow cooker and dot the banana slices on top. Cover with the remaining batter.

Stir the boiling water together with the golden syrup, rum and vanilla essence, pour over the batter and cover with the lid.

Cook on high power for 2–2½ hours or until the spongy top is cooked.

Serve with lashings of whipped cream and/or ice cream.

crust

3 cups self-raising flour
175 grams butter, chilled and diced or grated
About ½ cup milk
1 egg

filling

1 cup demerara sugar
2 teaspoons vanilla essence
250 grams butter, chilled and grated
1 lemon, well-washed

sussex pond pudding

serves 6–8
preparation time **30 minutes**
cooking time **4 hours, high only**

A lemon softens slowly in a generous mound of butter and sugar that melts to a golden pool of sweet lemon sauce, all encased in a simple dough, making one truly delicious family pudding. Serve a little of the lemon with each portion if wished.

Turn the slow cooker on to low to pre-warm while gathering and preparing the ingredients. Place an upturned saucer into the base of the slow cooker. Generously grease an 8-cup capacity pudding bowl.

Sift the flour into a second bowl. Rub in the butter until the mixture looks like breadcrumbs. Make a well in the centre. Beat the milk and egg together and pour into the well. Mix together with a knife to make a firm, scone-like dough. Add more milk if required.

Turn out onto a lightly floured bench and bring together. Roll out to a large 30-cm circle. Cut a quarter of the dough out in a wedge-shaped piece and set aside.

Press the larger piece into the prepared pudding basin, pressing the cut edges firmly together.

Rub the sugar and vanilla essence together and toss with the butter. Place half the sugar and butter mixture into the dough-lined bowl.

Prick the lemon all over with a fork and sit it in the sugar and butter mixture. Scatter the remaining sugar and butter around and on top of the lemon.

Gently re-knead the remaining piece of dough, rolling it out to a circle shape wide enough to cover the top of the pudding. Roll over the top and press the edges together to seal, firmly enclosing the filling.

Lightly grease one sheet of baking paper and make a pleat across the centre. This will allow space for the pudding to rise. Place on top of the pudding bowl and secure with string. Make a pleat in a piece of foil and place on top of the baking paper. Secure with string.

Sit the basin on top of the saucer in the slow cooker. Pour sufficient boiling water into the slow cooker until it comes three-quarters of the way up the sides of the pudding basin.

Cover with the lid. Cook on high for 4 hours.

Carefully remove the pudding basin from the slow cooker and remove the foil and baking paper. Turn upside down onto a serving plate. (The centre will drop in – don't panic.) Dust liberally with icing sugar before serving with custard or cream.

allyson's tip

- Loop a couple of lengths of string over the top of the pudding basin and under the string that secures the foil layer to make a handle. This will make lifting the pudding basin out of the hot slow cooker easier at the end of the cooking time.

6 tablespoons treacle, lightly warmed
2 cups flour
¼ cup brown sugar
2½ teaspoons ground ginger
100 grams butter, chilled and diced
1 teaspoon baking soda
¾ cup milk
2 eggs

ginger & treacle pudding

serves 8
preparation time **15 minutes**
cooking time **3–4 hours, high only**

Treacle is one step darker than golden syrup. Its molasses-like flavour gives this steamed pud a rich flavour. Serve with a rum-flavoured custard or whipped cream for a fabulous winter pudding.

Turn the slow cooker on to low to pre-warm while gathering and preparing the ingredients. Place an upturned saucer into the base of the slow cooker, this will act as a trivet. Lightly grease an 8-cup capacity pudding basin.

Pour 2 tablespoons of the treacle into the base of the pudding basin and set aside.

Into a large mixing bowl sift the flour, brown sugar and ginger. Rub in the butter until the mixture resembles breadcrumbs, and make a well in the centre.

In a jug, beat together the baking soda, milk and eggs. Pour into the well and gradually stir together. Stir in the remaining treacle towards the end. Do not over-mix as the pudding will peak when it cooks.

Turn the soft cake mixture into the prepared pudding bowl. Lightly grease one sheet of baking paper and make a pleat across the centre. This will allow space for the pudding to rise. Place on top of the pudding bowl. Secure with string. Make a pleat in a piece of foil and place on top of the baking paper. Secure with string.

Sit the pudding on top of the saucer. Pour 2 cups of boiling water into the slow cooker. The water should come about halfway up the sides of the bowl. Cover with the lid.

Cook on high for 3–4 hours.

Remove carefully from the slow cooker and remove the foil and baking paper. Check to see if the pudding is cooked. If not, quickly re-cover with the baking paper and foil and return to the slow cooker for a further 30 minutes or until cooked.

Turn out onto a plate to serve. Leftovers are great the next day, pan-fried in a knob of butter and served with ice cream.

variations

- Use golden syrup in place of treacle.
- Ginger can be replaced with cardamom, cinnamon or mixed spice.
- Add a little mixed peel and the grated rind of a lemon or orange.
- Add about ¼–½ cup currants and grated orange rind.

3 cups self-raising flour
¼ cup cocoa
100 grams butter, chilled and diced
1 cup sugar
2 cups milk
2 eggs
2 teaspoons vanilla essence

chocolate sauce
3½ cups boiling water
½ cup dark rum or coffee liqueur
1 cup sugar
¼ cup cocoa

rich chocolate self-saucing pud

serves 8
preparation time **15 minutes**
cooking time **2 hours, using high and low**

I am sure this is every kid's favourite pudding. It's that luscious smooth sauce hiding under a rich chocolate sponge and then there's the addition of ice cream or cream to help it slide down with a 10/10 yum factor. And it is very easy to cook in a slow cooker, ideal for days where you want to put a pud on for the family and then run out the door to do something.

Turn the slow cooker on to low to pre-warm while gathering and preparing the ingredients.

Sift the flour and cocoa into a bowl. Rub in the butter until the mixture resembles fine crumbs.

Stir in the sugar and make a well in the centre.

Beat the milk, eggs and vanilla essence together and mix into the dry ingredients using a holed spoon to form a stiff batter.

Into the pre-warmed slow cooker, put the boiling water, rum or coffee liqueur, sugar and cocoa and stir to dissolve the cocoa.

Carefully spoon the batter evenly into the slow cooker and cover with the lid.

Cook on high for 1 hour then turn to low for a further 1 hour.

Serve hot with ice cream and cream.

caramel sauce
1 litre boiling water
¾ cup sugar
75 grams butter, diced

pudding
2½ cups flour
2 teaspoons baking powder
2 teaspoons baking soda
2–3 teaspoons mixed spice
1½ cups sultanas
1 cup currants or raisins
1 cup brown sugar
1¼ cups milk
50 grams butter, melted

fruit & caramel self-saucing pud

serves 10–12
preparation time **15 minutes**
cooking time **4–5 hours, using high and low**

This recipe is a favourite of a good friend's mother, who found it in a magazine somewhere some time ago and has kept it torn out of the mag in her recipe scrapbook for years. Whoever the original author was, I thank you, it's divine. It is ideal for a large family gathering as it will easily serve 10–12.

Turn the slow cooker on to low to pre-warm while gathering and preparing the ingredients.

Stir the water, sugar and butter together until the sugar has dissolved and the butter melted. Pour into the pre-warmed slow cooker and cover with the lid.

Sift the flour, baking powder, baking soda and mixed spice into a large bowl. Stir in the sultanas and currants or raisins and brown sugar and make a well in the centre.

Pour the milk into the well and, using a wooden spoon, stir gradually to form a thick batter, free of flour lumps. Once all the milk has been added, stir in the butter.

Spoon the batter evenly into the hot sauce and cover with the lid.

Cook on high for 1 hour and then turn to low for a further 3–4 hours. Do not lift the lid for the first 2 hours of cooking time. Serve warm with whipped cream.

variations

- In place of sultanas and currants or raisins, use your favourite combination of dried fruits.
- Add the grated rind of 1 orange to the batter, and maybe a small handful of mixed peel.

allyson's tip

- For slow cookers with a 'keep warm' function, this pudding, once cooked, can be kept warm for an extra 1–2 hours and still be delicious when served.

1 cup self-raising flour
1 cup fresh white breadcrumbs
1–1¼ cups currants
¼ cup caster sugar
75 grams butter, chilled and grated
grated rind 1 lemon
½ cup milk

vanilla custard
2 tablespoons cornflour
½ cup cream
¼ cup caster sugar
4 egg yolks
2 teaspoons vanilla essence or paste
2 cups milk

spotted dog with custard

serves 4–6
preparation time **15 minutes**
cooking time **2–2½ hours, high only**

Roly-poly puddings are pretty much classic, old-fashioned British pudding fare, originally being made from suet and not butter and cooked in a floured cloth, though today they are often baked. Spotted Dick, strictly speaking, has the currants or raisins in the centre of the dough, while Spotted Dog has them throughout! Being a steamed pudding, it will cook well in the slow cooker.

Turn the slow cooker on to low to pre-warm while gathering and preparing the ingredients. Place a plate long enough to sit in the base of the slow cooker and pour in 2 cups of boiling water. Lightly grease a 45-cm length of baking paper and sit greased-side up on top of a longer piece – about 50-cm in length – of foil.

Into a wide bowl, stir together the flour, breadcrumbs, currants, sugar, butter and lemon rind and make a well in the centre.

Stir in the milk to make a moist batter-like dough.

Turn the dough onto the centre of the baking paper and shape into a long sausage, about 40 cm long. Bring the edges of the baking paper together and fold loosely to seal, leaving plenty of room for the pudding to expand when cooking. Repeat with the foil.

Sit the parcel, folded side uppermost, on top of the plate in the pre-warmed slow cooker. The water should come about halfway up the sides of the pudding. Add more boiling water from the kettle if required, but do not submerge the pudding in water.

Cook on high for 2–2½ hours. To check if the pudding is cooked, just pull open the foil and baking paper a little and check that the pudding is cooked and does not have any raw areas of dough left. If there are raw areas, re-seal and continue to cook for a further 30 minutes.

Serve the spotted dog with a heavenly sized serving of vanilla custard.

vanilla custard
In a saucepan stir together the cornflour, cream, caster sugar, egg yolks and vanilla essence until smooth. Gradually add the milk and then cook, stirring regularly over a medium heat until the custard is smooth and thick. Remove from the heat and allow to cool.

index